JEROME

Jerome (*c*.AD 347–420) was the father of the Latin Bible, the Vulgate, and brought the traditions of classical rhetoric and Christian exegesis more closely together than any other early Christian writer. A major intellectual force in the early church, he mediated between eastern and western theology. His novelistic lives of the saints encapsulated Christian aspirations in an attractive literary form. As an ascetic and an often irascible mentor to many Christian men and women, he shaped the ideals of Christian chastity and poverty for generations.

Through a representative selection of translated works from Jerome's voluminous output, Stefan Rebenich analyses the saint's career as a Christian writer, his social and theological context, and his role in the public discourse on orthodoxy and asceticism. Combining informed and accessible commentary on the extracts with some provocative reassessments, the book will help readers to a more balanced portrait of a complex and brilliant, if not always likeable, man.

Stefan Rebenich is Lecturer in Ancient History at the University of Mannheim.

THE EARLY CHURCH FATHERS
Edited by Carol Harrison
University of Durham

The Greek and Latin Fathers of the Church are central to the creation of Christian doctrine, yet often unapproachable because of the sheer volume of their writings and the relative paucity of accessible translations. This series makes available translations of key selected texts by the major Fathers to all students of the early Church.

CYRIL OF JERUSALEM
Edward Yarnold, SJ

EARLY CHRISTIAN LATIN POETS
Carolinne White

CYRIL OF ALEXANDRIA
Norman Russell

MAXIMUS THE CONFESSOR
Andrew Louth

IRENAEUS OF LYONS
Robert M. Grant

AMBROSE
Boniface Ramsey, OP

ORIGEN
Joseph W. Trigg

GREGORY OF NYSSA
Anthony Meredith, SJ

JOHN CHRYSOSTOM
Wendy Mayer and Pauline Allen

JEROME

Stefan Rebenich

London and New York

First published 2002
by Routledge
11 New Fetter Lane, London EC4P 4EE

Simultaneously published in the USA and Canada
by Routledge
29 West 35th Street, New York, NY 10001

Routledge is an imprint of the Taylor & Francis Group

© 2002 Stefan Rebenich

Project management and typeset in 10/12pt Garamond by Steven Gardiner Ltd
Printed and bound in Great Britain by T J International Ltd, Padstow, Cornwall

British Library Cataloguing in Publication Data
A catalogue record for this book is available
from the British Library

Library of Congress Cataloging in Publication Data
A catalog record for this book has been requested

ISBN 0–415–19905–0 (hbk)
ISBN 0–415–19906–9 (pbk)

FÜR GERLINDE

CONTENTS

CONTENTS

PREFACE

Jerome is a familiar figure in literature and art. We all know him with a lion at his feet, and, with biblical manuscripts in Latin, Greek, and Hebrew in his study, he is depicted as a desert hero or as a cardinal. Throughout the ages, changing images have characterized this father and doctor of the church.

The aim of this book, however, is to reflect upon and revise some elements of the traditional portrait of Jerome that even today determine his representation across various denominational and ideological borderlines. Thus, on the one hand, the saint is venerated as trilingual translator and commentator and praised as an ascetic virtuoso, while, on the other, he has frequently been described as ill-tempered and attacked as the spiritual seducer of noble ladies. Most scholarly contributions still focus on his individual characteristics, both positive and negative. I will, instead, emphasize Jerome's position in Christian society of the fourth century AD, his archetypical career as a provincial parvenu, his social and theological networks, and his role in the public discourse upon orthodoxy and asceticism. Thus, it is to be asked how Jerome, a traditionally educated Christian intellectual, was able to succeed as an exponent both of the ascetic movement and of Nicene orthodoxy, as a translator and a commentator of the Bible, and as a mediator between eastern and western theology. The book proposes to elucidate some of the determining factors in Jerome's literary and theological success, and his self-invention as a heroic hermit and brave fighter against Origenist heresy.

I have profited much from the great strides modern scholarship on Jerome has made in various fields. We are now able to reconstruct his translations of the New and Old Testament and to assess his linguistic competence; our understanding of his philological and exegetical methods has improved; his literary theory and practice has been more clearly defined; his dependence as an amazingly productive exegete on both Greek and Latin predecessors has been discussed; new light has been shed on many chronological questions; the Hebrew traditions within his oeuvre have become apparent; many of his writings have been critically edited, translated into modern languages, and copiously annotated. French scholars in particular – among them Yves-Marie Duval, Roger Gryson, and Pierre Jay – have studied some of Jerome's biblical commentaries in great detail, whereas Neil Adkin, in a profusion of articles, has discovered many reminiscences from both pagan and Christian authors, and has promoted textual criticism of Jerome. In the last decade, Jerome's correspondence with Augustine has attracted special attention, and his circle of female ascetics has been closely examined. I owe much to many of these contributions and to the studies of Tim Barnes, Peter Brown, Henry Chadwick, Elizabeth Clark, Jacques Fontaine, and John Matthews, either on Jerome and his contemporaries, or on the social and cultural milieu of his times. But, it should be stressed that this book is not meant to be an exhaustive synthesis of increasingly specialized and diversified research. I have rather presented a sketch of what I think is essential to understand and appreciate: the saint's life and writings. Readers familiar with my earlier work on Jerome will realize that I have synthesized my doctoral dissertation on *Hieronymus und sein Kreis*, published ten years ago in German, and some of my other contributions to the international debate about Jerome.

A final word may be said concerning the translations. A selection of writings from an author as prolific as Jerome must always be biased. But I hope the reader will get at least an idea of the wide spectrum and amazing variety of Jerome's literary production. I have decided not to render once again the famous texts that have often been quoted and translated (e.g. letter 22 on the Preservation of Virginity, letter 108 on the Death of Paula, or the Life of Paul the First Hermit), but rather to translate some important, but less well-known passages. I have repeatedly relied upon the text of the *Nicene and Post-Nicene Fathers*, which I have altered now and then, since it is an established translation that has influenced many modern English versions. The commentary is written for a non-specialist audience. The short introductions, however, place the texts within Jerome's oeuvre and reflect upon the scholarly discussion.

Over the years, I have received help and encouragement from friends and colleagues who have read bits and pieces of what I have published on Jerome. Some of them have also commented on earlier drafts of this book. In particular, I should like to thank Peter Heather, Adam Kamesar, Wolfram Kinzig, Neil McLynn, and

Mark Vessey. Many thanks too to Katja Bär and Christian Bechtold, who have read and improved the typescript. John Matthews and Peter Heather gave me the opportunity to discuss some parts of the biographical introduction in a classics seminar at Yale University in spring 2000; the audience made many helpful observations and suggestions that have been gratefully received. Tomas Hägg kindly invited me to a meeting of the *Nordiskt patristiskt textseminarium* at Bergen in May 2000 to give a paper on Jerome's desert period and to study the correspondence between Jerome and Augustine. I should like to express my gratitude to the university of Bergen and the participants of the seminar for a highly stimulating, but at the same time enjoyable stay in Norway. Last, but not least, it is my pleasurable task to thank Carol Harrison and Richard Stoneman, who asked me to write this book many years ago and waited patiently for the typescript. They have also saved me from many errors and much inelegance.

Stefan Rebenich   March 2001
Mannheim

Part I

INTRODUCTION

1

FROM STRIDON TO AQUILEIA

Between Career and
Conversion

Men of letters often make their way into the civil service.

Symmachus

At the end of the fourth century AD, Jerome contemplated writing a history in which he would show how the church during this period 'increased in influence and in wealth but decreased in virtue'.[1] In the course of his lifetime, Jerome experienced the rapid transformation of the Christian church in Roman society and the Christianization of the imperial government. After the end of the Great Persecution (311) and especially from the moment of Constantine's promotion of the new religion (312–13), the Christian communities acquired legal privileges and financial benefits from the emperor. The bishops, who received rights of civil jurisdiction, gained much power and influence in the cities. More and more members of the urban and provincial elites were attracted by the prospect of an ecclesiastical career, and many of the ordinary people in the cities were Christianized by the second half of the fourth century. Christian communities flourished, new churches were erected, institutions of charity were founded. Christian culture, based upon the Bible and traditional learning, became more elaborate, better-off Christians travelled to the holy places in Palestine, and the ascetic movement fascinated many true believers.

At the same time, Christian congregations all over the Roman Empire were fragmented through religious divisions. Violence and intimidation were frequent, and many cities saw riots over the election of a bishop.[2] In Africa, where Christianity was strong, the dispute between Catholic and Donatist parties forced Constantine to intervene soon after he became senior ruler (312). The conflict started when the latter group refused to accept the bishop of Carthage in about 311 on the grounds that his consecrator had surrendered the Scriptures in the

Diocletianic persecution. In spite of several interventions of the state, the schism persisted during the fourth century. During his reign, Constantine was also confronted with the teaching of Arius, a priest of Alexandria, who distinguished the divine status of God the Father from that of the Son. His doctrine was strongly opposed and condemned by other theologians. The contending parties, however, appealed to Constantine who summoned, in 325, the Council of Nicaea (now Iznik) to settle the dispute. There, the opponents of Arianism defined the Catholic faith in the consubstantiality of Father and Son, using the famous term *homoousios*. The emperor took an active part in the discussion since his policy was to unite the Christian church to the secular state in order to stabilize the newly unified Empire. Thus, he enforced the *homoousios* formula, condemned Arius, and deposed two insubordinate bishops. But, soon, Constantine began to waver and banished some prominent advocates of the Nicene Creed. Therefore, the Arian question was not solved and remained open until Theodosius implemented a strictly Nicene definition of orthodoxy at the beginning of the 380s.

When Jerome was born in 347,[3] Athanasius, the ferocious chief opponent of Arianism, had just returned from exile to his see in Alexandria. The influence of Constantine's son, Constans, who ruled the western part of the Empire, helped to restore him against the will of his brother Constantius, emperor in the east, who openly embraced Arianism.[4] Jerome grew up in an obscure town called Stridon, which was located somewhere on the border between the Roman provinces of Dalmatia and Pannonia and within easy reach of Aquileia and Emona (Ljubljana/Laibach).[5] Later, when he ardently campaigned for asceticism, he complained about the rusticity and religious indifference that were to be found in his own country: 'Men's only God is their belly. People live only for the day, and the richer you are the more saintly you are held to be.'[6] Although Jerome's parents were Christians, who took care that he had been, as a baby, 'nourished on Catholic milk',[7] he was not baptized as a child in Stridon, but as a young man in Rome. In those days, baptism was postponed until maturity, or even until one's deathbed, for fear of the responsibilities incurred by it. Augustine and Jerome's friends, Rufinus and Heliodorus, are parallel cases.[8]

Jerome's father Eusebius, like so many other parents, both Christian and pagan, invested in the tuition of his son to prepare the ground for a future career. The family owned property around Stridon and was well off; slaves belonged to the household and nurses took care of the children. We hear of a younger brother named Paulinianus and a sister. Later, Jerome recalled to memory how he romped about the young servants' cells, how he spent his holidays in play, and how he had to be dragged like a captive from his grandmother's lap to the lessons of his enraged teacher.[9] Jerome may have attended the elementary school in his hometown. The syllabus was rather modest and consisted of reading and writing and some arithmetic. We know from Augustine's *Confessions* that late antique teaching was not very sophisticated. Pupils were forced to chant 'One and one are two, two and two are four'; the main stimulus was the *ferula* (the cane), and educational theory focused on coercion and punishment.[10] 'Who is there who would not recoil in horror and choose death, if he was asked to choose between dying and going back to his childhood!'[11] Jerome would certainly have joined in the lamentation of the aged bishop of Hippo.

Still, the detestable experience of primary school was the first step towards the advanced education that was the privilege of the elites of the Roman Empire, and a classical training was of vital importance for recruitment into the imperial bureaucracy. Ambitious and affluent parents were prepared to send their children first to the school of the *grammaticus*, who advanced the study of language and literature, and then, at the age of fifteen or sixteen, to the rhetor, who introduced the students into the theory and practice of declamation. There were, of course, remarkable regional and social differences in these schools. Whereas Augustine's father, a member of the municipal council of Thagaste in Numidia, was hardly able to pay for his son's education in North Africa, Jerome was allowed to go to Rome to attend the classes of the best teachers the Latin speaking world could provide. Many years later, Jerome mentioned in a letter to a young monk from Toulouse that the latter's mother, when sending her son to Rome, spared no expense and consoled herself for her son's absence by the thought of the future that lay before him.[12] Jerome's father was also prepared to make the economic sacrifice, since he was convinced that exclusive tuition would be the key to his son's success. Three other young provincial careerists joined Jerome in Rome: his friend Bonosus, who came from Stridon or a neighbouring village, Rufinus of Concordia (close to Aquileia), and Heliodorus of Altinum. All of them were Christians, enjoyed their student life, but also visited the shrines of the martyrs and the Apostles on Sundays.[13] After they had finished their studies, the fellow-pupils remained in close contact.

In 'the renowned city, the capital of the Roman Empire',[14] Jerome was taught by the famous grammarian Aelius Donatus,[15] and then went to a Roman school of rhetoric. His student years in Rome were essential to his intellectual formation. All his later work reveals the brilliant pupil who is proud of his language, style, and dialectic. He closely studied the classics and may have picked up some Greek.[16] Whether he had already followed lectures on philosophy in Rome is difficult to say. But when he left the *Urbs*, he was undoubtedly well acquainted with the traditional canon of Latin authors who are ubiquitous throughout his oeuvre. Jerome also started to build up with immense zeal and labour his own library, which, though initially restricted to classical authors, soon also housed Christian texts.[17]

The provincial parvenu shared his bibliophily with Christian senators, who stored in their libraries copies of classical texts and magnificent manuscripts of the Bible.[18] Rome, the centre of the old senatorial aristocracy, also offered Jerome the possibility of getting in touch with influential friends, *amici maiores*, who were always important for social promotion. He and his friends from northern Italy met the young aristocrat Pammachius, who belonged to the illustrious *gens Furia*, and perhaps Melania the Elder, whose husband was prefect of Rome from 361 to 363. Both Jerome and Rufinus profited through all their life from the contacts with the Christian nobility of Rome that they had established during their years of study at the end of the 350s and the beginning of the 360s.

It was now up to Jerome, *bene uti litteris*, as Augustine once said,[19] to make the best out of his education. Hence, Jerome, after his graduation, moved, together with his friend Bonosus, to Augusta Treverorum (Trier). Although Jerome does not tell us the motives for this journey to Gaul in his later writings, there cannot be any doubt that the two young men intended to make careers in Trier, which was at that time both an imperial residence and an administrative centre. In Ausonius' *The Order of Famous Cities*, written *c.*388–9, Trier comes sixth, after Rome, Constantinople, Carthage, Antioch, Alexandria, and just ahead of Milan.[20] The tetrarchs had based the Gallic prefecture there, and, throughout the fourth century, it accommodated various emperors and their entourages. Valentinian I, who was elected emperor in Nicaea in February 364, reached Trier in October 367, where he concentrated on frontier defence, fought against the Alamanni, and rebuilt the fortifications on the Rhine. Soon after his arrival, Ausonius, who had been teaching grammar and rhetoric in Burdigala (Bordeaux) for 30 years, was summoned to Trier and appointed tutor of the emperor's son and heir, Gratian. Valentinian was known for promoting professors and bureaucrats, and, after his death in 375, Ausonius went on to enjoy a remarkable career, securing family and friends positions of influence at the imperial court. He himself gained a praetorian prefecture and the consulship of 379.[21]

The ambitious and talented son of a rich landowner in Stridon must have hoped that the liberal arts he had studied in Rome would help him to get a post in the imperial bureaucracy. Such an appointment was the passport to success and ascent into the governing classes. It seems that Jerome decided to go to the right place at the right time. Valentinian's court was an important cultural and political centre in the west and a catalyst of social mobility, where an exclusive group of new functionaries was formed. Service at court promised economic success and social prestige, offered relative security, and could even promote the 'courtier' to the highest ranks of the Empire.

As we know, Jerome did not end as a bureaucrat at the imperial court. The intended career was abruptly stopped through a religious awakening. What happened? Once again, we have no testimony from Jerome himself, who only mentions some years later that he purchased Christian texts and theological treatises for his ever-growing library.[22] A revealing account of a conversion at Trier is also to be found in Augustine's *Confessions*: that of two court officials, *agentes in rebus*, who, while walking through the gardens on the fringe of Trier, happened to meet two hermits who possessed a copy of the *Life of Antony* by Athanasius.[23] The two friends were captivated by the inspirational biography and spontaneously decided to embrace an ascetic life, giving up their worldly employment (*militia saecularis*) to serve God. 'What is our motive in doing service? Can our hopes in court rise higher than to be friends of the emperor (*amici principis*)?' they asked, and came to the conclusion that they should 'become a friend of God (*amicus dei*).'[24] It has been suggested that the office-holders mentioned in Augustine were Jerome and Bonosus.[25] This ingenious hypothesis cannot be confirmed, especially since Augustine's stylized story describes an exemplary conversion. But Jerome's withdrawal from the imperial service may be imagined in a similar way. In Trier, he could have come across the popular Latin version of the *Life of Antony*, which spread through the west, and may have experienced new forms of Christian living in an area where, in those days, the first monasteries were founded.

His dedication to the ascetic life was a major event, powerful and overwhelming. But, in his later work, Jerome did not reflect upon his conversion. Instead, he describes another episode that has always fascinated later generations: his famous dream. We find an impressive account of this event in letter 22, which encouraged the young

Roman lady Eustochium to devote herself to virginity and warned her against overestimating the relevance of classical education:

> Many years ago when, for the kingdom of heaven's sake, I had cut myself off from home, parents, sister, relations, and, what was harder, from the dainty food to which I had been accustomed, and when I was on my way to Jerusalem to wage my warfare, I still could not bring myself to forego the library which I had formed for myself at Rome with great care and labour. And so, miserable man that I was, I would fast only that I might afterwards read Cicero. After many nights spent in vigil, after floods of tears called from my inmost heart in recollection of my past sins, I would once more take up Plautus. And when at times I returned to my right mind and began to read the prophets, their style seemed rude and repellent. With my blinded eyes I could not see the light; but I attributed the fault not to them, but to the sun. While the old serpent was thus making me his plaything, about the middle of Lent a fever attacked my weakened body, and while it destroyed my rest completely – the story seems hardly credible – it so wasted my unhappy frame that my bones scarcely held together. Meantime, preparations for my funeral went on; my body grew gradually colder, and the warmth of life lingered only in my poor throbbing breast. Suddenly I was caught up in the spirit and dragged before the judgment seat of the Judge; and here the light was so bright, and those who stood around were so radiant, that I cast myself upon the ground and did not dare to look up. I was asked to state my condition and replied: 'I am a Christian.' But he who presided said: 'You lie, you are a follower of Cicero and not of Christ (*Ciceronianus es, non Christianus*). For where your treasure is, there will your heart be also (cf. Matthew 6.21).' Instantly, I became dumb, and amid the strokes of the lash – for he had ordered me to be scourged – I was even more severely tortured by the fire of conscience, considering with myself that verse, 'In the grave who will give you thanks?' (Psalm 6.5). Yet for all that I began to cry and to lament, saying: 'Have mercy upon me, O Lord: have mercy upon me.' Amid the sound of the scourges my voice made itself heard. At last the bystanders, falling down before the knees of him who presided, prayed that he would have pity on my youth and that he would give me opportunity to

repent of my error, on the agreement that torture should be inflicted on me, if I ever again read the works of gentile authors. Under the stress of that awful moment, I should have been willing to make still larger promises than these. Accordingly I took an oath and called upon his name, saying: 'Lord, if ever again I possess worldly books or read them, I have denied you.' After taking this oath I was dismissed and returned to the upper world. There, to the surprise of all, I opened again eyes so drenched with tears that my distress served to convince even the incredulous. That this was no sleep nor idle dream, such as often mock us, I call to witness the tribunal before which I fell down and the verdict which I feared. May it never be my lot again to come before such a court! I profess that my shoulders were black and blue, that I felt the bruises long after I awoke from my sleep, and that henceforth I read the books of God with a greater zeal than I had previously given to the books of men.[26]

Domine, si umquam habuero codices saeculares, si legero, te negavi – 'Lord, if ever again I possess worldly books or read them, I have denied you.' It is obvious that Jerome lied – without blushing in embarrassment. Of course he read pagan authors after his vow.[27] Still, this dramatic story, full of classical rhetoric, might reflect a real experience, which Jerome later inserted into and embellished in his treatise on virginity. The exact setting and date of the celebrated dream is controversial. Some place it at the beginning of the 370s at Antioch on the Orontes, others three or four years later in the desert of Chalcis. There is, however, reason to think that this episode occurred in Trier when Jerome realized that his initial ambitions of a secular career, and his new yearning for an ascetic life, could not come together.[28] His conversion was followed by the radical negation of his former conduct and implied the revocation of his classical (i.e. 'gentile') education and the subsequent study of the Bible and Christian authors. The dream's narrative, in other words, focuses on the one consequence of the ascetic reorientation that was most agonizing for Jerome, who was a traditionally trained intellectual and highly talented writer. We may conclude that this magnificent piece of showmanship refers to Jerome's decision to serve God taken in Trier in about 370.

After his conversion, Jerome stayed for some time in northern Italy. We are not able to reconstruct his itinerary and the chronology of this period, but, from the scattered evidence, it can be deduced that he wished, and tried, to live a life according to ascetic ideals, and established contacts with like-minded Christians. Thus, he got in touch with a monastic circle at Aquileia, the capital of the province of Venetia and Istria. After Rome and Trier, it was again an urban centre that attracted Jerome. Others followed in due course: Antioch on the Orontes, Constantinople, and Rome again. The first decades of his life were formed through stays in major cities and imperial residences.

During the second half of the fourth century, northern Italy and southern Gaul saw the growth of the ascetic movement and the development of monastic life. Church politicians, pilgrims, and exiles – Athanasius and Peter of Alexandria, Hilary of Poitiers and Eusebius of Vercelli – either leaving or returning from the east brought a wealth of information into the west and conveyed different eastern models of ascetic living. The eremitic tradition of asceticism represented by the Latin translation of the *Life of Antony* mentioned above now became immensely influential. Ascetic conduct turned out to be more austere, seclusion from communal life was demanded, and spiritual perfection in solitary contemplation required. The contemporary debate on orthodoxy and the Arian conflict also had a strong impact on the ascetic movement, since the fight against heresy and self-imposed ascetic perfection were interrelated, and ascetic propaganda was manipulated for ecclesiastical politics. In this environment, a new type of church politician appeared: the 'monk-bishop'. As we can, for instance, deduce from the *Life of Martin* by Sulpicius Severus, the *moine-évêque* combined pastoral and ascetic life, defended the orthodox tradition, and was vested with spiritual authority.[29] Jerome's further career, which led him to become one of the most influential Christian writers of his time, is only to be understood in the context of the gradual emergence of occidental monasticism.

From an entry in Jerome's *Chronicle*, we learn that, in the year 374, a group of clerics founded a monastery in Aquileia. Their monastic programme was perhaps influenced by the coenobitic community that Eusebius, the bishop of Vercelli, had introduced upon his return from exile.[30] Jerome and his friends communicated with ascetic clerics and monks in the region of Aquileia, Vercelli, Concordia, and Emona.[31] A very close acquaintance was the presbyter Chromatius, a learned scholar, who seems to have lived together with his relatives in an informally organized ascetic community. Chromatius' widowed mother denied herself a second marriage, and his sisters vowed themselves to virginity. Such quasi-monastic households were popular at this time among pious Christians in northern Italy. Chromatius' brother, the deacon Eusebius, instructed Rufinus, Jerome's fellow-student, for baptism.[32] At the beginning of the 370s, Aquileia was a stronghold of Nicene orthodoxy and the bishop Valerian gained much influence, since Milan, the nearby imperial residence, was controlled by the Homoeans, an Arian party that was led by the bishop Auxentius.[33] Even after having moved to the east, Jerome remained in touch with the Aquileian circle, whose other members were the archdeacon Jovinus, the subdeacon Niceas, and the monk Chrysocomas. After his conversion, Jerome immediately built up a network of influential clerics based upon ascetic commitment and orthodox zeal. The form and intention of these personal contacts remained traditional. The ascetically orientated Christians from the educated classes, like their pagan compeers, banded together with their social equals and looked for powerful patrons. Old friends were used for establishing new friendships. Jerome's seventh letter to Chromatius and his family shows that the combination of the ascetic profession and the battle against heterodoxy was the principal constituent of this interconnection. What Jerome missed in his own country, he found in Aquileia: 'Though every day you confess Christ by keeping his commandments, you have added to this private glory the public fame of an open confession, and it was by your efforts in the past that the poison of the Arian heresy was expelled from your city.'[34]

During his stay in northern Italy, Jerome intensified his commitment to the ascetic movement and became acquainted with divergent patterns of ascetic living. Some Christians stayed together as clerics in monastic or quasi-monastic groups, some founded coenobitic communities fulfilling ascetic commitment, and others pursued their religious perfection in eremitic privation. The ascetic convert sought a form of ascetic living that appeared to him to be acceptable. At the same time, his new companions in Aquileia introduced him to the correlation between Christian learning, asceticism, and orthodoxy (i.e. the Nicene definition of orthodoxy). All those not willing to endorse his interpretation of a Christian life were ostracized, like the rustic inhabitants and lukewarm Christians of his hometown Stridon. Prepared in such a way, Jerome decided suddenly to go on a pilgrimage to Jerusalem.

2

ANTIOCH AND CHALCIS
The Making of an Ascetic Champion

La force de ses tentations me fait plus d'envie que sa pénitence
ne me fait peur.

Nicolas Chamfort

In the early 370s, Jerome, accompanied by some friends, left northern
Italy and set out for the east. Trouble with his relatives, who may
have been deeply disappointed at the complete failure of his secular
career, and quarrels within the Aquileian group of devout clerics
about the best possible form of ascetic self-fulfilment forced Jerome
to embark on a pilgrimage to the east and to Jerusalem. He decided
to take his large personal library of pagan authors and Christian texts
with him. Jerusalem, a Mecca of Christian pilgrims for some time
already, was beginning to attract monastic and ascetic aspirants.[1] But
the would-be *monachus perfectus* got only as far as Antioch on the
Orontes. He reached the residence of the eastern emperor Valens as a
broken man, exhausted and fever-stricken – in his own words: 'Syria
presented itself to me, as a secure haven to a ship-wrecked sailor.'[2]
The haven was the household of his wealthy and powerful friend
Evagrius, whom he had met earlier in Aquileia and who now
received him with open arms and provided him with a roof.[3]
Evagrius of Antioch ranked among the class of local councillors
(*curiales*) and joined the imperial service where he exerted some influence. After he was dismissed from his provincial office, he entered the
church and was ordained a priest by the bishop Eusebius of Vercelli,
who brought him to Italy where he got involved in various ecclesiastical affairs. For a Greek speaker, he had an extraordinary command
of Latin and translated into his language the *Life of Antony*. Evagrius'
example illustrates the continuation of a secular career in the
church: in 388, he was made bishop of his native city Antioch. Such

an ecclesiastical 'reorientation' was not exceptional for a man of his standing and wealth.

The rich patron Evagrius, who had supported Jerome, his protégé, in northern Italy, returned to his home in Antioch on a diplomatic mission from Damasus, bishop of Rome. There is reason to think that Jerome and his friends travelled together with Evagrius through the Balkans, Greece, Thrace, and Asia Minor to Antioch. In the comfortable Antiochene household, however, the planned pilgrimage to Jerusalem was to be postponed indefinitely. Jerome, having regained his health and good temper, instead improved his understanding of spoken and written Greek, the language of the urban elites, studied philosophical and theological treatises from Evagrius' well-equipped library, learnt more about the sophisticated controversies concerning the doctrine of the Trinity then troubling the eastern churches, and – after some rather pleasant months – secluded himself in the desert of Chalcis to practise asceticism.

The following two or three years in the wilderness are supposed to have transformed the ascetic neophyte into an ascetic champion. Ecclesiastical art, devotional literature, and modern scholarship have created the image of a penitent recluse.[4] 'Like the other hermits he earned his daily living as a craftsman in the sweat of his brow,' wrote Georg Grützmacher, Jerome's Protestant biographer, at the beginning of the twentieth century.[5] The Catholic Ferdinand Cavallera was at least disposed to believe that 'la solitude de saint Jérôme' was 'plus encore morale que matérielle,'[6] and J. N. D. Kelly, representing the Anglican church, thought that Jerome found his home in 'a natural cave in the rocks', where he experienced 'the harsh reality' of a troglodyte.[7] All of these accounts of Jerome's ascetic *secessus* are misleading since they unhistorically try to harmonize his desert stay with the concept of total isolation practised by eastern hermits and pictured, for example, in Athanasius' *Life of Antony* and in Theodoret's *Historia religiosa*. Jerome himself described, and praised, the self-denying eastern asceticism in his amazingly popular and entertaining novels on various desert heroes. His primary emphasis was on the need for poverty and withdrawal, and he was inviting western readers to join what amounted to a new society, and to feel no longer at a loss about their ascetic aspirations, but to follow the firm example set by ascetic pioneers.

Let us first discuss Jerome's domicile. Chalcis, also called Chalcis ad Belum or, in the language of the native population, Qinnesîn ('eagle's nest'), lies on the border between northern Syria and the region west of the Euphrates.[8] Today, some ruins of the acropolis, lower town, and cemetery are still extant. In Jerome's time, Chalcis was an important strategic point in the Roman defence system of the province of Syria and an economic centre, through which major caravan routes passed. It was located 55 miles east-south-east of the Syrian capital Antioch and 17 miles south-west of Aleppo (Haleb/Berrhoea). So, it has been argued that Jerome exposed himself to the scorching sun in the menacing desert which began a few miles to the south-east of Chalcis.[9]

His own letters written in this period, however, portray a different reality. They give ample evidence that, during his stay in the *solitudo Syriae Chalcidis*, he was never completely secluded from the outside world. He was still in touch with Evagrius, who often visited him and served as a postman delivering letters and parcels.[10] Jerome maintained his correspondence with his friends at Aquileia, exchanged epistles with Florentinus, a wealthy western monk residing in Jerusalem with whom he had corresponded from Antioch,[11] and he wrote two excited letters to Damasus asking for theological advice and spiritual direction.[12] Obscure as he then was, Jerome mentioned his *patronus* Evagrius, who was an ideological confidant of the Roman bishop. Jerome also ensured that a runaway slave of Florentinus was sent back to his master. Moreover, he made several efforts to acquire interesting books. In a letter, for example, he asked Florentinus to have their mutual friend Rufinus send him the commentaries of Reticius, bishop of Autun, on the Song of Songs, and return the transcript of Hilary's explanation of the Psalms and work *On the Synods* that he had copied for him at Trier. Next, he begged Florentinus to get transcribed by a copyist certain books he did not possess. As compensation, Jerome offered to provide any work, especially on Scripture, he desired: 'And since, through the Lord's bounty, I am rich in volumes of the sacred library, you may command me in turn. I will send you what you please; and do not suppose that an order from you will give me trouble. I have pupils devoted to the art of copying (*habeo alumnos, qui antiquariae arti serviant*).'[13] The sentence makes you think twice. Jerome must have lived in quite a spacious hollow to store his expanding collection of *codices* and to supervise young assistants, or protégés, who were copying manuscripts there. Not only *alumni*, but also *fratres* joined his solitude.[14] Apart from copying manuscripts, Jerome was also concerned with writing. Perhaps his *Life of Paul the First Hermit* should be assigned to the desert period, although a reasonable case can be made for dating the work later.[15] All this information reminds us of monks' cells excavated in Egypt, which were rather underground atrium-style houses, 'with rooms, a court, a well, and other amenities, including cool rooms for the storage of bread, movable doors, and even glass in some windows.'[16]

Jerome also took language lessons. First, he made himself familiar with Syriac, the native tongue of the peasants and the monks in his neighbourhood: '*hic enim aut barbarus semisermo discendus est aut tacendum est*: For hereabout you must either learn the barbarous gibberish or else keep your mouth shut.'[17] Further, he began to study Hebrew: 'I betook myself to a brother who before his conversion had been a Hebrew and asked him to teach me his language. Thus, after familiarising myself with the pointed style of Quintilian, the fluency of Cicero, the seriousness of Fronto and the gentleness of Pliny, I now began to learn the alphabet again and practise hissing and breath-demanding words.'[18] Although this passage was written more than thirty years later, at a stage when Jerome ostentatiously celebrated his knowledge of Hebrew and carefully depicted himself as *vir trilinguis* to defend his authority as a translator and commentator of Scripture, I cannot see any reason to mistrust his assertion that an anonymous Jewish convert taught him the elements of Hebrew in the desert of Chalcis.

Finally, Jerome became involved in the heated debate over the Trinity that divided the church at Antioch into three factions. The schism in the metropolis also shook the *hinterland* and disturbed the monastic and ascetic communities in Jerome's vicinity. Asked to express his position, Jerome first manoeuvred and then supported Paulinus, who himself was backed by Evagrius[19] and who refused to cooperate with the rival orthodox party at Antioch led by Meletius. But, before he declared himself for Paulinus, Jerome had referred to the authority of the bishop of Rome whom he effusively praised and to whom he promised his loyalty.[20]

Obviously, the priests, monks, and hermits around Chalcis considered Jerome an unwelcome guest. When he preached the consubstantial Trinity, they ostracized him; when he subscribed to their statement of belief, they did not trust him. In the end, even the orthodox majority accused him of being a heretic. He bitterly complained: 'Every day I am asked for my confession of faith, as though when I was regenerated in baptism I had made none. I accept their formulas, but they are still dissatisfied. I sign my name to them, but they still refuse to believe me. One thing only will content them, that I should leave this place. I'm on the point of departure. [. . .] It is preferable to live among wild beasts rather than with Christians such as these.'[21] People were annoyed by this western partisan of Paulinus, who continued his correspondence throughout the world and was joined, amazingly enough, by a group of copyists and was supported by the Antiochene *curialis* Evagrius. No wonder that all they wanted was for Jerome to go away – and, eventually, he, with his close friends, made the journey back to Antioch.

An unbiased examination of Jerome's contemporary evidence about his brief period in the desert of Chalcis shows that he did not live the life of a heroic hermit incessantly struggling against vices and sensuality. He did not take up residence in the most inaccessible wilderness, but in a place where he could maintain relations with his patron and with Italian friends and establish new contacts. His residence was obviously situated on the road that led from Antioch to Chalcis. It is very likely that he stayed at an estate of Evagrius' called Maronia, less than thirty miles from Antioch.[22] The property probably belonged to the district of Chalcis and was perhaps located on a rocky plateau that runs south of the town of Imma and is known by the name *Jebel Baricha*. The rich Antiochene priest Evagrius, who sympathized with the ascetic movement, seems to have allowed Jerome, along with his friends and *alumni*, to practise their ascetic ideals in Maronia.

But, how does this hypothesis fit with Jerome's description of his desert domicile as solitude (*solitudo*), desert (*desertum*), and wilderness (*eremus*). What do these words mean? They refer to a place where Jerome could realize his ascetic proposal (*propositum*), and they underline the contrast with the tumultuous urban life that Jerome had experienced, and enjoyed, in Antioch and in other major cities of the Roman Empire. '*Interpretare vocabulum monachi, hoc est nomen tuum: quid facis in turba, qui solus est*: Consider the meaning of the word "monk", that is your name: What are you doing in the crowd, who should stay alone?'[23], he wrote to Heliodorus at Altinum in northern Italy, urging him to join him in the desert. Some years later, he advised Paulinus of Nola: 'Abandon cities and their throng, live on a small patch of ground, seek Christ in solitude.'[24] The perfect monk has to avoid the busy cities, the *urbium frequentia*,[25] and retire to a calm refuge where, 'far away from the crowds (*procul a turbis remotus*),'[26] he can find God through prayer and contemplation. In his ferocious polemic *Against John of Jerusalem*, written in 397, Jerome stated that he had forsaken the famous city of Antioch to weep over the sins of his youth and draw upon himself the mercy of Christ '*in agris et in solitudine*: in the countryside and in solitude.'[27] The great Syrian metropolis, after Rome and Alexandria the third largest city in the *oikoumene*, with nearly 200,000 inhabitants, offered a thrilling life and many sophisticated pleasures; but it was no place for an ambitious ascetic novice. So, Jerome exchanged his urban *vita activa* in Antioch for a *vita contemplativa* in the *hinterland*, which he called solitude and desert.

For the same reason, John Chrysostom left Antioch in 375 to join a monastic community on Mount Silpius close to the city and to bring himself to perfection under the guidance of an old Syrian. The rejection of the body implied the rejection of the *patria*, 'A monk cannot be perfect in his own country,'[28] and the rejection of the *civitas*, the urban centre of ancient civilization. The true ascetic, Jerome suggested, must break completely with his family, renounce all his possessions, and, above all, live in solitude: 'Those living in a city are not Christians (*quicumque in civitate sunt, Christiani non sunt*).'[29] From the beginning of antiquity, urban living had distinguished the civilized from everything savage, rustic, and barbarous. Jerome's withdrawal from Antioch implied a reversal of the traditional values he had previously held.

Although his interpretation of asceticism involved many features typical of the east, and especially of Egypt, Jerome felt attracted to the company of others, to 'the heavenly family here on earth.'[30] Among the various competitive forms of ascetic life, Jerome thus decided against the radical seclusion and repudiation of the world, an idea later propagated in some of his writings. In Chalcis, or Maronia, he settled to live in a coenobitic community, a style of living with which he was familiar from Aquileia. His sojourn in the *solitudo Chalcidis* anticipated his later life in Bethlehem where the monasteries founded by Paula and himself followed the 'western', more moderate forms of asceticism, which were, for instance, also practised in the communities of Paulinus in Nola, of Augustine in Cassiciacum, of Martin in Ligugé, and of Melania in Jerusalem.

The examination of Jerome's contemporary evidence about his brief period in Chalcis, then, makes the traditional picture of his desert solitude, still popular among pious Christian as well as critical scholars, obsolete.

When the dogmatic disputes had finally spoilt his pleasure in solitude, he made the journey back to Antioch where he was ordained priest, followed the lectures of Apollinaris of Laodicea, who introduced him to scriptural exegesis, and probably learnt of Origen's writings.[31] After the disillusionment of the desert, it was again the cities that attracted him. There, the predominance of Christianity allowed more and more wealthy people to preserve their virginity or widowhood, to study the Bible, to support the poor with alms, and, not least of all, to entertain the wandering ascetic. After Antioch,

Constantinople and Rome were the next stages in Jerome's ecclesiastical career.

Later in his life, however (i.e. from the time of his stay in Rome), Jerome carefully integrated his limited ascetic experience in the desert of Chalcis into the radical ascetic concept that he spread among aristocratic Roman ladies. These women had established what were virtually domestic nunneries in their palaces on the Aventine, where the small communities of noble ladies and their household slaves vowed themselves to chastity and biblical study, fasted, and neglected their clothing. Jerome was determined not merely to theorize about the ascetic life, but to give practical advice about the protection of virtue. He encouraged ascetic seclusion, sexual abstinence, and biblical reading, but he also tolerated the quasi-monastic communities in the aristocratic households. 'Let her find in the busy city the desert of the monks (*in urbe turbida inveniret heremum monachorum*).'[32]

It was only when powerful opposition forced him to leave Rome, in summer 385,[33] that he shifted his ground again. In a letter, he described in great detail the attraction and beauty of rural life. There is nothing like this in Rome, with its hurry, the fury of the arena, the madness of the circus, the profligacy of the theatre, not even in the daily meetings of pious matrons. He quoted Tertullian '*habeat sibi Roma suos tumultus*'.[34] Here, a frustrated Jerome is revelling in reminiscence of an existence far removed from urban civilization. But his willingness to tolerate a city life was not abandoned, only modified. In several letters written in Bethlehem, he did not cease praising the household asceticism he had encountered in Rome. Paulinus of Nola, the Roman lady Furia, Salvina, daughter-in-law of the powerful Moorish officer Gildo and resident in Constantinople, and others in Gaul and Spain: they were all to practise ascetic perfection at home. Although he stressed that the essence of monastic life is poverty and solitude, away from the city,[35] he often recommended household asceticism and coenobitic life as worthy preparation for the eremitic life and, sometimes, for ordination to the priesthood. It was not theological insecurity, as has been suggested,[36] that led Jerome to different answers to the question: 'How should an ascetic live?', but the individual expectations and requests of his audience. Jerome's concept of ascetic life was not only theologically motivated, but also aimed at winning the supporters and patrons who were always essential for him.

In Rome, he had started propagating his qualities as an ascetic master and spiritual leader. Whereas the interpretation of virginity proposed by Cyprian, Damasus, and Ambrose was stamped with the authority of episcopate,[37] Jerome had to refer to his personal experience to enforce his discourse. Thus, he summarized his period in the wilderness in a passage often quoted:[38]

> Oh, how often, when I was living in the desert (*heremus*), in the vast solitude (*vasta solitudo*), scorched by the burning sun, which offers monks a savage dwelling place, how often did I imagine myself back among the pleasures of Rome. I used to sit alone because I was filled with bitterness. My unshapely limbs were covered in sackcloth and my skin from long neglect had become as black as an Ethiopian's. Tears and groans were every day my portion; and if sleep chanced to overcome my struggles against it, I bruised my bare bones, which hardly held together, against the ground.

He had no companions but scorpions and wild beasts. He slept on the bare ground, drank only water, and spurned cooked foods as an unacceptable luxury. He mortified a body tormented by visions of dancing girls. He subdued his rebellious flesh with weeks of fasting.

> I remember [Jerome continues] crying out for days and nights together; and I ceased not from beating my breast till tranquillity returned to me at the Lord's rebuke. I used to dread my small cell as though it knew my thoughts. Stern and angry with myself, I used to make my way alone into the desert. Wherever I saw hollow valleys, rough mountains, steep cliffs, there I made my place of prayer and tortured my unhappy flesh. The Lord himself is my witness, that, after I had shed many tears and had fixed my eyes on heaven, I sometimes found myself among angelic hosts. And in joy and gladness I sang: 'We will run after you because of the savour of your good ointments.' (Song of Songs 1.3).

This touching portrait impressed not only the Roman ladies, but also generations of clergymen, artists, and scholars. It is found in the most famous of all his letters, *de virginitate servanda*, addressed to the young Roman aristocrat Julia Eustochium. In fact, a fairly large treatise, this *epistola* lays down the motives that should inspire those who devote themselves to a life of virginity, and also the rules by which they ought to regulate their daily conduct. It is brilliant in style, full of rhetorical display, and deals with a whole variety of related themes. The letter must be read in the context of the ascetic campaign that Jerome was carrying on in 383 and 384, with the approval of the Roman bishop, not only among his circles of devout ladies but in Rome at large. Jerome was using this epistle as a platform for setting out his challenging programme of female asceticism, and also for presenting himself as an expert in ascetic guidance. He therefore denounced his numerous rivals, who were also competing for the favour and fortunes of the Roman *patronae*, as would-be Christians, worldly clergy or charlatans posing as ascetics. And he depicted his desperate struggle for perfection and against temptation when he dedicated himself to the ascetic life. Eloquent reminiscences of his time in the desert of Chalcis and his famous dream and outright rejection of classical culture[39] are inserted in the letter. Elsewhere, he even gave an ascetic explanation of his initiative to learn Hebrew: 'When I was a young man walled by the solitude of the desert, I could not resist the promptings of vice and the fire of my nature. I tried to crush them by repeated fasting, my mind was in a turmoil with sinful thoughts. To bring it under control, I made myself the pupil of a Christian convert from Judaism.'[40]

Since only a man of rich ascetic experience could obtain the position of an ascetic guide to noble men and women, Jerome did not hesitate to recast the story of his desert solitude in Chalcis so that it smoothly fitted into the ascetic ideas and practices he passionately campaigned for in Rome and, later, in Bethlehem. Acceptance of his theological and ascetic competence was vital to his ambitious literary programme. Jerome, the Christian *litteratus* and the hermit of Chalcis, wanted to make himself the spiritual leader of wealthy Christian intellectuals in the western part of the Empire, who in their turn were able to support Jerome and, later, his monastic community in Bethlehem. His brilliant showmanship as an ascetic champion who had started his impressive career in the wilderness of Chalcis has been so successful that, for more than 1,600 years, scholars have been deceived by the picture of the learned ascetic in his barren cell in the *solitudo Syriae Chalcidis*.

3

CONSTANTINOPLE

The Formation of a Christian Writer

I awoke one morning and found myself famous.

Lord Byron

On 27 February 380, the emperor Theodosius issued an edict that made the Nicene teaching of the bishops Damasus of Rome and Peter of Alexandria compulsory for all his subjects. Henceforth, the only form of Christianity to be tolerated was the one that acknowledged the full, undivided divinity of Father, Son, and Holy Spirit.[1] In the same year, while suffering from a serious illness, Theodosius decided to be baptized in Thessalonica. On 24 November 380, he entered Constantinople and, immediately after his arrival, took measures against the Arian bishop Demophilus. When the latter refused to subscribe to an orthodox, that is, Nicene Creed, Theodosius did not hesitate to depose him and to entrust the churches of the eastern metropolis to Gregory of Nazianzus. Some weeks later, on 10 January, 381, Theodosius addressed a rescript to the Praetorian Prefect Eutropius depriving the heretics – the Photinians, the Arians, and the Eunomians are mentioned *expressis verbis* – of their consecrated places of assembly and handing them over to the representatives of the *Nicaena fides*.[2] Then, in May, he convoked a council of all eastern churches in Constantinople, which was meant to approve his ecclesiastical politics.[3]

This contemporary background allows us to understand Jerome's journey to, and residence in, the eastern capital at the beginning of the 380s.[4] Contrary to what has often been supposed, he had no intention of carrying on the literary and theological studies begun in Antioch.[5] We should not infer from Jerome's subsequent allusions to his preceptor and teacher Gregory of Nazianzus that his sojourn to Constantinople was an educational leave.[6] In his later writings, Jerome, depicting himself as Gregory's pupil, made much of the authority of the learned and, we may add, orthodox Cappadocian Father, in the hope of reducing the critics of his scholarship and orthodoxy to silence. The contemporary ecclesiastical and political implications of their first meeting were thus thrust into the background; not surprisingly perhaps, since they did not at all fit the image Jerome later promoted of himself, which was that of a secluded scholar.

Ecclesiastical affairs and ambitions led him to the Golden Horn. It has been convincingly suggested that Jerome's decision to go to Constantinople was also influenced by his effort to back Paulinus, the bishop of the uncompromising ultra-Nicene minority in Antioch.[7] Jerome had committed himself to Paulinus, by whom he was ordained priest and whose influential partisan Evagrius was also Jerome's patron. Although leading western bishops like Damasus of Rome and Ambrose of Milan had long since ostracized his opponent Meletius, the leader of the larger Nicene community in Antioch, and openly supported Paulinus,[8] the latter's position in Antioch and in the eastern part of the Empire was rather weak. Thus, Paulinus was in desperate need of influential friends to boost the prestige of the tiny Antiochene congregation and its controversial bishop. What better place was there to promote Paulinus' claims than Constantinople, especially when it was loudly rumoured that a great council to solve the theological disputes of the east was shortly to be held there?[9]

Jerome did not hesitate to plead Paulinus' cause in words and writings, even though the emperor recognized Meletius of Antioch as a compromise candidate of the majority of eastern theological factions and appointed him president of the council. A masterpiece of Jerome's propaganda for Paulinus was his translation and continuation of Eusebius' *Chronicle*, which was probably composed during his stay in Constantinople.[10] Jerome accused Meletius of apostasy from the true faith (*recta fides*), and styled Paulinus the only catholic bishop of Antioch. Two Arian bishops, he wrote, introduced Meletius to Antioch, but Paulinus was ordained bishop by the orthodox Lucifer of Cagliari who himself met the approval of two other confessors. Trickily, Jerome disguised the fact that Lucifer acted precipitately and without authorization. At the same time, he alleged that Meletius supported the position of an Arianizing party – the Macedonians – and thus opposed the teaching of the western churches and of Alexandria. The message of Jerome's *Chronicle* is obvious: the bishop of the Antiochene catholics could be none other than Paulinus.[11]

Shortly before and during the assembly, which was later to be recognized as the Second Ecumenical Council, Jerome had an opportunity to meet various important theologians and church politicians. He took it with both hands. He became acquainted with Gregory of Nazianzus, who was appointed bishop of Constantinople and replaced Meletius as president of the council after the latter's sudden death. Gregory in turn acted as a mediator in establishing new connections for Jerome. Thus, he met Gregory of Nyssa[12] and Amphilochius, bishop of Iconium in Cappadocia and cousin of Gregory of Nazianzus.[13] In Constantinople, therefore, the ambitious westerner made contact with important representatives of Nicene theology – and orthodoxy – in the east.

At the same time, and with Gregory's assistance, Jerome came to know members of the imperial court. In 400, when he had been living in Bethlehem for more than a decade, he wrote a consolatory letter to Salvina,[14] daughter of Gildo, the governor of Africa who had revolted against the western government in 397 and been killed in the following year. Salvina's recently deceased husband, Nebridius,[15] was a nephew of Flaccilla, first wife of Theodosius the Great and mother of the reigning emperors Arcadius and Honorius. His father, also called Nebridius, held high offices.[16] While city prefect of Constantinople, he married Olympias, who came from one of the leading senatorial families of the eastern capital. Soon after their nuptials, he died. Jerome emphasized in his letter to Salvina that the elder Nebridius was a close friend of his.[17] He must have become acquainted with him during his stay in Constantinople between 380 and 382 and secured the confidence of an official who was about to attain an influential post in the imperial administration. Although we have no evidence that their relations were as close as Jerome later pretended, the case of Nebridius and his family nevertheless proves that Jerome, from the time of his stay in Constantinople, had access to the Christian elite of the eastern part of the Empire.

We may note, too, that members of the senatorial aristocracy were devoting themselves to the ideals of asceticism then being propagated in the Empire. Nebridius' second wife Olympias has already been mentioned.[18] After her husband's death, Theodosius I intended to marry her to a Spaniard from his family, but she declined. Olympias instead sold her estates in the provinces and founded the first monastic community for women at Constantinople in one of her houses, although members of her class were strongly opposed to her new conduct. Educated by Theodosia, sister of Amphilochius of Iconium, Olympias supported John Chrysostom and was ordained deaconess by Nectarius, previously *praetor* and then bishop of Constantinople, who succeeded Gregory of Nazianzus in the imperial see. Jerome, for his part, met Amphilochius in Constantinople. This example illustrates the multiple interrelations between Christian aristocrats, intellectuals, and clergymen who had adopted the Nicene definition of orthodoxy and devoted themselves to the ascetic ideals. It is also worth mentioning that Nebridius' son by his first marriage is praised for his outstanding ascetic virtues, his contempt of wealth and his charitable relief of the poor. His widow, Salvina, is advised by Jerome to honour his memory by refusing a second marriage and practising strict asceticism.[19]

Nebridius was not an isolated case. Other distinguished members of the Theodosian court took a fancy to the ascetic movement and lavished favours upon its intellectual representatives.[20] There are good grounds for believing that Jerome, during his stay in Constantinople, succeeded in establishing new contacts with powerful friends and subsequently with Spanish associates of the emperor Theodosius, like the Praetorian Prefect of Italy in 395, Nummius Aemilianus Dexter, who received the dedication of his *De viris illustribus*.[21] Nebridius and others granted their favour and benevolence to Jerome, regarding him as an ambitious man who was capable of propagating ascetic ideas and Nicene dogma in fine-sounding language. In later years, these relations were crucial for Jerome's ambitious literary projects, his ascetic community in Bethlehem, and his survival in the bitter quarrels with Rufinus during the Origenist controversy. The case of Evagrius has illustrated the function of spiritual support and material assistance for spreading theological concepts and new forms of living. Jerome's stay in the eastern part of the Roman Empire at the end of the 370s and the beginning of the 380s thus exemplifies the function of traditional patronage structures in the theological and ascetic discourse of the fourth century.

Jerome's arrival at Constantinople around the year 380 was almost perfectly timed. Once again in his life, he was in the right place at the right moment. Theodosius had just begun to enforce his religious policy against paganism and Christian heresies and to strengthen links with exponents of Nicene orthodoxy. Members of the court society of Constantinople gave financial and ideological support to the ascetic movement and posed as influential patrons of the intellectual avantgarde of asceticism. But, how did Jerome succeed in calling the attention of the Christian court society of Theodosian Constantinople to his person? Certainly, Jerome could promote himself as the protégé of the Antiochene grandee Evagrius and of the 'Nicene' bishop Paulinus. But, this personal network cannot fully explain his impressive ecclesiastical career in the aftermath of the council of Constantinople. It must furthermore be noted that, during his time in the east, Jerome laid the foundation of his recognition as a Christian scholar and writer. We should hence be well advised to have a look at the major works that Jerome composed in Constantinople and, beyond that, in the eastern part of the Roman Empire, to define their target groups and to comprehend the reasons for their immense success.

In the *Life of Paul the First Hermit*, Jerome described the exemplary ascetic virtues and achievements of his protagonist and invited the reader to imitate the saintly hermit.[22] As the title proclaims, the object of the booklet is to prove that the famous Antony, who was believed to have been the first hermit, had in fact had a predecessor in Paul of Thebes (in Upper Egypt). A literary masterpiece, skilfully composed and extremely entertaining, the *vita* obviously enjoyed great popularity immediately upon its publication.[23] Deliberately revising the ideals of Athanasius' *Life of Antony*, which had been freely translated into Latin by Evagrius, Jerome insisted that Paul, unlike Antony, had received an excellent traditional training. It is obvious that the *Life of Paul the First Hermit* was addressed to a public of educated Christians who were themselves interested in the ascetic movement. Jerome, in a brilliant antithesis, characterized the expected audience at the end of his work:

> I may be permitted at the end of this little treatise to ask those who do not know the extent of their possessions, who adorn their homes with marble, who string house to house and field to field, what did this old man in his nakedness ever lack? Your drinking vessels are of precious stones; he satisfied thirst with the hollow of his hand. Your tunics are trimmed with gold; he had not the clothing of the meanest of your slaves. But on the other hand, poor though he was, Paradise is open to him; you with all your gold will be received into Gehenna. He, though naked, yet kept the robe of Christ; you, clad in your silks, have lost the vestures of Christ. Paul lies covered with worthless dust, but will rise again to glory; over you are raised costly tombs, but both you and your wealth are doomed to burning. Have a care, I pray you, at least have a care for the riches you love. Why are even the grave-clothes of your dead made of gold? Why does not your vaunting cease even amid mourning and tears? Cannot the carcases of rich men decay except in silk?[24]

Jerome's *Life* is evidence for a monastic practice of belles-lettres[25] that combined religious edification and ascetic instruction with pleasant entertainment. After Jerome had made his public debut as an author with the exciting story of the miraculous rescue of the Christian woman of Vercelli,[26] he turned to the *lecture à la mode*[27] of the Christian upper classes, imitating the literary model and success of the *Vita Antonii* and its Latin translations. By virtue of its literary qualities and the fact that Jerome had written the life of the supposed first hermit, the *Vita Pauli* was able to replace the earlier Latin versions of the Athanasian biography, which had so far been the only accessible writings on this topic in the western part of the Empire. Jerome's fame as a writer of the ascetic movement was founded upon his first *Life* and later increased through the other two *Lives*, the *Vita Hilarionis* and the *Vita Malchi*, and many relevant treatises and letters. The contemporary genesis of an occidental monasticism explains Jerome's first best-seller. For he was the first Christian writer to respond to the lack of an authentic Latin monk's biography.

Although the book was sent to his aged friend Paulus of Concordia in northern Italy and although Jerome pretended to have adopted a simple style,[28] we may assume that this work delighted the western associates of the Theodosian court at Constantinople who took an interest in ascetic literature. Jerome tried to reach the same group of potential benefactors with another genre, his Latin translations of Greek theological writings. His immense success in this field had four reasons. First, the Latin west was then by no means able to match the abundant Greek Christian literature. Second, the theological discourse of the fourth century intensified academic interest in Greek scholarship, and it became necessary for westerners to tackle the complex philosophical and theological systems of the Greek Fathers. Third, more and more Latin-speaking Christians turned to ascetic ideals originating in the east. Finally, the number of intellectuals in the western Empire, who had a good command of both Latin and Greek, was steadily declining.[29] Jerome thus continued the practice of some earlier western bishops, like Eusebius of Vercelli and Hilary of Poitiers, who were exiled in the east during the Arian controversy and had succeeded in conveying Greek theological concepts to the west through their translations. Since Jerome mastered Greek and had familiarized himself with Greek Christian literature, he was able to put Latin-speaking Christians greatly in his debt as an *interpres Christianus*.

Jerome commenced this career by translating into Latin Origen's thirty-seven homilies on Isaiah, Jeremiah, and Ezekiel. In a dedicatory letter to his friend Vincentius, who was the first recipient of his version of the homilies on Ezekiel, Jerome drew an outline for a translation of Origen's exegetical work, to 'make available to Roman ears the man who, in the judgement of Didymus, blind but so clear-sighted, is second only to the Apostles as teacher of the churches.'[30] Unfortunately, he continues, a serious affliction of his eyes, caused by continuous reading, prevented him from executing the job, which was also made more difficult by the 'the lack of stenographers (*notariorum penuria*), since shortage of cash has removed this aid too.'[31] This ambitious programme, which was never carried out because Jerome became occupied with other projects, needed Vincentius' financial support. Paying the bill for stenographers was an important task of wealthy sponsors, who were also responsible for copying and disseminating the writings they paid for. Vincentius, however, was presbyter in Constantinople[32] and came, like Jerome, from the western Empire, as may be deduced from his request for a translation of Origen's work into Latin. Thus, he was associated with the Latin-speaking orthodox Christians of Constantinople and able to propagate Jerome's versions among the westerners at the Theodosian court. Vincentius may also have paid the *notarii* whom Jerome needed in order to translate the fourteen homilies on the prophet Jeremiah, completed some time previously, and Eusebius' *Chronicle*. The latter work is also dedicated to Vincentius and to a certain Gallienus who is otherwise unknown.[33]

Jerome not only translated into Latin the *Chronicle* of Eusebius of Caesarea (i.e. its second part, the synchronistic tables of relevant pagan and Christian dates), but added a continuation of the work from 327 to 378, ending with the death of the emperor Valens. He also enlarged the Eusebian work, inserting events and names that were of interest to western readers.[34] Modern scholarship has tried to reconstruct Jerome's sources for these supplements.[35] With the translation and continuation of Eusebius' *Chronicle*, however, Jerome for the first time made a chronologically structured compendium of world history from Abraham down to the year AD 378 available to Latin Christianity. Up to this date, the western church possessed no work that could be compared to the outstanding chronographical achievement of the bishop of Caesarea. The immediate success of Jerome's *Chronicle* among Latin-speaking Christians causes no surprise. As in the case of the *Life of Paul*, Jerome responded to the lack of, and need for, a certain genre in the Christian literature of the Latin west and undertook to supply the want by imitating a Greek model. But he was not content to present a world history to Latin readers that, in accordance with Eusebius' work, claimed the superiority of the Jewish–Christian tradition. His *Chronicle*, especially its supplements, had to meet the expectations of a well-defined audience. Jerome, therefore, inserted the names of Latin authors, Roman emperors, and Christian bishops, and mentioned religious, political, and military events of the western Empire. He did not leave it at that. In addition to new entries of general interest, he included numerous other details which, at first sight, seem to be irrelevant, biased, subjective, and gossipy. Jerome has often been blamed on this score.[36] This criticism, however, ignores the fact that the additional entries were deliberately fitted into the Latin chronicle in order to attract certain kinds of reader; they are, in other words, the precondition of its literary success.

By stigmatizing some eastern bishops, like Meletius, as Arian heretics, Jerome adopted the position held by the majority of politicians and theologians of the Latin church.[37] The *Chronicle* depicts the heroic struggle of orthodox bishops and clergymen, who did not submit to threats and banishments of heretical emperors, against Arianism. Moreover, Jerome notes various events relating to the history of asceticism and monasticism[38] and thus responds to the interest in these new forms of living, which became increasingly popular among Christian men of letters in the western Empire during the later fourth century. The references to miscellaneous and miraculous phenomena, such as hailstorms and curious rain showers,[39] are simply meant to entertain the reader. The inclusion of celebrated Latin authors and of illustrious contemporary orators, rhetoricians, and grammarians,[40] who quite often came from Gaul, reflects the literary and intellectual preferences of an educated audience. Finally, there is a considerable number of entries that highlight important patrons and personal friends, like Pompeianus, an ancestor of his 'dearest Evagrius',[41] or Jerome's Roman *praeceptor*, the grammarian Donatus,[42] or the circle of friends living together in a monastic community in Aquileia 'like a band of blessed ones' (*quasi chorus beatorum*),[43] or Florentinus, Bonosus, Rufinus, who are honoured through their monastic life (*insignes monachi habentur*),[44] or Rufinus' rich *patrona* Melania the Elder.[45]

Jerome's purpose in translating and supplementing Eusebius' *Chronicle* is easily understood. He composed a chronological compendium that served the needs of Christian *litterati* in the western Empire who maintained the position of Nicene orthodoxy and sympathized with the ascetic movement. His additions observed their literary taste and their theological experience. Vincentius and Gallienus, the dedicatees and the 'friends', who are mentioned in the *Chronicle*, were encouraged to spread the work. Jerome's literary concept of a Latin chronicle could win many benefactors at once.[46]

But Jerome flew even higher. His masterpiece of propaganda was to reach the court of Theodosius. At the end of the preface, Jerome reveals that he has ended with the sixth consulship of the emperor Valens and the second of the emperor Valentinian II (i.e. the year AD 378), since he has 'reserved the remaining period of Gratian and Theodosius for a wider historical survey.'[47] The announcement of a separate description of the reign of Gratian and Theodosius (i.e. of a new imperial history), at such a prominent place perfectly fits with Jerome's aspirations to be successful as a best-selling Christian author in the Latin west. This statement directed the attention of the western entourage of Theodosius to a man of great literary talent, of some ascetic experience and firm convictions. Perhaps Jerome had high hopes in those days of obtaining access to the inner circle of the emperor's friends (*amici imperatoris*) and thereby promoting his ecclesiastical career. The *Chronicle*, however, is by no means a 'tumultuous work', as it is called in the preface.[48] This *captatio benevolentiae* should not obscure the fact that the work is coherent and that the presentation of the material is convincing. Jerome used his alleged *opus tumultuarium* to advance the causes of Nicene orthodoxy and Christian asceticism. To all those who identified themselves with the *fides catholica* and the ascetic movement, Jerome presented himself through his *Chronicle* as a highly capable author, worthy of support.

Finally, Jerome, during his time in the eastern Empire, tried to make a reputation for himself not only as a biographer and a translator,[49] but also as an exegete.[50] He published a short treatise on the vision that Isaiah had of God and of the two Seraphim, one of whom touched the prophet's mouth with a glowing coal (Is. 6, 1–9). It has come down in two letters, and some of the manuscripts give the Roman bishop Damasus as addressee.[51] Whether Jerome had already sent the *tractatus* from Constantinople to Rome, or whether he added the heading *Ad Damasum* during his time in the western capital or even later, cannot be decided. But, it should be noted that this little study had the special purpose of displaying a learned commentator of the Bible. Jerome mentioned the various readings of the Septuagint and other Greek versions of the Old Testament, referred to the Hebrew original, and discussed the Hebrew meaning of the names Seraphim and *Jahve Sabaoth*. The exegesis, however, seems to be strongly dependent on earlier expositors, especially Origen, and prompts doubts as regards the author's theological and exegetical originality. Nevertheless, Jerome seems to have been aware at this early time of the importance of a return to the Hebrew text of the Old Testament.[52]

Jerome thus began the literary production for which he was and still is distinguished in the eastern part of the *Imperium Romanum*. He appeared as a well-read exegete with a profound command of languages, as a talented translator of Greek theological works, and as a capable author of ascetic and monastic literature. Thanks to his linguistic competence, Jerome was able to adopt eclectically the works of Greek Christian writers and to endow the Latin west with new literary genres. At the same time, he wanted to make himself the favourite author of wealthy Christian intellectuals, who in their turn were able to support his ambitious projects and ensure his advancement. The foundation of his career as an advocate of the ascetic movement and of Nicene orthodoxy, as a translator and commentator of the Bible, and as an intermediary between western and eastern theology was laid in the Eastern Empire, in Antioch, Maronia, and, above all, Constantinople. After his early and immediate success as a leading western protagonist of eastern religious piety, Jerome decided to make a profession as a Christian writer.

4

ROME

High-Flying Hopes and Deep Fall

> I would have wished him a wife; so many things he would
> have written in a different way.
>
> Martin Luther

In the late summer of 382, Jerome, the ambitious Christian author, left Constantinople, where he had translated into Latin Eusebius' *Chronicle* and established relations with many influential church politicians and even with the imperial court. He accompanied Paulinus of Antioch and Epiphanius of Salamis as interpreter and adviser. They were heading for Rome to attend a synod that Ambrose of Milan had persuaded the Emperor Gratian to convoke.[1] Paulinus intended to protest at the court of the Roman bishop Damasus against the decision of the council of Constantinople that had approved his rival Meletius. Once the eastern delegation reached Rome, they were accommodated by families of the senatorial aristocracy. Epiphanius was a guest of the young widow Paula who, like her relative Marcella, had transformed her household into a domestic nunnery. There had been some form of western asceticism in Rome before Jerome arrived. During the fourth century, patterns of ascetic life exercised in Rome evolved under the influence of visitors from the east, especially through Athanasius, who spent some years in Rome during his second exile, and his successor Peter of Alexandria. Thus, the ascetic family homes, where a life of prayer and chastity was common, were often transformed into monastic communities.[2]

Although the synod was a failure, Jerome stayed on in Rome when Paulinus and Epiphanius returned to the east some months later. In the following four years, Jerome made a brilliant career, which ended abruptly in 385. First, the clever monk and multilingual scholar was noticed and favoured by bishop Damasus, who relied upon him for information about the complex ecclesiastical affairs of the Greek east.[3] Jerome is likely to have worked in the ecclesiastical archive, which was reorganized and housed in a new building under Damasus. He may have been responsible for drafting the official correspondence with the Greek churches, and perhaps Damasus asked him to comment upon synodal interpellations and inquiries from the eastern part of the Empire. Later generations have therefore depicted him as the bishop's secretary. Years later (409), Jerome himself wrote: 'I was helping bishop Damasus of Rome with his ecclesiastical correspondence and writing his answers to the questions referred to him by the councils of the east and west.'[4]

Damasus also consulted him on the interpretation of difficult points of Scripture,[5] encouraged him to translate Greek theologians like Origen and Didymus,[6] paid the bills for copyists, and, most important, commissioned him to revise the Latin text of the Gospels according to the Greek original:

> You urge me to make a new work out of an old one, and, as it were, to sit in judgement on the copies of the Scriptures now scattered throughout the whole world, and, because they differ from one another, you ask me to decide which of them agree with the Greek original. The labour is one of love, but at the same time both perilous and presumptuous; for in judging others, I must be myself judged by all; and how can I dare to change a language that is old and carry the world back in its hoary old age to the early days of its infancy? Is there a man, learned or unlearned, who will not, when he takes the volume into his hands, and perceives that what he reads does not suit his settled tastes, break out immediately into violent language, and call me a forger and a profane person for having the audacity to add anything to the ancient books, or to make any changes or corrections therein? Now there are two consoling reflections which enable me to bear the odium – in the first place, the command is given by you who are the supreme bishop; and, secondly, even on the showing of those who revile us, readings at variance with the early copies cannot be right. For if we are to pin our faith to the Latin texts, it is for our opponents to tell us which, for there are almost as many forms of texts as there are copies. If, on the other hand, we are to glean the truth from a comparison of many, why not go back to the original Greek and correct the mistakes introduced by inaccurate translators, and the blundering

alterations of confident but ignorant critics, and, further, all that has been inserted or changed by copyists more asleep than awake?'[7]

Jerome anticipated in this preface the criticism that his new translation of the Bible met in Rome and, later, in Bethlehem. For the moment, the powerful Roman bishop protected his challenging literary projects. But, Damasus also took a fancy to his protégé since both of them were disseminating the ideal of virginity and chastity in their writings. Damasus' sister, too, had dedicated herself to an ascetic life. The elegant style, the linguistic competence, and the ascetic zeal of the prolific author fascinated the bishop, who himself wrote fine epigrams, which are still extant in the Roman catacombs. They met with Jerome's approval: 'Damasus, bishop of Rome, had a fine talent for making verses and published many brief works in heroic metre.'[8]

Damasus opened the door for him to noble ladies who practised chastity in their family homes. Within a short period, Jerome became the centre of an ascetic circle that included Marcella, Asella, Lea, Paula and her daughters Blesilla and Eustochium. His letters and threnodies, which give touching portraits of late Roman women, illustrate their role in the conversion of the Roman aristocracy and have excited scholarly controversy concerning the extent to which the ascetic movement contributed to the emancipation of the *feminae clarissimae*.[9]

What could Jerome himself offer to attract the matrons' attention? First of all, he was able to convey the ascetic concepts of the east in fine-sounding language. A marvellous example of his rhetorical campaign for asceticism is his famous letter, more precisely, his treatise 'On the preservation of virginity' (*De virginitate servanda*) addressed to Eustochium,[10] but aimed at a wider audience, in which he praised the virgin as the Lord's bride, laid down exact rules for her daily conduct and defined virginity as the highest level of asceticism. Classical allusions, biblical references, extensive borrowing, and ascetic examples are the central elements of his literary style.[11] But, it was not sufficient to combine Scripture and classical literature and to give practical advice. Jerome had to rewrite the story of his limited ascetic self-experience. He integrated the episode in his handbook in which Eustochium was told to remain in the safety of her home, to avoid ostentation, to be submissive to the guidance of an older man of sanctity, and to be surrounded by a pious *familia*, whose life and daily tasks she shared completely:

I would not have you court the company of married women or visit the houses of the high-born. I would not have you look too often on what you despised when you desired to be a virgin. Even if women of the world plume themselves if their husbands are judges or in other high positions, even if an eager crowd of visitors flocks to greet the wife of the emperor, why should you insult your husband? Why should you, God's bride, hasten to visit the wife of a mere man? [...] Avoid men also when you see them loaded with chains and wearing their hair long like a woman's, contrary to the Apostle's precept, not to speak of beards like those of goats, black cloaks, and bare feet braving the cold. All these things are plain signs of the devil. [...] Let your companions be those who are pale of face and thin with fasting, approved by their years and their conduct.[12]

In this treatise, as in other epistles, Jerome encouraged ascetic seclusion, sexual abstinence, fasting, and scriptural meditation.[13] He urged the superiority of virginity to marriage and the monastic to civic life, advocated the renunciation of one's property, recommended prayer and Bible reading, and gave dietary advice. In Rome, Jerome established himself as an educated churchman and developed to the full his interpretation of the ascetic life. His experience in the desert of Chalcis contributed to his contemporaries' image of Jerome as a spiritual teacher and ascetic exemplar. At the same time, he sought to reconcile Christian virtues with the traditional primacy of the Roman senatorial aristocracy: 'Learn in this respect a holy arrogance (*sancta superbia*); know that you are better than all of them.'[14] Ascetic virtues now guaranteed the superiority of the Roman ladies and transcended their noble origin. While pagan relatives strongly opposed their conversions to asceticism, Jerome Christianized aristocratic competitiveness and emphasized that the holy women of asceticism surpassed the old nobility of birth and office: 'Noble in family, she was much nobler still in holiness (*nobilis genere, sed multo nobilior sanctitate*).'[15] The better part of mankind, to use Symmachus' definition of the senatorial aristocracy,[16] still identified itself by impressive genealogies, immense fortunes, overwhelming prestige, and social munificence; Jerome just added ascetic values, above all sexual renunciation and virginity.

Moreover, the *Christiani senatus lumina*, the lights of the Christian senate,[17] were captivated by Jerome's linguistic and exegetical competence. Not only did he legitimize his ascetic concepts through scriptural commonplaces taken from the Song of Songs and the

Pauline Epistles, Jerome also presented himself as a learned commentator on the Bible. Special attention should be directed to his correspondence with the Roman aristocrat Marcella, who herself published studies on the Old and New Testament and whose exegetical–theological expertise attained a remarkably high intellectual level. Marcella, having been widowed at an early age, held firm to her decision, against the resistance of her family, to live an ascetic life and to group around herself, in her house on the Aventine, a circle of like-minded Christian women.[18] She may have paid Jerome for some of his treatises on the interpretation of difficult biblical passages and the meaning of Hebrew words.

As in his ascetic papers, Jerome borrowed extensively from earlier theological writers. But his plagiarism did not damage his image. He knew how to incite 'the ardent love of the divine Scriptures'[19] and even persuaded some of his senatorial friends to learn Hebrew. His most challenging project was the adaptation of Origen for Latin readers. He continued his propaganda for the great Alexandrian scholar, which he had already spread in Constantinople. In his letters to Marcella, Jerome, without any reservation, applauded Origen for his Old Testament scholarship and his philological recourse to the Hebrew original. He celebrated Origen's restless biblical work and criticized Latin writers for ignoring Origen's outstanding theological legacy:

> Do you see how the labours of this one man have surpassed those of all previous writers, Greek and Latin? Who has ever managed to read all that he has written? Yet what reward have his exertions brought him? He stands condemned by his bishop, Demetrius, only the bishops of Palestine, Arabia, Phoenicia, and Achaia dissenting. Rome consents to his condemnation, she convenes her senate to censure him, not – as the rabid hounds who now pursue him cry – because of the novelty or heterodoxy of his doctrines, but because men could not tolerate the incomparable eloquence and knowledge which, when once he opened his lips, made others seem dumb.'[20]

Jerome emulated the role that the Alexandrian Biblicist played in the eastern churches, and depicted himself as a Latin Origen.[21] Like his paragon, he wrote on a wide range of topics. His instruction for the preservation of virginity became so famous, or notorious, that, according to Rufinus, even pagan readers copied it.[22] He also abandoned his former plan of writing a history of the Empire under Gratian and Theodosius the Great, especially since the Roman aristocrats did not seem to be very fond of historiographical work.[23]

His 'taskmaster' and 'slave-driver' Marcella,[24] and some senatorial men like Jerome's fellow-student Pammachius and the latter's friend Oceanus, combined the ascetic vocation and the *lectio divina* under Jerome's intellectual guidance. The representatives of the higher echelons in the city of Rome propagated the ideals of an ascetically orientated Christianity to which they themselves had subscribed. Jerome provided theoretical legitimation and practical advice. His traditional education, brilliant style, linguistic capacity, and his knowledge of Greek theology made him popular with the senatorial aristocracy of Rome who were also responsible for spreading his work. His *epistulae* and *tractatus*, like those of other contemporaries, were not only written for discussion within private circles, but copied and circulated, and thus attained wide publicity and guaranteed ideological as well as material support. The exploitation of effective sources of influence and patronage enabled Jerome to realize his ambitious literary plans and to communicate his programme of *studia scripturarum* combining ascetic reading and Greek exegesis.

Jerome could have enjoyed life in Rome. He was on good terms with some powerful patronesses and patrons, and Damasus also protected him. With all due modesty, Jerome later described his position in the bishop's entourage as follows: 'I was the spokesman of Damasus.'[25] And he added: 'Men called me saintly; men called me humble and eloquent.' Almost everybody would have judged him worthy of the highest office in the church.[26] But he did not become bishop of Rome. His militant campaigns for asceticism not only brought him admirers and supporters, but also enemies in many places. The oriental ascetic ideas and practices Jerome propagated vigorously offended pagan aristocrats and moderate Christians. With the same ardour and harshness, he crusaded against luxury of the better-off, coquetry of matrons, worldliness of the clergy, and hypocrisy of monks. His sharpest weapon was satire.[27] Impressively, he expressed his indignation about wealthy widows and avaricious priests:

> Look at them as they ride in their capacious litters, a row of eunuchs walking in front of them, look at their red lips and their plump bodies, you would not think that they had lost a husband, you would fancy they were seeking one. Their houses are full of flatterers, full of guests. The very clergy, who ought to inspire them with respect by their teaching

and authority, kiss these ladies on the forehead, and then stretch out their hands – so that, if you did not know, you would think they were in the act of blessing – and to take wages for their visit (*salutatio*). The widows meanwhile, seeing that priests cannot do without them, are lifted up with pride; they know by experience what a husband's rule is like, and they prefer the liberty of widowhood. They call themselves chaste nuns, and after an immoderate dinner they dream of the Apostles.[28]

Jerome also ridiculed a noble lady standing in the basilica of the blessed Peter with a band of eunuchs in front of her. She exercised humility in public and was giving money to the poor, a coin apiece, 'with her own hand to increase her reputation of sanctity'. Each beggar received a penny. When an old woman ran forward to get a second coin, she received not a penny but the lady's fist in her face, 'and for her dreadful offence she had to pay with her blood.'[29] These citations describe the ecclesiastical patronage wielded by Christian women of the Roman senatorial aristocracy who welcomed their new clerical clientele for the formal morning call paid by the client on his patron (*salutatio*) and supported the poor through alms and welfare work. These ascetic aristocrats thus amalgamated their traditional liberality and public beneficence with the new Christian command for charity.

In Rome, as in other cities of the Roman Empire, there was tough competition among bishops, priests, and monks for the favour of noble women. Damasus had been so successful in establishing contacts with wealthy Christian ladies that his opponents called him 'the matron's ear-pick' (*auriscalpius matronarum*).[30] Quite a few servants of God owed their promotion within the clerical hierarchy to the influence of women.[31] When Damasus' predecessor Liberius was exiled by Constantius, Roman *nobiles feminae* asked the emperor when he visited Rome in 357 to permit the bishop to reoccupy his see.[32] In 370, an imperial rescript was addressed to Damasus that penalized legacy-hunting clergymen who, under the pretext of religion, misused the confidence of rich matrons to obtain their donations.[33] No wonder that the pagan city prefect Vettius Agorius Praetextatus said to Damasus in sport: 'Make me bishop of Rome, and I will be a Christian.'[34] A pagan historian like Ammianus Marcellinus also commented upon the ostentatious luxury of the new ecclesiastical elite sarcastically: 'They can ride in carriages, dress splendidly and outdo kings in the lavishness of their table.' They would be 'truly happy', he appended, if they were to despise urban life 'and follow the example of some provincial bishop' whose self-restraint in food and drink, rough clothes, and downcast eyes demonstrate to the supreme deity and his true worshippers the purity and modesty of their lives.[35]

Christian intellectuals and clerics entered into rivalry with other Christian groups for material and ideological backing granted by the Christianized elite of Rome. Jerome was certainly a talented and successful *cliens*, but he was just one among many others. His aggressive polemic against 'certain worthless creatures (*quidam homunculi*)', 'two-legged asses (*bipedes aselli*)' and 'mercenary priests (*nummarii sacerdotes*)'[36] among the holy brethren also reflects the harsh struggle for powerful and propertied *patronae*. And every inch of the ground was contested. Valentinians, Marcionites, Sabellians, Manichaeans, Luciferians, and other heterodox movements agitated in Rome. Domestic circles like the one of Marcella integrated heretical and orthodox groups.[37] Theological treatises and ascetic manuals were disseminated. Hardly any Christian author in the second half of the fourth century failed to write about virginity.[38] Competing programmes circulated in the quasi-monastic households of ascetic ladies. Jerome attacked not only worldly clergy, but also divergent theoretical and practical concepts of a Christian way of life. Helvidius, for instance, who denied the perpetual virginity of Mary and defended Christian marriage against celibacy, was dismissed in a ferocious pamphlet.[39] Virgins and widows visiting married women's houses were called idle and inquisitive.[40] Novatianists and Montanists were ostracized.[41] Special emphasis was put on the *monachisme hippie* (hippy monasticism)[42] of the *agapetae* or *subintroductae* (i.e. of women who lived together with men in spiritual marriage):

> Whence come these unwedded wives, these new types of concubines, these, as I will call them, one-man harlots? They live in the same house; they occupy the same chamber and often the same bed, and yet they call us suspicious if we think anything is wrong. A brother leaves his virgin sister; a virgin, slighting her unmarried brother, seeks a brother in a stranger. Both alike pretend to have but one object, to look for spiritual consolation among strangers; but their real aim is to indulge in sexual intercourse.'[43]

But Jerome, too, came under fire. His tactless pen and his ascetic zeal outraged many of the Roman clergy. Some accused him of having changed the Lord's words with his new translation of the Gospels.[44] Some were disgusted by his discourse on virginity, like Damasus' successor Siricius, a former Roman deacon. Jerome's spiritual influence on high-ranking women aroused suspicion; rumours arose. He complained that the disgrace of a false charge was laid upon him. 'I am said to be a scandal, a slippery turncoat and a liar using Satan's art to deceive others.'[45] The Roman patricians were not amused by one of Jerome's favourite topics, that Roman ladies should forget their social standing, renounce their traditional habits, neglect their clothing, and perform their servants' job; they were asked to carry water, hew wood, trim lamps, light fires, sweep floors, clean vegetables, lay tables, and wash dishes.[46] Such a lifestyle stood in sharp contrast to the traditional expectations of class and birth. The renunciation of family property for various charities was opposed by non-ascetic members of the kinship. Finally, the aristocratic clan feared that Jerome's campaign for chastity would prevent their wives and daughters from fulfilling their vocation of motherhood and thus securing the family tradition. Hence, they slandered Jerome as a sorcerer and a seducer who 'should be transported to the ends of the earth'.[47] When Blesilla, Paula's eldest daughter, who was persuaded to live a life of abstinence after her husband's death, died three months after her conversion, it was murmured that the young widow had died from fasting. At the funeral, her mother was carried out fainting and the crowd whispered: 'How long must we refrain from driving these detestable monks out of Rome? Why do we not stone them or hurl them into the Tiber? They have misled this unhappy lady; that she is not a nun from choice is clear.'[48]

When Damasus, his patron, died on 11 December 384, a powerful opposition forced Jerome to leave Rome. There is reason to think that a council of the Roman clergy was summoned to exile the ascetic fomenter who in later days calumniated the 'senate of the Pharisees' that drove him from Rome.[49] Perhaps Ambrose participated in this meeting; at least the influential bishop of Milan did not grant his benevolence to the fallen priest, who was deeply disappointed by this and, some years later, accused Ambrose of having plagiarized Didymus' treatise 'On the Holy Spirit' for his own work on the subject. Jerome teased his rival as an ugly crow who adorned himself with borrowed plumes, and continued to heap venomous attacks upon him.[50] In summer 385, Jerome finally boarded ship in Portus, the harbour of Rome, to sail to the east. He was never to see the city he now called Babylon[51] again.

Modern scholarship has often overestimated Jerome's position within the Christian society of Rome in the 380s by relying upon his own testimony, in which he depicts himself as an influential 'spiritual guide and scriptural teacher of a remarkable group of Roman ladies.'[52] In fact, his position was never unchallenged. Jerome was a highly controversial exponent of extreme ascetic conduct. The evidence provided in the letters written during his stay in Rome, and later in Bethlehem, shows that the Roman topography of the ascetic movement was complex and became even more complex when non-ascetic Christian groups were integrated into the discourse of dissent. Students of the Christian communities in Rome in the second half of the fourth century, or of the Roman noble women mentioned by Jerome, would therefore be well advised not to reproduce Jerome's self-invention. Marcella was much more emancipated than Jerome wanted to lead posterity to believe. It is certainly clear that she discussed Montanist ideas, read the writings of many prominent Christian authors, formed her own opinions in theological and church–political matters and corresponded with various prominent theologians of her day. Jerome was reckoned among her theological counsellors, but he was by no means the only one who profited intellectually and financially from this remarkable Roman lady.

5

BETHLEHEM (I)

The Origenist Controversy

Yesterday, all my troubles seemed so far away.
John Lennon/Paul McCartney

Having left Rome in August 385, Jerome set out for the east again and, after an edifying tour of the holy places, established himself in Bethlehem in 386. During the following three years, Jerome, sponsored by the Roman aristocrats Paula and Eustochium, who had followed him into exile, founded a monastery, a convent, and a hospice for pious travellers. Servants, who had accompanied the illustrious group, were now enlisted as the first monks and nuns.[1] The withdrawal to Bethlehem did not imply renunciation of the world. The decision to settle at the birthplace of Christ and to build Paula's convent next to the Church of the Nativity promised a lively exchange with wealthy western visitors from the east and the west, who received a warm welcome at the hospice.[2] Sometimes, Jerome even complained about masses of pilgrims distracting him from work.[3]

His forced departure from Rome was in no way followed by the collapse of the ascetic network carefully constructed by Jerome during his stay in Rome. Letters, treatises, commentaries, and handbooks were addressed to influential Italian patrons like Marcella and Pammachius, who paid for the copyists and secured the distribution of Jerome's work. Messengers were sent on special missions delivering orders and inquiries and keeping Jerome in touch with the Christian circles of the western world. Their main task was to maintain communication between Palestine and Italy. His Roman friends were also in contact with ascetic groups in northern Italy, Gaul, and Spain whom Jerome approached after he had taken up residence in Bethlehem.[4]

His works of this period responded to the intellectual needs and literary interests of a constantly increasing number of Christians of birth, eloquence, and wealth, as Jerome himself once pointedly remarked;[5] that is, of ecclesiastical and secular dignitaries, who advocated the theological tenets of the *fides catholica* and supported the ascetic movement. From among such people – men and women whose prestige and influence, according to Paulinus of Nola, rested on honour, education, and possessions[6] – the supporters of the ambitious author were recruited. The bond of ascetic and orthodox friendship was now strengthened by an exchange of letters.

At Bethlehem, the erudite monk was occupied with the translation of Greek theologians, above all of Origen, and started to compose learned handbooks and commentaries on the Scripture and to translate the Old Testament into Latin from the original languages.[7] He wrote the *Life of Hilarion*, a native of Thabata near Gaza and son of pagan parents, who allegedly founded the first monastic community in Palestine. Hilarion was said by Jerome to have been known for his biblical learning and his literary education and mirrored Jerome's perception of himself as the ideal monk–scholar.

In 392 or 393, Jerome published his *Lives of Famous Men*, which contains 135 Christian authors from Peter to himself. In fact more a catalogue, as Erasmus had already noted, than a literary history, it was meant to demonstrate to the ignorant pagan public that the church had men of great learning. This handbook of ecclesiastical writers, which was dedicated to his powerful friend Nummius Aemilianus Dexter, followed the model of Suetonius. It named Greek, Latin, and Syriac authors, included heretics and even mentioned Jews and the pagan Seneca.[8] In another work, Jerome unleashed his venom against the monk Jovinian, who denied the superiority of virginity and widowhood to marriage and maintained that extreme abstinence did not make an ascetic champion holier than those baptized Christians who lived a normal life. Like Helvidius, he questioned the perpetual virginity of Mary. 'The Epicurus of Christians' was attacked in two books (*Against Jovinian*), which caused some annoyance at Rome, not only among Jovinian's adherents but also in the ascetic circles that were shocked by the violence of Jerome's polemic.[9]

Jerome was working day and night, corresponding with many Latin-speaking Christians, explaining obscure scriptural passages, giving pastoral advice, and fighting against heterodoxy. 'The heretics hate him, because he never desists from attacking them; the clerics hate him, because he assails their life and crimes. But beyond doubt, all the good admire and love him [...] He is always occupied in reading, always at his books with his whole heart: he takes no rest day or night; he is perpetually either reading or writing something,' a friend of Sulpicius Severus remarked after visiting Jerome in Bethlehem.[10] Jerome, the workaholic, would have thoroughly enjoyed such a portrayal of himself.

Just as Jerome had established himself in Palestine as learned oracle of western Christianity, the Origenist controversy broke out and seriously threatened his carefully erected reputation. The bitter quarrels about the orthodoxy of Origen's teaching would not be settled in Jerome's lifetime.[11] It was not until 553 that the debate came to an end, when the doctrine of the great Alexandrian theologian of the third century was anathematized by the Second Council of Constantinople. The first phase of the controversy was inaugurated by Epiphanius in 393, who was bishop of Salamis, the largest city of Cyprus, and a fierce fighter for the Lord's glory. His campaign in defence of orthodoxy was crystallized in his vitriolic *Panarion*, also known as the *Refutation of all the Heresies*, in which he banished every doctrine, from the beginning of the church, that he considered heretical. Jerome had met the militant heresy-hunter during his first stay in the east and then accompanied him to Rome in 382. On their route to the holy places, Jerome and Paula stopped in Cyprus, where they enjoyed the bishop's hospitality.

Almost twenty years after he had inserted Origen in his catalogue of heresies, Epiphanius was prepared to extirpate Origenism and decided to start in Palestine, his native country. Jerusalem was known to be a stronghold of Origenist teaching, where the clergy were fond of reading the works of Origen. Jerome's friend Rufinus and his patroness Melania the Elder, who had settled on the Mount of Olives, circulated Latin translations of his writings and were ready to oppose Epiphanius. In 393, they refused to sign a formal abjuration of Origen's errors, which the bishop of Salamis may have initiated. 'I do not accuse or change my teachers', Rufinus replied.[12]

And Jerome? Had he not just praised Origen's 'immortal genius'?[13] Had he not, in his collection of letters to Marcella,[14] announced that Origen's scholarship exercised a continuing fascination on him and reinforced his claim to be his Latin successor? Now, Epiphanius pointed his finger at Origen as 'the spiritual father of Arius and the root and parent of all heresies'.[15] Jerome caved in. Overnight, as it were, he changed his mind and was converted from an ardent admirer into a zealous opponent. Scholarship has tried hard to explain Jerome's dramatic volte-face, which also had considerable implications for his friendship with Rufinus. Some have argued that Jerome wanted to please Epiphanius.[16] But, it seems more likely that Epiphanius' witch-hunt disturbed him severely. If the Alexandrian theologian were condemned, then it was to be feared that he, the Latin Origen, would be banned along with him. That would have been the end of his far-reaching literary ambitions and the community in Bethlehem.[17] In the following years, therefore, Jerome tried hard to dissociate himself from Origen and to refute the charge of Origenism.

Probably in mid-September 393, Epiphanius visited Jerusalem and wanted to obtain a condemnation of Origen from its bishop, John. He was not very successful. The young clergymen ridiculed his request to 'denounce the perverse doctrines of Origen', jeered at 'the silly old man', 'grinned like dogs, wrinkled their noses, scratched their heads, and nodded to one another'.[18] The quarrel with the bishop of Jerusalem soon became worse when, in early summer 394, a frustrated Epiphanius ordained Jerome's brother Paulinian presbyter without calling in John in whose diocese Bethlehem lay. Jerome poured oil on to the fire when he translated a letter of Epiphanius into Latin, in which the latter vindicated his condemnation of Origen. Thus, the conflict, which so far had been limited to the east, was exhibited to western readers,[19] and Jerome was charged with having mistranslated the original Greek letter. John was disgusted with these machinations and Paulinian's ordination gave him a most welcome formal cause to intervene. Without further ado, he excommunicated Jerome and the insubordinate monks troubling the peace in Palestine and obtained a sentence of exile against Jerome from the imperial authorities.[20] There is some reason to think that the powerful official Rufinus, then Praetorian Prefect of the East, was involved in the proceedings; his assassination at the end of November 395 may have prevented the banishment from being carried out. And certainly the attention of the government was at that time likely to be directed to the incursions of the Huns into Asia Minor and not to an obscure ecclesiastical case in the Holy Land.

The debate over the nature of the Origen's teaching divided the monasteries of Palestine and aggravated the tensions between various nationalities and different ascetic groups. Origenism had so far been a subject of theological discussion, but was now transformed into an ecclesiastical and even political issue. It was a struggle for power. Elitist networks were involved in the controversy from the very beginning. Powerful friends and influential patrons served on both sides as advocates for the literary exponents of the debate and ensured the dissemination of polemical and theological statements. The controversy had become an international affair. It has been conjectured that this debate cost Jerome his friendship with Rufinus. But the rift may have occurred earlier, when the latter disapproved of Jerome's decision to

translate the Old Testament from the Hebrew original.[21] There was
also a certain amount of rivalry between the monasteries in Bethlehem
and Jerusalem, and Palladius, in his *Lausiac History*, pointed at the ill
will and envy between the groups.[22] Both Rufinus and Jerome were
anxious not to discourage wealthy patrons from supporting their communities and suppressed every possible doubt about their orthodoxy.
In 395, Jerome wrote to Paulinus of Nola, the offspring of a noble
Aquitainian family, who had just decided to lead a monastic life at the
tomb of St Felix at Nola in Campania. He warned him not to come to
Jerusalem, which he described as a worldly city full of prostitutes,
actors, and idlers.[23] Some months earlier, when he had still hoped to
persuade Paulinus to live in Bethlehem, he had lampooned his
powerful monastic antagonist on the Mount of Olives as Melania's
handmaid and theological ignoramus: 'Others – I blush to say – learn
of women what they are to teach men; and as if even this were not
enough, they boldly explain to others what they themselves by no
means understand.'[24]

When a letter of John, in which the bishop described in great detail
his view of the debate and Jerome's sudden change of heart, was read
in Rome and weakened his case, he answered with his most aggressive
pamphlet *Against John of Jerusalem* (397). Two or three years earlier
(394–5), Augustine launched his first attack against Jerome.[25] He
first questioned Jerome's exegesis, in his *Commentary on Galatians*, that
Paul's confrontation with Peter at Antioch (Gal. 2,11–14) was staged
to serve the expectations of both the Gentile and the Jewish Christians.
Then, he raised the issue of the authority and veracity of the Septuagint
and expressed his doubts about Jerome's decision to go back to the
Hebrew original when translating the Old Testament into Latin.[26] In
both instances, Jerome's approach had been influenced by Origen's
biblical scholarship, so that Augustine's enquiry forced Jerome to
define his relation to the Origenist tradition. When his first letter
failed to find its way to Bethlehem, Augustine asked Jerome again
and explicitly to specify Origen's false doctrines.

Some time later, in about 397, he reiterated, in greater detail, his reservations against Jerome's interpretation of the controversy between
Peter and Paul in Antioch and insisted that Jerome should provide
him with 'an explicit account of Origen's errors, which prove that a
man of his stature departed from the true faith.'[27] And he asked
Jerome to correct his views on Galatians, to 'sing a palinode.'[28] One
can imagine Jerome's perturbation when the epistle by the bishop of
Hippo reached him only after a long odyssey and by chance: a friend
of his had found a copy on an Adriatic island and learnt that Jerome's

enemies in Italy thoroughly enjoyed reading Augustine's letter. Wild rumours even said that he had written a book against Jerome![29] It took Augustine quite some time and effort to make plausible that he did not intend to provoke Jerome, but he still insisted that the latter should 'prove conclusively (*certa ratione*)' that he had interpreted the passage from the Apostle's letter accurately.[30] Jerome was not very willing to discuss the matter and supposed that Augustine had other motives:

> Friendship ought to be free from all suspicion and one should be able to talk to a friend as to a second self. Some of my friends, vessels of Christ, many of whom live at Jerusalem and in the holy places, suggested to me that this had not been done by you with complete frankness, but through desire for praise and fame and popularity, intending to become famous at my expense; that many might know that when you challenge me, I am afraid, and that when you, a man of learning, write to me, I keep quiet like an ignorant man, now that someone has been found who knew how to stop my garrulous tongue.[31]

Augustine was obviously not impressed by Jerome's learning and age. In his letters, which were read and copied in the circles of western Christianity, he openly questioned Jerome's orthodoxy. When challenging Jerome to recant, Augustine violated the conventions of Christian friendship based upon agreement in theological issues.[32] The exchange and publication of letters constituted and maintained complex networks, which were defined through friendship (or enmity). Augustine's sharpest weapon was his matter-of-fact opposition and friendly tone. Was there a better method to put pressure on the famous master of polemics? Indeed, Augustine's honey-coated sword (*litum melle gladium*)[33] was extremely difficult to parry, especially at a moment when Jerome was desperately struggling for his survival in the Origenistic controversy. Some ten years later, they were fighting side by side against Pelagianism,[34] politely discussing the origin of the human soul and the interpretation of James 2.10. Now, conformity and unanimity were displayed and they praised each other for their orthodox perseverance in the campaign against the heretics:

> You are famous throughout the world; the Catholics respect you and honour you as the second founder of the ancient

faith, while (and this is a sign of greater glory) all the heretics hate you and persecute me with equal hatred.[35]

At Easter 397, however, John of Jerusalem and Jerome were reconciled through the mediation of Theophilus of Alexandria who, at that time, was still a supporter of Origenism. But the peace did not last long. In the same year, Rufinus returned to Rome, where he began his literary production for the sake of Origen's rehabilitation, maintaining that unscrupulous forgers were interpolating dogmatic absurdities and heretical fallacies into the works of Origen. His translation of the *Apology* of Pamphilus and his own treatise on *The Falsification of the Books of Origen* were supposed to corroborate this theory. It was obvious that his accusations were directed against Epiphanius, who incessantly struggled to unmask the Alexandrian theologian as a heretic. In 398, Rufinus published in Rome his Latin translation of Origen's major study *On First Principles* or *Peri Archon*. In the preface, he explained his theory of translation, a topic Jerome, too, had dealt with some time before. The issue of falsifying the original and forging orthodox doctrine incited the discourse 'on the principles of good translation',[36] Thus, Rufinus:

> Wherever I have found something in his books contrary to the truth concerning the trinity which he has in other places spoken in a strictly orthodox sense, I have either omitted it as something foreign and interpolated, or set it down in terms agreeing with the rule of faith which we find him constantly assenting to. There are things, no doubt, which he has developed in somewhat obscure language, wishing to pass rapidly over them, and as addressing those who have experience and knowledge of such matters; in these cases I have made the passage clearer by adding words which I had read in other books of his where the matter was more fully treated. But I have added nothing of my own; I have only given him back his own words, though I have taken these words from other passages.'[37]

Rufinus further declared that he would continue the job, and the method, of a well-known 'brother' and 'colleague', who had rendered seventy homilies of Origen into Latin and announced even more translations to incite in everybody an avid desire for reading Origen. It was not too difficult to identify the anonymous translator to whom this request was made by bishop Damasus. Jerome's Roman circle,

who had by questionable methods secured the first draft of the translation, were immediately alarmed and sent a copy to Bethlehem, long
before Rufinus had it ready for publication. They asked Jerome to
publish his own version and added maliciously that Rufinus manipulated Jerome's reputation to spread the work of Origen.[38]

Jerome, having received his friends' message, did not hesitate to get
down to work. In 399, he published a literal translation of Origen's
On First Principles, which was, together with two letters, sent to
Rome. The one was destined for Rufinus, the other for his agents
Oceanus and Pammachius.[39] Whereas the epistle to Rufinus was
rather moderate in tone, the letter to his Roman allies, which was
written for public circulation, admitted and defended his former admiration of the Alexandrian theologian, but then impugned Origen's
propagators and charged them with heresy. Although he gave no
names, the attack was rightly considered to be directed against
Rufinus, who never received Jerome's personal letter since Jerome's
friends decided to withhold it.[40]

The controversy reached its climax when one year later (400) a
council at Alexandria convoked by Theophilus, who had, in the
meantime, become an apostate of Origenism, condemned Origen, the
'hydra of heresies', and, largely for political motives, expelled from
their monasteries the four monks who led the Origenist movement in
Egypt and were called 'Tall Brothers'. Jerome effusively congratulated
the Alexandrian patriarch on the success of his crusade against
Origenism,[41] and translated into Latin a series of paschal and synodical
letters in which the errors of Origen were listed and refuted.[42] In
Italy, however, the situation was still unsettled. There, Melania (who
had returned from the Holy Land in 400) and Rufinus were uniting
and enlarging their forces. The Roman lady used her far-reaching rela-
tionships throughout the western world, and even in Constantinople,
to promote the case of her protégé. We know that the ecclesiastical
politicians Chromatius of Aquileia, Gaudentius of Brescia, Siricius of
Rome, and Simplicianus of Milan were prepared to support them. A
war of propaganda was in progress: 'Why do you write books addressed to others against me, and spread them by your satellites
through the whole world?' Jerome asked later.[43]

On Jerome's side there were to be found Pammachius, Oceanus,
Marcella, who supported her Roman client (*cliens*) after some
hesitation,[44] and one Eusebius of Cremona, who carried incriminating
documents 'round to private houses, to ladies, to monasteries and to
Christian men one by one.'[45] The circles were linked through family
ties, patronage, ascetic devotion, and orthodox profession. Each side

aimed at winning new allies. Rufinus hoped for some time to attract Anastasius, bishop of Rome, as combatant, to whom he addressed a short treatise defending his position.[46] Also, John of Jerusalem wrote to his Roman colleague urging him to back Rufinus.[47]

The public debate between Jerome and Rufinus, which was followed by an ever-growing audience, culminated in two large apologetical works. First, Rufinus published his *Apology against Jerome* in two books (401), in which he clearly, but tediously, demonstrated Jerome's erstwhile and dogmatically untroubled admiration of Origen, his efforts at disguising the dependence on Origen in his commentary on the Epistle to the Ephesians[48] and his violation of the solemn oath he had sworn to the Judge that he would never again possess or read wordly books.[49] In addition, Rufinus defended his translation of *On First Principles*.[50] Jerome did not wait to possess a copy of the apologia. When rumours reached him, he sat down to write his polemical answers. His *Apology* (401) combined self-defence and assault and is another masterpiece of polemic. The argument is less compelling. Evidently, Rufinus replied in a private letter asking Jerome to put an end to his onslaughts and threatening him with disclosures and even a lawsuit. Jerome came back with a third, extremely vitriolic book of *Apology* (402): 'How can you dare to say that you are speaking as a Christian, not for display but for edification, when you set yourself in mature age to say things against your equal which a murderer could hardly say against a robber, or a whore against a prostitute or a buffoon against a farce-player?' At the end, he suggested an agreement on his terms: 'If you desire peace, lay down your arms. I can be at peace with one who shows kindness; I do not fear one who threatens me. Let us be at one in faith, and peace will follow immediately.'[51] Augustine was right in concluding that the controversy had ruined an exceptional friendship.[52]

Rufinus did not reply. He did not need to. His backing was strong enough to withstand Jerome's attacks, whose inconsistent handling of the debate had enlarged the number of his enemies, who also criticized his new translation of the Bible and his ascetic verve. The Renaissance scholar Sabellicus was surely wrong to observe that the writings of Rufinus were 'as the strumming of a flea to the trumpeting of the Indian elephant.'[53] His position as an original writer and successful translator could not be challenged by Jerome. At the invitation of Paulinus of Nola, for instance, he wrote a commentary on the *Benedictions of the Twelve Patriarchs*.[54] Jerome, on the contrary, continued to calumniate Rufinus by nasty sobriquets. He loved to call his former friend 'the scorpion', 'the gross swine,' and the 'grunting pig'

(*Grunnius*).[55] Even after Rufinus' death in 410, he rejoiced: 'The Scorpion lies under the soil of Sicily. [...] The many-headed hydra has at last ceased to hiss against me.'[56] Other enmities too were pursued. After a visit to Bethlehem, Vigilantius, a presbyter of Aquitaine, had attacked Jerome as an Origenist. Jerome replied with two letters and his *Against Vigilantius* (406), in which he nicknamed his opponent 'Dormitantius' (i.e. 'sleepyhead'), blamed him for repudiating the cult of relics, the observation of vigils, celibacy, and monasticism in south-west Gaul. 'Vigilantius has again opened his fetid lips and is vomiting out a torrent of filthy venom upon the relics of the holy martyrs,' Jerome observed, and recommended: 'The doctors should cut out his tongue or he should be put under treatment for insanity.'[57]

The outbreak of the controversy over Origen's orthodoxy moved Jerome to condemn his old hero and to deny, or at least play down, his earlier admiration. After 393, he tried to disconnect his literary programme from the Origenian *persona* and manoeuvred himself into a difficult situation that became even more difficult, since the great variety of the topics Origen dealt with led to a rather vague concept of Origenism, which could be applied to different theological positions. Jerome's solution, which artificially separated Origen's scriptural exegesis from his theological doctrine, did not convince everybody:

> Origen is a heretic, true; but what is that to me, who do not deny that he was heretical in very many points? He erred about the resurrection of the body, he erred about the condition of souls, he erred by supposing it possible that the devil may repent, and – an error more important than these – he declared in his commentary upon Isaiah that the Seraphim mentioned by the prophet are the divine Son and the Holy Ghost. If I did not allow that he erred or if I did not daily anathematize his errors I should be partaker of his fault. For while we receive what is good in his writings we must on no account bind ourselves to accept also what is evil. Still in many passages he has interpreted the scriptures well, has explained obscure places in the prophets, and has brought to light very great mysteries, both in the Old and in the New Testament. If then I have translated what is good in him and have either cut away or altered or ignored what is evil, am I to be regarded as guilty on the score that through me the Latins receive the good in his writings without knowing anything of the bad?[58]

Jerome, however, could weather out the severe crisis not because he had the better arguments and more vigorous polemic on his side, but because his Italian network provided financial means and personal resources throughout the controversy. Thus, the Origenist controversy is not only a story of personal rivalry, hostile insinuations, and rhetorical aggression, but also a splendid example of the social setting of a late antique Christian debate.

Jerome's character and doctrine remained disputed,[59] and only few contemporaries would have agreed with the Spaniard Hydatius who, continuing Jerome's *Chronicle* in the second half of the fifth century, characterized his predecessor as follows:

A man outstanding in all respects, left innumerable volumes of his work. He was highly skilled in Hebrew letters and it is written that he meditated constantly, both day and night, upon the law of the Lord. To the very end he pounded with the adamantine hammer of truth the sect of Pelagius along with its originator. His greatly esteemed works against these and other heretics are extant.'[60]

6

BETHLEHEM (II)

The Biblical Scholar

The great Jerome, the only scholar in the church universal
who had a perfect command of all learning both sacred and
heathen.

Erasmus

Albrecht Dürer, in an engraving of 1492, depicted the learned ascetic
and the translator of the Old and New Testament in his study dealing
with Latin, Greek, and Hebrew versions of the Bible.[1] Still, today,
Jerome's name is linked with Hebrew scholarship and, of course, the
Vulgate.[2] But, we must not forget that the passionate controversies
in Jerome's days about his rendering of the Old Testament *iuxta
Hebraeos* (i.e. according to the Hebrew text), and hence about the inspiration of the Septuagint and the Old Testament canon, had the consequence that the merit of his translations, including the Gospels, was
recognized only long after his death. Not until the ninth century was
his work accepted, and, even then, up to the thirteenth century,
monks and priests were still copying and reading the Old Latin
versions of the Scriptures. In Jerome's lifetime, his translation would
not even supersede the *Vetus Latina* in Italy, though Rome was the
place where he started to propagate his new interpretation with the
ideological and financial help of influential friends, who also maintained a large staff of copyists. Augustine, Cassiodorus, and Gregory
the Great, to give only three examples, used both versions at the same
time. And, in practice, the text of the Vulgate quickly became corrupted with passages taken from the Old Latin Bible. Among the
three oldest Gospel manuscripts of the Vulgate that date back to the
fifth century, there is only one that has not borrowed elements from
the *Vetus Latina*; the other two manuscripts have hybrid texts.[3]

Modern scholarship has been able to reconstruct Jerome's translations of the New and Old Testament. It has thus emerged that he

only revised the text of the Gospels, but not of Acts, the Epistles, and Revelation. The passages Jerome himself cites from these books of the New Testament very often differ from the text of the Vulgate. And in his commentaries on the Pauline Epistles to Philemon, the Galatians, the Ephesians, and Titus, which were written in 386 (i.e. shortly after the alleged revision of the New Testament[4]), Jerome never referred to his own translation, but only criticized an anonymous Latin interpreter on several occasions. His statement in *Famous Men* that he had translated the whole New Testament from Greek into Latin[5] might at best be understood as an intention that was never fully realized, unless one is prepared to explain it as another testimony to his amazing showmanship. The Vulgate version of Acts, the Pauline Epistles, and Revelation is now ascribed to an author working in Rome at the end of the fourth century; modern editors of the Old Latin versions in particular are prepared to identify this translator with Rufinus the Syrian, who is said to have been a friend of Jerome and Epiphanius of Salamis until he, at the beginning of the fifth century, went over to the Pelagian movement.[6]

Jerome, as we have already seen,[7] started his revision of the Bible with the translation of the Gospels during his stay in Rome. There, he also corrected the Latin text of the *Psalter* according to the Septuagint and boasted of his substantial corrections. Shortly after his settlement in Bethlehem, judging by his own testimony, he undertook to revise the *Psalter* again, but now according to the *Hexapla*, the edition of the Old Testament produced by Origen, in which the Hebrew text, a transliteration into Greek characters and four Greek versions were arranged in parallel columns. That important work Jerome could consult in the nearby library of Caesarea in Palestine.[8] The revised version was dedicated to Jerome's aristocratic friends, Paula and Eustochium.[9] Finally, about 392, he declared that he had translated the *Psalter* from the Hebrew text.[10]

Immediately after his arrival in Bethlehem, Jerome started work on a first version of the Old Testament, which was based upon the text of the Septuagint, more precisely on the Hexaplaric text of the Septuagint. The revision of the *Psalter* was followed by the *Book of Job*, which was also dedicated to Paula and Eustochium.[11] We also have the prefaces to the *Books of Solomon* (i.e. *Proverbs*, *Ecclesiastes*, and the *Song of Songs*), and to the *Chronicles*.[12] The text of these books, however, has not survived. Despite some isolated remarks suggesting that he had revised the whole canon of the Old Testament according to the Septuagint,[13] it is reasonable to assume, as Georg Grützmacher has already insisted, that Jerome's revision based upon the Septuagint and the *Hexapla*, respectively, only included the above-mentioned books of the Scriptures.[14]

This work had to remain unfinished since Jerome increasingly devoted himself to the Hebrew original or 'Hebrew verity (*Hebraica veritas*)'. About 390, convinced of the superiority of the Hebrew text, he started on a new Latin version of the complete Old Testament *iuxta Hebraeos*. Both the relative and the absolute chronology of his translations of the books of the Old Testament are controversial. In *Famous Men*, he states, 'I translated the Old Testament from the Hebrew.'[15] This is, along with the corresponding remark on his rendering of the New Testament, most certainly an exaggeration since, in his own preface to Joshua, Jerome said that he finished the translation of the Old Testament according to the Hebrew text about 405.[16] It appears that up to 392–3, Jerome had translated only the *Psalter*, the *Prophets*, the *Books of Samuel* and *Kings*, and *Job*.[17] The remaining books of the Hebrew canon, as well as the deuterocanonical books *Judith* and *Tobit*, were translated in the following fourteen years or so.

The prefaces, but also the commentaries and many epistles demonstrate the occasion, intention, technique and theory of translation, and especially the criticism his new translations of the Old Testament provoked.[18] The recourse to *Hebraica veritas* was firmly rejected by those who, like Epiphanius or Rufinus, recognized the Septuagint as the only true and legitimate, divinely inspired version of the Old Testament. In addition, those, like Augustine, who had doubts about the authority of the Septuagint nevertheless joined the critics, because the text was familiar to the congregation and a translation from the Greek version was checked more easily than one from the Hebrew original.[19]

The new Latin version of the Bible was an attempt at providing an educated Christian audience with a scholarly and accurate translation that also pleased the literary taste of an audience that was familiar with classical literature.[20] But, criticism forced Jerome to back it up with a vast programme of commentaries, dedicated to his Roman patrons, yet written for a wider public. His immense exegetical output was not only an answer to the growing need for intellectual studies on the Scriptures, but also part of his strategy of defending his new Latin Bible. At the same time, he tried to reconcile Christian exegesis with pagan literary standards.

He commented on many books of the Christian Bible and added special treatises, such as his *On Hebrew Names*,[21] the *Book of Places*,[22] and the *Hebrew Questions*.[23] The extent of Jerome's dependence, as an amazingly productive exegete, on both Greek and Latin predecessors is apparent. Again, Origen emerges as the inspirer of Jerome's textual criticism and exegesis of Scripture, even after the outbreak of the Origenist controversy. Vigilant readers among his contemporaries often discovered that Origen was his model. Jerome replied: 'What they consider a reproach, I regard as the highest praise, since I desire to imitate Origen who, I doubt not, is acceptable to all wise men.'[24] When Rufinus charged him with having plagiarized heterodox arguments in his commentary on the Epistle of Paul to the Ephesians, Jerome justified his method:

> What I have done in that and other commentaries is to develop both my own opinion and that of others, stating clearly which are heretical and which catholic. This is the common rule and custom of those who undertake to explain books in commentaries: They give at length in their exposition the various opinions, and explain what is thought by themselves and by others.[25]

In writing his commentaries, Jerome borrowed from virtually all the Christian biblical exegesis that was available to him.[26] But, he consulted Jewish advisers as well, who also assisted him in translating the Bible into Latin. Recent research has rightly stressed that Jerome as biblical scholar learned from Jewish exegesis at least as much as from Origen. Jerome's concept of *Hebraica veritas* was dependent on the help of Jewish scholars and exegetes.[27]

In fact, Jerome's approach to the works of preceding and contemporary writers was in no way different from his approach to secular literature. Many, if not most of the authors and their works he cited were quoted second-hand.[28] Even in Jerome's lifetime, Rufinus laughed at the amazing number of philosophers, historians, and poets whose works he pretended to have studied. Thus, Rufinus inquired how it could be possible that Jerome had read letters of Pythagoras, given that probably no single work of this philosopher had been preserved.[29] Jerome's reply was poor: 'I was speaking not of the books but of the tenets, with which I was able to acquaint myself through Cicero, Brutus, and Seneca.'[30]

Recognition of the extent of Jerome's carefully disguised plagiarism and patchwork method has naturally prompted doubt about his theological and exegetical originality. For that reason, many students of Jerome, in the last decades, have formed a negative opinion of the *doctor ecclesiae*. But, Jerome was entirely in line with the contemporary practice of both Christian and pagan authors when he extracted the writings of preceding authors. And, in the Latin west, he played an important role as an intermediary of Greek and Hebrew exegesis. Jerome's exegetical importance can properly be compared with the theological importance of Augustine.

The image of a learned exegete of Holy Scripture, promoted by Jerome himself, was absolutely necessary to obtain authority among, and support from, well-to-do Christians. Very much to the point here was his reputation as *vir trilinguis*, which underlay recognition of his prestige as a translator and commentator of Scripture, both by contemporaries and later generations. Hence, it is not surprising that, from the time of his stay in Rome, Jerome repeatedly and carefully depicted himself as a 'trilingual' scholar with a command of Latin, Greek, and Hebrew.[31] He also reports, of an earlier stage of his life in the desert of Chalcis, that he spoke fluent Syriac,[32] and often mentions that he was translating from the 'Chaldee' (i.e. from Aramaic).[33] Jerome was able to celebrate his knowledge of languages since hardly any of his contemporaries could come near to rivalling him:[34] his knowledge of the Hebrew tongue receives special mention in the literature of the time.[35] Although modern scholars have sometimes questioned Jerome's command of the language, a close examination of the evidence makes it more than likely that he at least knew some Hebrew.[36] I would conjecture that his Hebrew was at the same level as his Aramaic, which he could read and understand better than he could speak it.[37] He had perhaps only received elementary instruction in both languages. The numerous references to Hebrew scholars, among whom one, Baranina, is mentioned by name,[38] and Hebrew sources confirm that Jerome did not only have access to the Jewish tradition through Greek authors, but was in direct contact with Jews, who were helping him in translating the Old Testament and in solving exegetical problems. It was their excellence that enabled Jerome to propagate and to defend his notion of the Hebrew verity. Throughout almost all his time in Bethlehem, he was able to consult Jewish scholars; their importance is proved not least by the fact that Jerome spared no expense to employ them. Thus, he remarked: 'What trouble and money it cost me to get Baranina to teach me during the night.'[39] The bills for the language lessons and Hebrew scholars were, of course, paid by Jerome's wealthy sponsors.

Jerome's new Latin translation raised serious suspicions, as the famous incident of the gourd shows.[40] In Jonah 4.6, in the Hebrew text, a plant is mentioned called *qîqājôn*, which on God's command grew up fast in order to throw its shade over Jonah. Jerome translated the Hebrew word as *hedera*, ivy. As a result, he was heavily criticized in Rome because the Old Latin Bible rendered *qîqâjôn* as *cucurbita*, gourd, rather than Jerome's ivy. For that reason, an influential Roman opponent, probably a member of the senatorial aristocracy, accused him of sacrilege.[41] Jerome, driven onto the defensive, tried to refute the charge both by personal polemics and botanical, as well as philological, expertise. The plant, called *ciceia* in Syriac and Punic, he explained, was a fast-growing bush, which was to be found especially in dry places in Palestine; the Latin tongue had no equivalent so that, to avoid a new word, he had translated the expression with *hedera*, ivy, following the Greek versions of the *Hexapla*, which have *kissós* (ivy), and not with *cucurbita*, gourd, found in the Septuagint and the Old Latin version.[42] The new translation had not been criticized for linguistic, but for theological reasons: Jerome was attacked because his translation differed from the traditional (i.e. divinely inspired) reading of the Bible.

The affair was not settled then. Rufinus, in his *Apology*, sarcastically advised his readers that upon the ancient tombs the gourds should, for Jerome's sake, be replaced by ivy.[43] In Africa, too, the new rendering was found disturbing. The bishop of Oea (Tripoli) in Tripolitania had adopted Jerome's new translation of Jonah.[44] But, when the passage was read out in a church of his diocese, a tumult broke out since the word ivy was unfamiliar – the congregation expected the traditional gourd. It was even rumoured that the text was forged. Thus, some resident Jews were consulted who pronounced against Jerome's translation explaining that the reading of the Hebrew manuscripts corroborated the translation found in the Septuagint and the Old Latin version. As a result, the bishop had to erase the word. Augustine, who recorded the story, was seriously disturbed by the news of a protesting flock and tied up this event with his criticism of Jerome's translation of the Old Testament from the Hebrew. Jerome, in his reply, argued that the whole matter had been resolved for a long time, referred to the detailed philological and botanical observations in his commentary on Jonah, and, finally, assailed the Jews who 'through malice or ignorance (*malitia vel inperitia*)' pronounced in favour of the Septuagint. He concluded that his version was in correspondence with the Hebrew manuscripts.[45] In this case, a group of 'traditionalists' evidently challenged Jerome's 'modernizing' translation and accused him of an obvious mistranslation after consulting Jewish scholars, probably rabbis. In his refutation, Jerome defended his translation of *qîqâjôn* and countered criticism of his linguistic proficiency by emphasizing that he had conferred with Jewish experts, who had offered their assistance with difficult textual problems.[46]

But the most perilous charge Jerome had to face while translating the Old Testament according to the Hebrew text lay in the argument that he was abandoning the divinely inspired version of the Septuagint and thus Judaized the Old Testament. His decision for *Hebraica veritas* and the Jewish exegesis led to the accusation that he was deviating from Christian tradition. It was precisely this point that Rufinus made in his *Apology against Jerome*:

> This action is yours, my brother, yours alone. It is clear that no one in the church has been your companion or confederate in it, but only that Barrabas whom you mention so frequently. What other spirit than that of the Jews would dare to tamper with the records of the church which have been handed down from the Apostles? It is they, my brother, you who were most dear to me before you were taken captive by the Jews, it is they who are hurrying you into this abyss of evil.[47]

Jerome's campaign for the superiority of the Hebrew text threatened his entire programme of *studia scripturarum*. His dissenters even forged a letter, in which Jerome was said to have condemned his new Latin version from the Hebrew; when this document circulated in Africa, his Roman supporters were seriously disturbed.[48] The strong opposition might explain Jerome's different, even inconsistent remarks on the Septuagint, which are not only contingent upon the time but also upon the addressee of the work.[49] There is no doubt that Jerome himself considered his translation of the Old Testament from the Hebrew superior to the Septuagint and even to the text of the Hexaplaric Septuagint, since his rendering followed the original more closely. Time and again, he asked his readers to compare his version with the Septuagint and, if necessary, to consult Jewish scholars. But, since the sharp criticism, which his successively published Latin translations of the Old Testament evoked, could be silenced neither through ardent polemic nor through careful reasoning, Jerome developed a flexible response to vilification. On the one side, he justified his recourse to *Hebraica veritas* by adducing philological and theological arguments. Thus, he tried to provide his friends and patrons, who were responsible for propagating his works, with arguments to prove the supremacy of his version. On the other side, he repressed his underlying reservations and criticism and sometimes acknowledged the Hexaplaric text, even the Septuagint, whenever it was necessary to repulse the attacks of those who, like Rufinus, considered the Septuagint and consequently the Old Latin versions to be inspired by God, and therefore went on charging Jerome with heresy. This accusation was no less serious than the charge that he adhered to Origenism. Jerome had no choice but to fight against both charges in order to defend his reputation and his authority as a translator and commentator of the Bible.

When Jerome died on 30 September 419 or – more likely – 420, he had produced an immense oeuvre. Next to Augustine, he was the most prolific of all Christian Latin authors in the ancient world. Later generations venerated him as a trilingual theologian and praised him as an ascetic virtuoso. But, he has also been attacked as a person of weak character and extremely nasty temper and as the spiritual seducer of aristocratic women. Yet, Jerome should also be understood as a provincial parvenu who made a brilliant career as a Christian writer. His literary talent, his ascetic self-invention, a strong feeling for self-promotion, many innovative writings, and an extraordinary command of languages enabled him to succeed at last as a literary exponent both of the ascetic movement and of Nicene orthodoxy, as a biblical scholar, and as a mediator between eastern and western theology. Jerome is thus a remarkable example of social mobility and intellectual achievement in the Christian society of late antiquity.

Part II

TRANSLATIONS

7

THE NOVELIST

Letter 1 to Innocentius

INTRODUCTION

Jerome's first epistle has been harshly criticized by modern scholars. The story of the miraculous rescue of a Christian woman falsely condemned to death for adultery is said to be the very modest debut of a literary novice (Monceaux [1933] 90; cf. Cavallera [1922] i 28; Berschin [1986] 134), full of 'exaggerated pathos', 'uncritical credulity', and with a 'flair for brutally realistic description' (Kelly [1975] 40; cf. as early as Grützmacher [1901–8] i 144 and Norden [²1909] ii 650f.). However, a thorough examination of the text by Scourfield (1983) 32–138 has proved once again that it is a highly mannered piece combining classical quotations, Old Testament reminiscences, rhetorical stratagems, and vivid descriptions for the one purpose of glorifying the faith of a woman who is characterized as a martyr. Hence, it is not surprising that there are some affinities with Christian hagiographic literature. The woman withstands excruciating torments, calls God to witness, and looks up to heaven while being tortured. The governor grows more and more furious seeing her endurance, and two different executioners are driven to despair by their unsuccessful efforts to behead her. Finally, the devil comes up in the person of the headsman to look for the corpse. Obviously, it is not Jerome's intention to give a report of a true incident, and there is no need to interpret the story allegorically (cf. Grützmacher [1901–8] i 145). 'The significance of the events at Vercellae lay for him not in the unfairness of the trial and the summary execution, nor in any clash between Christianity and the state, but in the courage of the victim and the triumph of the Christian faith' (Scourfield [1983] 47). The author wants to demonstrate his capacity for writing the edifying account of a 'profane martyrdom' (Berschin [1986] 134; cf. Müller [1998] 208ff.).

The narrative of this remarkable event is cast in the form of a letter to Jerome's friend Innocentius, who belonged to the group of ascetics Jerome joined in northern Italy. He, like Jerome, travelled to Antioch, where he died in the household of their wealthy patron, Evagrius, a few months after his arrival (cf. Hier. *ep.* 3.3.1). Yet, the Antiochene *curialis* (cf. Chapter 2) is the true addressee of the epistle. At the end, he appears as *deus ex machina*; his appeal to the emperor leads to the heroine's release. Moreover, his support for the Roman bishop Damasus and his fight against Arianism are praised. Jerome is therefore writing a panegyric to Evagrius, who played an important role as a semi-official representative of the western church in the east, defended the Nicene faith, and supported monastic communities and ascetic pilgrims such as Jerome himself and Innocentius. At the same time, Jerome is aiming to please a larger Latin-speaking audience enchanted by the new genre of 'hagiographical prose narrative' (cf. Fontaine [1988b] 326), which is also represented by Evagrius' Latin translation of the *Life of Antony*. (Evagrius had rendered Athanasius' famous biography into Latin during his visit to the west and dedicated it to Innocentius.)

Thus, Jerome's first letter served two purposes: it was an encomium for an influential patron whom Jerome had already won, or whom he intended to win, and it demonstrated the literary talent of an ambitious Christian writer who was just about to make a living out of writing in support of Nicene orthodoxy and the ascetic movement. Its success was remarkable. Even the author of the *Historia Augusta* may have used it for his anti-Christian polemics (Chastagnol [1972]).

The date of the first letter is controversial. Schwind (1997) argued that it was probably written after Jerome settled in Bethlehem (i.e. after 385), but he was immediately refuted by Müller (1998), who corroborated the accepted view that *epistula* 1 was written at the beginning of the 370s, either before Jerome left Aquileia for the east (cf. Rebenich [1992a] 71) or during his stay at Antioch (cf. e.g. Cavallera [1922] ii 13f.; Scourfield [1986]).

TEXT

1   You have often asked me, dearest Innocent, not to keep silent about the miraculous event that has happened in our time.[1] I have declined the request from modesty and, as I now learn by experience, with justice, believing myself to be incapable of it,[2]

because all human language is insufficient to the praise of heaven, and also because inactivity, like rust upon the intellect, has dried up any little power of eloquence that I once possessed. You on the other hand urged that in the affairs of God one must look not at the possibility, but at the courage, and that he who trusted in the Word would not find that words fail him.[3]

2   What then shall I do?[4] The task is beyond me,[5] and yet I dare not decline it. An unskilled passenger,[6] I am placed in command of a heavy cargo-vessel. A person who has never pulled an oar[7] on a lake, I am entrusted to the turmoil of the Euxine Sea.[8] I see the land sinking beneath the horizon, 'on every side is sky, on every side the sea'[9]; darkness lowers over the water[10] and in the black night of the storm clouds the waves are white with foam. You urge me to hoist the swelling sails, to loosen the sheets, and to take the helm.[11] Now I obey your command, and as love can do all things and the Holy Spirit is guiding my course, I may feel confident that I shall find comfort in either case. For, if the rough sea drives me to the desired haven, I shall be regarded as a navigator; if my rude diction runs aground amid the rough cross-currents of language, you may blame my lack of power, but you will not be able to question my good intentions.

3   Vercellae, then, is a Ligurian town,[12] situated not far from the foot of the Alps, once important, but now sparsely populated and lying half in ruins.[13] When the provincial governor[14] was holding his visitation there, a woman and her lover were brought before him accused by the husband of adultery, and he consigned them to the penal horrors of prison.[15] Shortly afterwards, excruciating tortures were inflicted to discover the truth.[16] When the blood-stained hook struck the young man's livid flesh and tore furrows in his side, the unhappy youth sought to avoid prolonged pain by a speedy death, and giving a false account of his own passions, he involved another in the charge. Thus it appeared that he was of all men the most miserable and that his execution was just for he left to an innocent woman no chance of self-defence.

But the woman was more couragous than her sex.[17] Although her body was stretched upon the rack,[18] and although her hands, stained with the filth of the prison, were tied behind her, she looked up to heaven with her eyes,[19] which alone the torturer had been unable to bind, and while the tears rolled down her face, cried: 'You are my witness, Lord Jesus, to whom nothing is hidden, who tries the reins and the heart.[20] You are my witness that it is not to save myself from death that I make the denial, but that it is to save myself from sin that I am unwilling to lie. And as for you, unhappy man,[21] if you are hastening to perish, why must you destroy two innocent persons? I also, myself, desire to die, desire to put off this hated body,[22] but not as an adulteress. I offer my throat, I welcome the gleaming sword without fear, so long as I take my innocence with me. He does not perish, who is triumphant in his death.'[23]

4   The governor, who had been feasting his eyes upon the bloody spectacle, now, like a wild animal that after once tasting blood always thirsts for it,[24] ordered her torture to be doubled, and cruelly gnashing his teeth, threatened the executioner with like punishment if he failed to extort from the weaker sex a confession which manly strength had not been able to keep back.

5   Help, Lord Jesus. How many tortures have been invented for this one creature of yours! Her hair is bound to a stake, her whole body is fixed more firmly on the rack, and fire is put to her feet.[25] The executioner jabs her on both sides, and even her breasts are not spared. Still the woman remains unshaken, and her spirit is free from the pain of her body; still enjoying a clear conscience she refuses to allow the tortures to vent their rage upon her.[26] The cruel judge rises, as if he were defeated. She still prays to the Lord. Her limbs are wrenched from their sockets, she only turns her eyes to heaven. Another confesses their common guilt. She, for the confessor's sake, denies it, and, in peril of herself, vindicates one who is in peril of his.[27]

6   In the meantime she has but one thing to say: 'Beat me, burn me, tear me in pieces. I have not done it. If you do not believe my words, the day will come when this charge will be carefully examined. I will have a judge to do me justice.' Exhausted by this time, the torturer was sighing and moaning;[28] nor could he find a place for a fresh wound. He shuddered to see the body he had torn, and his cruelty vanquished. Immediately, the governor was roused to new rage and cried: 'Why does it surprise you, by-standers, that the woman prefers torture to death? It takes two people, certainly, to commit adultery; and I think it more credible that a guilty woman should deny a crime than that an innocent young man should confess one.'

7   The same sentence, therefore, was passed on both, and the executioner dragged away the condemned pair. The entire populace poured out to see the sight, rushing out in a dense mass through the crowded gates, so that one might have thought the city was migrating. At the very first stroke of the sword the head of the

miserable youth was cut off, and the headless trunk rolled over in its own blood. Then came the woman's turn. She knelt down upon the ground, and the gleaming sword was lifted over her trembling neck. The executioner summoned all his strength into his trained right arm, but the moment it touched her body the deadly sword stopped short, and, lightly grazing the skin, merely scratched it sufficiently to draw a little blood. The striker became frightened by the failure of his hand; he is amazed that his right arm has been defeated, the sword becoming powerless, and whirled it for a second stroke. Again the sword fell forceless on the woman, sinking harmlessly on her neck, as though the steel feared to touch the accused.[29] Thereupon the enraged and panting soldier[30] threw his cloak back over his shoulder. As he gave his full strength to the blow, he shook to the ground the brooch which clasped the edges of his garment, and not noticing this, he poised his sword for another stroke. 'Look,' said the woman, 'a gold pin has fallen from your shoulder. Pick up what you have earned by hard labour, that you may not lose it.'

8   I ask you, what is the source of such confidence? She has no fear of the death that threatens her. While she exults, when hit hard, the executioner turns pale. Her eyes do not see the sword, they only see the brooch. And as though to have no fear of death were not enough, she does an act of kindness to her cruel enemy. And now the mystery of the Trinity[31] had rendered vain the third blow, too;[32] the soldier[33] was thoroughly terrified, and no longer trusting the blade put the point to her throat, with the idea that the sword which could not cut, might plunge into her body by the pressure of his hand. The sword – an amazing fact, unheard of throughout the ages – bent back to the hilt, and, as if looking at its master in its defeat, confessed its inability to strike.

9   Now, now let me bring to mind the example of the three children, who, amid the cool circles of the flames, sang hymns instead of weeping, and around whose turbans[34] and holy hair the flames played harmlessly.[35] Now let me recall the story of the blessed Daniel,[36] according to which the lions wagged their tails and were afraid of their prey.[37] Let Susannah also ascend to the minds of all in the nobility of her faith, who, after she had been condemned by an unjust sentence, was saved by a youth filled with the Holy Spirit.[38] Note that in both cases the Lord's mercy was not dissimilar; Susannah was freed by the judge that she might not die by the sword; this woman, who had been con-demned by the judge, was acquitted by the sword.

10 At last the populace takes up arms to defend the woman. People of every age and sex drive off the executioner. The crowd forms a circle around her and hardly anybody can trust what he has seen. The news of their action throws the adjacent city into confusion, and the entire force of the governor's attendants is mustered. The officer who is responsible for the execution of criminals bursts from their midst, and 'staining his grey hair with defiling dust',[39] exclaims: 'Is it my life you are seeking, citizens? Are you making me a substitute for her? If you are merciful, if you are clement, if you wish to save a condemned woman, surely I – an innocent man – ought not to perish.' His lamentable appeal took effect upon the crowd, they were all benumbed by the influence of sorrow, and there was a strange change of will. Before, it had seemed their duty to defend the woman, now it seemed their duty in a way to allow her to be executed.

11 Accordingly a new sword is fetched, a new executioner appointed. The victim takes her place, strengthened only with the favour of Christ. The first blow makes her quiver, beneath the second she is shaken, by the third she falls wounded to the ground. Oh, the majesty of the divine power to be extolled! She who previously had received four strokes without injury, now seems, for a moment to die, that an innocent man may not perish in her stead.[40]

12 Those of the clergy, whose duty it was,[41] wrap the blood-stained corpse in a linen sheet, dig out the earth and, piling up stones, prepare the customary tomb. Hastening its course, the sun sets, and by the mercy of the Lord the night falls swiftly and quickly.[42] Suddenly the woman's breast quivers, her eyes seek the light, her body is restored to new life. She breathes, she looks round, she gets up and speaks. At last she is able to cry aloud: 'The Lord is my helper. I will not fear. What can man do to me?'[43]

13 In the meantime an aged woman, supported by the funds of the church,[44] gave back her spirit to heaven from which she had received it.[45] And as though the course of events had been purposely ordered, her body took the woman's place in the tomb. In the twilight, the devil comes on the scene in the person of the executioner,[46] looks for the corpse of the woman who had been slain, and desires to have her grave pointed out to him. He thinks that she is still alive, for he is astonished that she could have died. The clergy show him the fresh turf and the earth that a little while ago had been heaped up; they reject his demands with words as follows: 'Come and dig up the bones[47] which have just been buried! Declare war anew against the tomb, and if that is

not enough, scatter the limbs to be mutilated by birds and beasts! Seven times struck by the sword, she must endure something more than death.'

14 Such hostile words throw the executioner into confusion, and the woman is secretly revived at home. And that the frequency of the doctor's visits to the church might not give occasion for suspicion, she has her hair cut short and is sent in the company of some virgins to a secluded country house. There she changes her dress for that of a man, and gradually scars form over her wounds. Yet after all these miracles the laws are still raging against her. How true it is that, where there is most law, there is also most injustice. [48]

15 See now to what point the order of events has brought me! We come to the name of our friend Evagrius. [49] If I were to suppose that I could describe his labour for Christ, I should only show my own folly; and if I decided to pass them over, I still would not be able to prevent my voice from crying out in joy. For who could fittingly proclaim that by this man's vigilance Auxentius, that nightmare of Milan, was buried even before he was dead, [50] and the bishop of Rome, [51] when almost entangled in the toils of faction, overcame his opponents and yet spared them in their defeat? But 'this I must leave for others to relate, shut out by envious straits of time and space'. [52]

I am content only to record the conclusion of the present story. Evagrius energetically seeks an audience with the emperor, [53] wearies him with his entreaties, softens him by the service he has done him, and gains his cause through his painstaking attention. The emperor restored to liberty the woman who had been restored to life.

8

THE THEOLOGIAN

Letter 15 to Damasus

INTRODUCTION

When Jerome arrived at Antioch in the early 370s, theological controversy had been turning the Syrian metropolis upside down for nearly half a century. No less than three candidates for the episcopal see and their pressure groups were fighting each other: Meletius, Paulinus, and Euzoius. The tensions increased when a fourth bishop, one Vitalis, was consecrated. The schism was not only a personal feud about political influence and economic resources, but reflected different notions of the doctrine of the Trinity. The Arian bishop, Euzoius, who was recognized by the imperial government of the east, refused to accept the Nicene doctrine of the consubstantiality of Father, Son, and Holy Spirit. He was opposed by Meletius, who had been transferred from the see of Sebaste to Antioch in 360, and advocated new theological concepts spread by the Cappadocian Fathers. So he, according to Basil of Caesarea's teaching, described the three divine persons as three *hypostaseis* (i.e. as three individual realities), to distinguish them from one another. But the formula 'three *hypostaseis* (ὑποστάσεις) in one *ousia* (οὐσία; 'substance')' was not yet everywhere considered to be a representation of the Nicene doctrine of the consubstantial (= ὁμοούσιος [*homoousios*]) Trinity. Especially, western theologians translating *hypostasis* (ὑπόστασις) by the Latin word *substantia* (substance) thought that their eastern colleagues were propagating the idea of three 'substances' when speaking of three *hypostaseis* in the Godhead. Hence, Meletius was accused of tritheism and failed to secure the backing of Athanasius, bishop of Alexandria, and Damasus, bishop of Rome, while Basil of Caesarea and the majority of the eastern bishops supported his claim.

Meletius was twice banished under the emperor Valens and was in exile when Jerome reached Antioch. His large anti-Arian community had to face the presence of two rival 'orthodox' groups at Antioch, who denied cooperating, and repudiated the Meletian interpretation of the Nicene Creed. One was led by the bishop Paulinus, who, consecrated by Lucifer of Cagliari and recognized by Athanasius and the west, insisted that in God there was only one *hypostasis*, the other by Vitalis, who shared the fundamentalist Christological position of Apollinaris of Laodicea and denied the complete manhood in Christ (cf. Cavallera [1905]; for the theological implications, cf. G. C. Stead, s.v. Homousios, *RAC* 16, 1994, 364–433 and J. Hammerstaedt, s.v. Hypostasis, *ibid.* 986–1035).

The monks living next to Jerome's retreat in the 'desert of Chalcis' (i.e. at Maronia) were also arguing about *hypostasis* and *ousia*, and urged Jerome to define his faith. In this situation, Jerome decided to appeal to the authority of the bishop of Rome and to ask 'the successor of the fisherman' for theological guidance. Undistinguished as he then was, Jerome mentioned his patron Evagrius, who had supported Damasus' claim to the episcopal see, put himself forward as as an agent of western thought, emphasized the primacy of the Roman episcopate and promised, as a Roman (*homo Romanus*), to obey Damasus' decision. He insisted that, according to the secular and ecclesiastical tradition, *hypostasis* is to be recognized as no different from *ousia* and translated both words by *substantia* (substance). The Meletians, the advocates of the three *hypostaseis*, were dismissed as Arians. With his elaborate letter full of rhetorical display and flattery, Jerome tried to attract the attention of the controversial Roman bishop, who promoted the supremacy of 'the apostolic see', showed sympathy for the ascetic movement, acknowledged men of cultivated interests, and, like Jerome, failed to understand the new theological developments of the east.

The first theological controversy Jerome became involved in reveals his weakness as a theologian. He preferred polemical simplification to subtle distinction, doctrinal conservatism to fresh ideas, rhetorical display to substantial argument, learned allusions to discursive ramifications, dogmatic reassurance to intellectual receptivity, and authoritative decision to independent judgement.

The letter was written during Jerome's stay at Maronia. The explicit reference to Evagrius, Jerome's patron at Antioch, and Damasus' ideological confidant in the east at that time, disproves Nautin's hypothesis ([1986], 304) that it was composed at Bethlehem in 387. For a closer analysis of the letter, cf. Comerford Lawler (1970), de Halleux (1984) 331ff., Rebenich (1992a) 108ff., and Conring (2001) 198ff.

TEXT

1   Since the East, disunited by the ancient rage of its people against each other, is bit by bit tearing into pieces the seamless robe of the Lord, 'woven from the top [throughout],'[1] and the foxes are destroying the vineyard of Christ,[2] so that among the broken cisterns that hold no water[3] it is difficult to discover where lay the fountain sealed and the garden enclosed,[4] therefore I think it my duty to consult the chair of Peter and the faith that has been praised by the apostolic mouth.[5] I now ask for food for my soul from that place whence I once received the vestment of Christ.[6]

Indeed, the wide space of the water and the large area of intervening land cannot keep me from my search for 'the pearl of great price.'[7] 'Where the carcass is, there will the eagles gather.'[8] After an evil progeny wasted their patrimony,[9] you alone keep the heritage of your fathers intact. There the land with fruitful soil gives back the pure seed of the Lord in a hundredfold profit;[10] but here the corn that is choked in furrows degenerates into darnel and oats.[11] Now the sun of righteousness[12] is rising in the west; in the east, Lucifer, who had fallen,[13] has set his throne above the stars.[14] 'You are the light of the world.'[15] 'You are the salt of the earth.'[16] You are vessels of gold and of silver.[17] Here are vessels of clay or of wood that wait for the rod of iron and the eternal fire.[18]

2   Yet, although your greatness terrifies me, your kindness invites me. From the priest I demand safety for the victim, from the shepherd the protection of the sheep. Away with all indignation! Let the grandeur of the Roman eminence withdraw. I speak to the successor of the fisherman and to the disciple of the cross. As I follow none but Christ as my leader, so I am united in communion with your holiness,[19] that is with the chair of Peter. I know that upon this rock the church is built.[20] Whoever eats the lamb outside this house is profane.[21] Whoever is not found in the ark of Noah, will perish when the flood prevails.[22]

For my sins I have betaken myself to this desert which lies on the confine between Syria and the barbarian region.[23] Therefore I cannot, because of the great distance between us, always ask of your sanctity[24] the holy thing of the Lord.[25] Consequently I follow here the Egyptian confessors, your colleagues,[26] and hide myself like a small boat under heavy cargo-vessels. I do not know Vitalis, I reject Meletius, I know nothing about Paulinus.[27]

Whoever does not gather with you, scatters,[28] that is, he that is not of Christ, is of Antichrist.

3   Just now, I am sorry to say, after the Nicene Creed, and the decree of Alexandria, in which the west has joined,[29] the Campenses,[30] that Arian brood, demand that I, a Roman,[31] accept the novel formula of three *hypostaseis*. Which apostles, I should like to know, have transmitted these doctrines? Which new Paul, teacher of the Gentiles, has taught it? We ask them what three *hypostaseis* are supposed to mean. 'Three persons subsisting,'[32] they answer. We reply that this is our belief. They are not satisfied with the meaning, they demand the word, because some venom is hidden in the syllables. We cry: 'If anyone does not acknowledge three *hypostaseis* as three *enhypostata*, that is three persons subsisting, let him be condemned!' And because we do not learn the words, we are counted heretics. But if anyone interprets *hypostasis* as *ousia* (substance) and does not say that in the three persons there is one *hypostasis*, he has no part in Christ and by reason of this confession we, like you, are branded with the stigma of union.[33]

4   Decide, I beseech you. If you agree, I will not fear to speak of three *hypostaseis*. If you prescribe, a new creed shall supersede the Nicene, and we, the orthodox members of the church, shall make a confession of faiths using the same terms as the Arians. In the whole range of secular learning *hypostasis* never means anything but *ousia*. And will anyone, I ask, be so sacrilegious as to speak of three substances?[34] There is only one nature of God, and this alone truly exists. For that which is subsistent is derived from no other source but is all its own. All other things, which have been created, although they appear to exist, do not exist, for there was a time when they were not, and that which once did not exist may again cease to be. God alone, who is eternal, that is, who has no beginning, truly bears the name of 'essence'.[35] Therefore also he says to Moses from the bush, 'I am that I am,' and again, 'He who is has sent me'.[36] At that time existed the angels, the sky, the earth, and the seas. And how can God claim for himself the name of 'essence', which was common to all? But because God's nature alone is uncreated,[37] and because in the three persons there subsists but one godhead,[38] which truly exists and is one nature. Whoever declares that there are three, that is three *hypostaseis*, tries under the name of piety to allege that there are three natures. And if this is true, why are we severed by walls from Arius, when in faithlessness we are united? Let Ursinus form a friendship with your holiness,[39] let Auxentius be associated with Ambrose.[40]

Far be it from the Roman faith! May the devout hearts of the people not be infected with so great a sacrilege! Let us be satisfied to speak of one substance and of three subsisting persons: perfect, equal, coeternal.[41] Let nothing be said, if you decide, of three *hypostaseis*, and keep to one. It arouses suspicion when different words are used for the same thing. Let us be satisfied with the aforesaid form of creed, or, if you think it right, write that we should speak of three *hypostaseis* and explain what we mean by them. I do not refuse your request, but, believe me, there is poison hidden under the honey. An angel of Satan has transformed himself into an angel of light.[42] They give a plausible interpretation of *hypostasis*; yet when I say that I understand the term in the same sense they declare me a heretic. Why are they so tenacious of a word? Why do they hide themselves under ambiguous language? If their faith corresponds to their interpretation, I do not condemn them for keeping it. If I belief what they themselves pretend to think, they should allow me to speak of their opinion in my own words.

5   I implore your holiness, therefore, by the Crucified, the salvation of the world, and by the consubstantial Trinity, to authorize me by letter either to repudiate or to accept this formula of three *hypostaseis*.[43] And lest the obscurity of the place where I live should puzzle the carriers of your letters, I pray you to address your reply to the presbyter Evagrius, whom you know very well.[44] At the same time also signify with whom I am to communicate at Antioch, because the Campenses, who are united with the heretics of Tarsus,[45] strive for nothing else than to preach the three *hypostaseis* in the traditional sense of the word, signed with the authority of communion with you.

9

THE CHRONOGRAPHER

Preface to the *Chronicle* of Eusebius

INTRODUCTION

About 380, Jerome, then staying at Constantinople, finished his work of translating, supplementing, and continuing Eusebius of Caesarea's *Chronicle*. He produced a chronologically arranged compendium of universal history from the birth of Abraham, dated in 2016 BC, to the year AD 378 (i.e. the death of the emperor Valens in the battle of Adrianople). Jerome's *Chronicon* was part of an ambitious programme. He 'launched out on a fresh branch of literary activity – translation. He now possessed a mastery of Greek, and with the guidance of well-informed friends was familiarising himself with Greek Christian litera-ture. He must have been struck by its vast extent and high quality, as compared with the Latin Christian literature that was available, and he certainly felt the impulse to introduce it to western readers' (Kelly [1975] 72).

The preface reveals that Jerome was already becoming aware of the manifold difficulties of translation. His introductory essay discusses pagan and Christian predecessors. First, Jerome evaluates Cicero's ren-derings of Greek texts into Latin and then moves on to the different versions of the Old Testament. This preface marks the beginning of his reflections on the best method of translation. In the following years, he elaborated his theory and argued that, except in the case of the Scriptures, the translator should always render the sense rather than the words; cf. especially his letter 57 with the learned commentary by Bartelink (1980).

The *Chronicle* is dedicated to Vincentius, a presbyter at Constant-inople, and to a certain Gallienus who is otherwise unknown. Vincen-tius also supported Jerome's translations of Origen and paid for stenographers and copyists. For their sake, some remarks are included about the technical features of the manuscript that Jerome had introduced in the interest of lucidity.

For a critical text of the preface, see R. Helm in *GCS* 47 = *Eusebius Werke* 7, [2]1956 ([3]1984), pp. 1–7. For a more detailed discussion of Jerome's *Chronicle*, see Chapter 3.

TEXT

Jerome to Vincentius and Gallienus, Greeting.

It has long been the practice of learned men to exercise their minds by rendering into Latin the works of Greek writers, and, what is more difficult, to translate the poems of illustrious authors though impeded by the requirements of verse. It was thus that our Tully[1] translated word for word whole works of Plato;[2] and after rendering Aratus into Latin hexameters,[3] he amused himself with Xenophon's *Oeconomicus*.[4] In this latter work the golden river of eloquence again and again meets with obstacles, around which its waters break and foam to such an extent that persons unacquainted with the original would not believe they were reading Cicero's words.[5] It is indeed a difficult thing to follow another man's lines and everywhere keep within the length of the original. It is a hard task to preserve in translation the elegance of what had been so well expressed in another language. Every word has its own meaning; I have no word of my own to convey the meaning, and while I am seeking to satisfy the sense I may go a long way round and accomplish but a small distance of my journey. Then we must take into account the intricacies of transposition, the variations in cases, the diversity of figures, and, lastly, the peculiar, and, so to speak, the native idiom of the language. A literal translation sounds absurd; if, on the other hand, I am obliged to change the order or the words themselves, I shall appear to have failed in the duty of a translator.

So, my very dear Vincentius, and you, Gallienus, whom I love as my own soul, I beg you, whatever may be the value of this hurried piece of work,[6] to read it with the feelings of friends rather than with those of judges. And I ask this all the more earnestly because, as you know, I dictated with great rapidity to my stenographer.[7] And how difficult the task is, the sacred records testify, for the distinctive quality is not preserved in the Greek version by the Seventy.[8] It was this that stimulated Aquila, Symmachus, and Theodotion,[9] and the result of their labours was to impart a totally different character to one and the same work; one strove to give word for word, another the general meaning, while the third desired to avoid any great divergence from the ancients. A fifth, sixth, and seventh edition,[10] though no one knows to which authors they are to be attributed, exhibit so pleasing a variety of their own that, in spite of their being anonymous, they have won an authoritative position. Hence, some go so far as to consider the sacred writings somewhat harsh and jarring to the ear; but these people are not aware that it is a translation from the Hebrew, and therefore, looking at the surface and not at the substance, they shudder at the squalid dress before they notice the splendid body which the language clothes.[11] In fact, what can be more musical than the Psalter?[12] Like the writings of our Flaccus[13] and the Greek Pindar it now flows in iambics, now resounds in alcaics, now swells into sapphics, now uses half a metrical foot.[14] What can be lovelier than the hymns of Deuteronomy and Isaiah? What more solemn than Solomon, what more perfect than Job? All these works, as Josephus[15] and Origen wrote, were composed in hexameters and pentameters and circulated among their own people. When they are read in Greek their sound is different; when in Latin they are utterly incoherent. But if any one thinks that the grace of language does not suffer through translation, let him render Homer word for word into Latin. I will go further and say that, if he will translate this author into the prose of his own language, the order of the words will seem ridiculous, and the most eloquent of poets almost mute.

What is all this getting at? I would not have you think it surprising if here and there we fail, if the language is halting or bristles with consonants or forms breaks between vowels or is constricted by condensation of the narrative, when the most learned among men have toiled at the same task. In addition to the general difficulty, which we have alleged to attend all translation, a peculiar difficulty besets us, inasmuch as the history is manifold, is full of barbarous names, the circumstances of which the Latins know nothing, dates which are impossible to disentangle, critical marks blended alike with the events and the numbers, so that it is almost harder to discern the sequence of the words than to come to a knowledge of what is related. Therefore I think you should take care that each portion should be preserved as written, including the range of colours employed, lest anyone should think that this device had been contrived for the sake of the irrational pleasure of the eyes alone, and should weave a labyrinth of error into the text in an attempt to escape the monotony of his job. So the midnight oil has been burnt over the work to distinguish the columns of regnal dates which were muddled by too great proximity through the use of red ink[16] and to preserve the colour at the same place throughout the pages.[17]

I am well aware that there will be many people who, with their customary fondness for universal detraction, will drive their fangs into this volume. Only those who write nothing at all escape from those critics. They will cavil at the dates, change the order, impugn the accuracy of events, winnow thoroughly the syllables, and, as is very frequently the case, will impute the negligence of copyists to the authors. I should have every right to tell them that they need not read the book, if they do not like it, but I would rather send them away in a calm state of mind, so that they may attribute to the Greek author the credit which is his due, and may recognize that any insertions for which we are responsible have been taken from other men of the highest repute. The truth is that I have partly done the job of a translator and partly that of a writer. I have with the highest fidelity rendered the Greek portion, and at the same time have added certain things which appeared to me to have been allowed to slip, particularly in the Roman history, which Eusebius, the author of this book, as it seems to me, only glanced at; not so much because of ignorance, for he was a learned man, as because, writing in Greek, he thought them of minor importance to his countrymen. So again from Ninus and Abraham, right up to the captivity of Troy, the translation is from the Greek only. From Troy to the twentieth year of Constantine[18] there is much, at one time added, at another included, which I have excerpted with great diligence from Tranquillus[19] and other famous historians.[20] The section from the aforesaid year of Constantine to the sixth consulship of the emperor Valens and the second of the emperor Valentinian[21] is entirely my own. Content to end here, I have reserved the remaining period, that of Gratian and Theodosius, for a wider historical survey; not that I am afraid of writing freely and truthfully about people who are still alive,[22] for the fear of God banishes the fear of man, but at a time when our country is still exposed to the fury of the barbarians everything becomes uncertain.[23]

10

THE EPISTOLOGRAPHER
Letter 31 to Eustochium

INTRODUCTION

Jerome's extensive collection of letters, which are the finest of Christian antiquity, is of greatest historical importance for his life and times. Erasmus of Rotterdam, the most renowned scholar of the Renaissance, was an admirer of Jerome and celebrated his epistolographical style (cf. Rice [1985] 116ff.). Jerome's epistles comprise a wide range of subjects: ascetic exhortation, theological polemics, defence of orthodoxy, consolation, monastic advice, pedagogical discourse, scriptural exegesis, historical digressions, ecclesiastical politics, moral edification, and personal invective.

Letter 31 to Iulia Eustochium, Paula's daughter, deals with a different matter. The young Roman aristocrat had sent some articles as a present on the festival of St Peter – bracelets, doves, a basket of cherries – and Jerome wrote to thank her for them, reflecting upon the allegorical meaning of the items received.

On the basis of this letter, Georg Grützmacher, Jerome's Protestant biographer, has labelled him as a 'salon confessor in the style of the abbés in the reign of Louis XIV' ([1901–8] ii 262). This characterization clearly fails to understand the function of *ep.* 31 and *ep.* 44 to Marcella, which has a similar theme (cf. Letsch-Brunner [1998] 169ff). The exchange of sophisticated gifts and a cultivated letter of thanks was part of the social interaction between Jerome and his noble patronesses (cf. Krause [1987] 26f.; A. Stuiber, *s.v.* Jeschen, K., *RAC* 10, 1978, 699ff.), and observes the traditional standards of communication within the educated elite, as the correspondences of Ausonius of Bordeaux and of Paulinus of Nola confirm (cf. Sivan [1993a] 72f.). Such a letter offered the golden opportunity of displaying classical and biblical erudition.

TEXT

1   The bracelets, the letter, and the doves are outwardly small gifts
which I have received from a virgin, but the affection which has
prompted them enhances their value. And since honey may not
be offered in sacrifice to God,[1] you have skillfully taken off their
cloying sweetness and – if I may say so – flavoured them with the
pungent taste of pepper. For nothing that is simply pleasurable
or merely sweet pleases God. Everything must have in it a sharp
seasoning of truth. Christ's passover must be eaten with bitter
herbs.[2]

2   A festival such as the birthday of St Peter[3] should be celebrated
with more gaiety than usual. Still our facetious speech must not
forget the limit set by Scripture, and we must not stray too far
from the boundary of our wrestling-place.[4] Ezekiel describes
how Jerusalem is adorned with bracelets,[5] Baruch receives letters
from Jeremiah,[6] and the Holy Spirit descends in the form of a
dove.[7] But I will give you, too, a pinch of pepper and remind
you of my former letter.[8] Take care that you do not forget to
adorn yourself with good works, for they are the true bracelets.[9]
Do not tear apart the letter written in your heart[10] as the profane
king cut with his penknife that delivered to him by Baruch.[11] Do
not let Hosea say to you as to Ephraim, 'You are like a silly
dove'.[12] 'Your words are too harsh', you will say, 'and hardly
suitable to the feast-day'. But you have provoked them by the
nature of your own gifts. So long as you put bitter with the
sweet, you must expect the same from me, harsh words, that is,
as well as praise.

3   However, you should not think that I wish to reduce the value of
your gifts. I also received a basket of fine cherries, blushing with
such a virgin modesty that I can fancy them freshly imported by
Lucullus himself. For it was he who, after his conquest of Pontus
and Armenia, first brought the fruit from Cerasus to Rome; and
the cherry tree is so called after its place of origin.[13] Now as the
Scriptures speak of a basket of figs,[14] but do not mention
cherries, I will use these instead to praise the gift.[15] May you be
made of fruits such as those which are set out before God's
temple and of which he says, 'Behold they are good, very
good.'[16] For the Saviour likes nothing that is half and half, and,
while he does not shun the cold and welcomes the hot, he tells us
in the Apocalypse that he will spit out the lukewarm.[17] Therefore

we must be careful to celebrate our holy day not so much with abundance of food as with exultation of spirit. For it is entirely preposterous to wish to honour a martyr by excess who himself, as we know, pleased God by fasting. When you have a meal always remember that eating should be followed by reading, and also by prayer.[18] And if, by taking this course, you displease some, repeat the words of the Apostle: 'If I yet pleased men I should not be the servant of Christ.'[19]

11

THE SATIRIST

Letter 40 to Marcella concerning Onasus

INTRODUCTION

'St. Jerome is the author of the final chapter in the brilliant volume of ancient satire, one of the chief glories of Latin literature' (Wiesen [1964] 264). Jerome is definitely the most important satirical author of Latin Christianity. He himself claimed to be a successor of Horace, Persius, and Juvenal (cf. *ep*. 50.5 and Wiesen [1964] 6ff.; Adkin [1994]). The following letter, which coarsely ridicules a priest called Onasus, is a *chef-d'oeuvre* of satire. Jerome carefully concealed his adversary's real name (*pace* Grützmacher [1901–8] i 281f.; Nenci [1995]) since the latter may have been an influential person whom he had met during his stay at Rome and who was insulted by Jerome's attacks against clerics also competing for aristocratic patronage. The name is taken from a passage of the Verrines, where Cicero speaks of Onasus of Segesta, a well-known and high-born man (Cic. *Verr*. 5.45.120; cf. Labourt ii [1951] 196; Preaux [1958]; Letsch-Brunner [1998] 124ff.). But Jerome had more reasons to use this *sobriquet*. Onasus is another form of Onesimus, 'the helpful', and Jerome cannot resist commenting sarcastically upon this meaning. The name also suggests *nasus*, nose, and throughout the letter his opponent's big and stinking nose is an object of mockery. Other satirists such as Horace, Persius, and Martial also make fun of noses (cf. Otto [1890] 238). Moreover, Onasus evokes both the Greek and Latin word for donkey, *ónos* and *asinus* (cf. Wiesen [1964] 203f.); therefore, this name is Jerome's hostile starting point to deride his rival's intellectual and rhetorical deficiencies. The letter intended, at the same time, to calumniate an influential adversary and to entertain an educated audience by a brilliant synthesis of biblical learning and satirical manoeuvre.

In another letter to Marcella, Jerome lamented 'What have I said with too great freedom? [. . .] Have I ever assailed anybody in too bitter terms?' (*ep.* 27.2.1). Even the most benevolent reader of the onslaught against Onasus will be surprised to read this fulsome apology. He may answer with Juvenal (*Sat.* 1.30): *difficile est saturam non scribere* – it is difficult not to write a satire.

TEXT

1   The medical men called surgeons are thought to be cruel, but really are pitiable.[1] Is it not pitiable to feel the pain of another's wounds and to cut away the dead flesh with the merciful knife? Is it not pitiable to show no horror at treating a malady which seems horrible even to the patient and to appear as an enemy? The order of nature is such that while truth is always bitter, pleasant vices are esteemed. Isaiah goes naked without blushing as a type of the future captivity.[2] Jeremiah is sent from mid-Jerusalem to the Euphrates, a river in Mesopotamia, and leaves his girdle to be ruined among hostile nations, the Assyrians and the camp of the Chaldaeans.[3] Ezekiel is told to eat bread made of mingled seeds and sprinkled first with man's and then with cattle's dung.[4] He looks upon his wife's death without shedding a tear.[5] Amos is driven from Samaria.[6] Why was all this, I ask? It was because spiritual surgeons who cut away the parts diseased by sin urged men to repentance.[7] The Apostle Paul says: 'I have become your enemy because I tell you the truth?'[8] And because the Saviour's words seemed hard, many of his disciples went away.[9]

2   So it is not surprising that we have offended many by exposing their faults. I have arranged to cut a foul-smelling nose; let him who suffers from a swelling tremble. I wish to rebuke a chattering small crow; let the fellow-crow realize that he is putrid.[10] But is there only one person in the Roman world 'whose nose is mutilated by a shameful wound?'[11] Is Onasus of Segesta alone in puffing out his cheeks like bladders and balancing hollow phrases on his tongue?[12]

I say that certain persons have, by crime, perjury, and false pretences, attained to a certain position. What is that to you, who know that the charge does not touch you? I laugh at the advocate who himself is in need of a defender; I jeer contemptuously at his eloquence which perfectly suits his silly shaped nose.[13] What does it matter to you who are such a good speaker? I want to attack mercenary priests.[14] Why are you, who are a rich man, angry? I wish to burn limping Vulcan in his own flames. Are you his guest or his neighbour that you try to save an idol's shrine from the fire? I like to laugh at ghosts, night-birds, eagle owls[15] and monsters of the Nile; and whatever I say, you take it as aimed at you.[16] At whatever fault I point the sharp end of my pen, you cry out that you are meant, you join issue and drag me into court and absurdly charge me with writing satires in plain prose!

So you really think yourself a fine fellow because you have a lucky name![17] Is not a grove called *lucus*, because the light does not break through it (*quod minime luceat*)?[18] Are the Fates called the 'sparers', because they spare no man? Are not the Furies called the 'gracious' (*Eumenides*),[19] and in common speech the Ethiopians 'silver-coloured people'? Still, if my description of faults makes you angry, I will sing of your beauty the words of Persius: 'May kings and queens desire you for their daughters, may the girls scramble for you. May roses bloom wherever you plant your foot!'[20]

3   I will give you, however, a word of advice. There are some things you must hide if you want to look your best. Let your nose not be seen upon your face and keep your mouth shut. You will then stand some chance of being thought both handsome and eloquent.

12

THE BIOGRAPHER

The *Life of Malchus the Captive Monk*

INTRODUCTION

The saints' lives of Jerome – the *Life of Paul the First Hermit*, the *Life of Malchus*, and the *Life of Hilarion* – are masterpieces of monastic romance. They were immensely popular and drew contemporary and later readers under their spell, although some questioned the author's reliability (cf. *Vita Hilarionis* 1 [*PL* 23, 30B]). Jerome adopted literary forms and narrative elements of pagan provenance, borrowed from the mythological lore of classical authors, and integrated many features that were meant to entertain an educated audience (cf. Reitzenstein [1906]; Coleiro [1957]; Kech [1977]; Fuhrmann [1977]; Rousseau [1978] 133ff.; Hamblenne [1993]; Bastiaensen [1994]; Huber-Rebenich [1999]; Rebenich [2000a]). The *Life of Malchus* is best described as a monastic novella concentrating on the monk's amazing peregrination. All Malchus wants is to preserve his virginity. The pamphlet is a 'paean in praise of life-long chastity' (Kelly [1975] 171). The protagonist has to go through many adventures: kidnapping, enslavement, forced marriage, despair, escape, persecution, until salvation comes in the form of a lioness.

We are still in need of a modern critical edition of the lives. Migne (*PL* 23, 17–62) reproduced Domenico Vallarsi's text from the eighteenth century. The recent editions of the *Vita Malchi* by Mierow (1961), and of the *Vita Pauli* by Kozik (1968) and Dégorsky (1987) do not always provide a better text and are to be used with caution; Kozik, for instance, censored the original version of the *Vita Pauli*, leaving out the story about the young martyr and the prostitute (chap. 3). For the manuscript tradition, see Oldfather (1943) and Lambert (1969–72) vol. ii, 459ff., No. 261ff.

TEXT

1   They who have to fight a naval battle prepare for it in harbours and calm waters by adjusting the helm, plying the oars, and making ready the hooks and grappling irons. They draw up the soldiers on the decks and accustom them to stand steady with poised foot and on slippery ground; so that they may not shrink from all this when the real encounter comes, because they have had experience of it in the sham fight. And so I who have long been silent[1] (because silence was imposed on me by one to whom I give pain when I speak of him) desire to practise myself by means of a small work, and as it were to wipe the rust from my tongue, so that I may be able later to write history on a wider scale. For I have purposed (if God grant me life, and if my detractors will at length cease to persecute me, now that I am a fugitive and shut up in a monastery) to write a history from the advent of our Saviour up to our own age, that is from the Apostles to the dregs of our time, and to show how and by whom the church of Christ received its birth and gained strength, how it grew under persecution and was crowned with martyrdoms; and then, after reaching the Christian emperors, how it increased in power and in wealth but decreased in virtues. But of this elsewhere.[2] Now let us explain what lies before us.

2   Maronia is a little village some thirty miles to the east of Antioch in Syria. After having many owners or patrons, at the time when I was staying as a young man in Syria, it came into the possession of my intimate friend, the bishop Evagrius, whose name I now give in order to show the source of my information.[3] There was at the place at that time an old man by the name Malchus, which in Latin we might render '*rex* (king)', a Syrian by nationality and tongue, in fact a genuine son of the soil. His companion was an old woman, very decrepit, who seemed to be on the verge of death. Both of them were so zealously pious and such constant frequenters of the church that they might have been taken for Zacharias and Elizabeth in the Gospel[4] but for the fact that John was not with them. With some curiosity I asked the neighbours what was the link between them; was it marriage, or kindred, or the bond of the spirit? All with one accord replied that they were holy people, pleasing to God, and gave me a strange account of them. Longing to know more I began to question the man with much eagerness about the truth of what I heard, and learnt the following story.

3   My son, said he,[5] I was a tenant farmer on a bit of ground[6] at
     Nisibis and was an only son. When my parents wished to force
     me into marriage, since I was the only survivor of their family
     and their sole heir, I said I would rather be a monk. How my
     father threatened and my mother coaxed me to betray my
     chastity requires no other proof than the fact that I fled from
     home and parents. Since I could not go to the East because Persia
     was close by and the frontiers were guarded by Roman soldiers, I
     turned to the West, taking with me some little provision for the
     journey, but merely sufficient to keep me alive. To be brief, I
     came at last to the desert of Chalcis which is situated between
     Immae and Beroea further south.[7] There, having found some
     monks, I placed myself under their direction, earning my living
     by the labour of my hands, and restraining the wantonness of the
     flesh by fasting. After many years the desire came over me to
     return to my native country while my mother was still alive (for
     my father, as I had already heard, was dead), to comfort her
     widowhood and then to sell the little property and give part to
     the poor, settle part on the monastery and (why should I blush to
     confess my faithlessness) keep some to spend in comforts for
     myself. My abbot began to cry out that it was a temptation of the
     devil, and that under a fair pretext the snares of the old enemy lay
     hidden. In other words, the dog was returning to his vomit.[8]
     Many monks, he said, had been deceived by such suggestions,
     for the devil never showed himself openly. He set before me
     many examples from the Scriptures, and told me that even Adam
     and Eve in the beginning had been overthrown by him through
     the hope of becoming gods.[9] When he failed to convince me he
     fell upon his knees and besought me not to desert him, not to
     ruin myself, not to look back after setting my hand to the
     plough.[10] Alas, miserable creature that I am, I conquered my
     adviser in a most miserable victory. I thought he was seeking not
     my salvation but his own advantage. So he followed me from the
     monastery as if he had been going to a funeral, and at last bade
     me farewell, saying, 'I see that you bear the brand of a son of
     Satan. I do not ask your reasons nor take your excuses. The
     sheep which forsakes its fellows is at once exposed to the jaws of
     the wolf.'[11]

4   On the road from Beroea to Edessa,[12] adjoining the public
     highway, is a solitary area through which nomad Saracens are
     always wandering back and forth. Through fear of them, travellers
     in those parts assemble in numbers, so that by mutual assistance

they may escape impending danger. There were in my company men, women, old men, youths, children, altogether about seventy persons. All of a sudden Ishmaelites[13] riding on horses and camels made an assault upon us, with their flowing hair bound with fillets and their bodies half-naked. They wore cloaks and broad military boots, and their quivers slung upon their shoulders. They brandished bows unstrung and carried long spears, for they had come not to fight, but to plunder. We were seized, dispersed, and carried in different directions. I, meanwhile, and far indeed from gaining possession of my inheritance and repenting too late of the decision I had taken, fell by lot, along with the woman of the company, into the service of the same owner. We were led, or rather carried, high upon the backs of camels through a vast desert, suspended rather than seated, every moment in fear of falling off. Flesh half raw was our food, camel's milk our drink.

5   At last, after crossing a great river, we came to the interior of the desert, where, being commanded after the custom of the people to pay reverence to the mistress and her children, we bowed our heads. Here, as if I were a prisoner, I changed my dress, that is, learnt to go naked, the heat being so excessive as to allow of no covering but a loin cloth. Some sheep were given to me to tend, and, in contrast to the evils I could have been subjected to, I found this occupation a comfort, for I seldom saw my masters or fellow slaves. My fate seemed to be like that of Jacob, and reminded me also of Moses; both of whom were once shepherds in the desert.[14] I lived on fresh cheese and milk, prayed continually, and sang psalms which I had learnt in the monastery. I was delighted with my captivity, and thanked God for His judgement, because I had found in the desert the monk's state which I was on the point of losing in my country.

6   But nothing is ever safe from the Devil. How manifold and unspeakable are his snares! Hidden though I was, his malice found me out. My master seeing his flock increasing and finding no dishonesty in me (I knew that the Apostle has given command that masters should be as faithfully served as God Himself[15]), and wishing to reward me in order to secure my greater fidelity, gave me the woman who was once my fellow servant in captivity. When I refused and said I was a Christian and that it was not lawful for me to take a woman to wife so long as her husband was alive (her husband had been captured with us, but carried off by another master), my owner was relentless in his rage, drew his

sword and began to menace me. If I had not without delay stretched out my hand and taken possession of the woman, he would have shed my blood on the spot.

By this time a darker night than usual had set in and, for me, all too soon. I led my bride into a half-demolished cave. Sorrow was bride's-maid. We shrank from each other but did not confess it. Then I really felt my captivity. I threw myself down on the ground, and began to lament the monastic state which I had lost, and said: 'Wretched man that I am! Have I been preserved for this? Have my sins brought me to this, that now with my hair turning grey I must lose my virginity and become a married man? What is the good of having despised parents, country, property, for the Lord's sake, if I do the thing I wished to avoid doing when I despised them? And yet it may perhaps be the case that I am in this condition because I longed for my native country. What are we to do, my soul? Are we to perish or conquer? Are we to wait for the hand of the Lord or pierce ourselves with our own sword? Turn the blade against yourself! I must fear your death, my soul, more than the death of the body. Chastity preserved has its own martyrdom. Let the witness for Christ lie unburied in the desert. I will be both the persecutor and the martyr.'

Thus I spoke and drew my sword which glittered even in the darkness, and turning its point towards me I said: 'Farewell, unhappy woman, receive me as a martyr not as a husband.' She threw herself at my feet and exclaimed: 'I beseech you by Jesus Christ, and adjure you by this hour of trial, do not shed your blood and bring its guilt upon me. If you are determined to die, first turn your sword against me. Let us rather be united upon these terms. Even if my husband should return to me, I would preserve the chastity which captivity has taught me. I would even die rather than lose it. Why should you die to prevent a union with me? I would die if you desired it. Take me then as the spouse of your chastity; and love more this union of the spirit than that of the body. Let our masters believe that you are my husband. Christ knows you are my brother.[16] We shall easily convince them we are married when they see us so loving.'

I confess, I was astonished and, much as I had before admired the virtue of the woman, I now loved her as a wife still more. Yet I never gazed upon her naked body. I never touched her flesh, for I was afraid of losing in peace what I had preserved in the conflict. Many days passed away in wedlock of this kind. Our marriage had made us more pleasing to our masters, and there was no suspicion of flight. Sometimes I was absent for even a whole month like a trusty shepherd of the flock traversing the wilderness.

7   After a long time, as I sat one day by myself in the desert seeing nothing but earth and sky, I began to turn things over in my thoughts, and among many others called to mind the companionship of the monks, and especially the look of the father who had instructed me, kept me, and lost me. While I was thus meditating I noticed a crowd of ants swarming over a narrow path. You might see them carrying loads larger than their own bodies. Some with the forceps of their mouths were dragging along the seeds of herbs; others were excavating the earth from pits and banking it up to keep out the water. One group, in view of approaching winter, and wishing to prevent their granary from sprouting through the dampness of the ground, were cutting up the seeds they had carried in; another with solemn lamentation were removing the bodies of the dead. And, what is stranger still in such a host, those coming out did not hinder those going in. Rather, if they saw one fall beneath his burden, they would put their shoulders to the load to give him assistance. In short that day afforded me a delightful entertainment. So, remembering how Solomon sends us to the shrewdness of the ant and quickens our sluggish faculties by setting before us such an example,[17] I began to tire of captivity, and to yearn for the cells of the monastery, and longed to imitate those ants and their doings, where toil is for the community, and, since nothing belongs to any one, all things belong to all.

8   When I returned to my bed, my wife met me. My look could not dissemble the sadness of my heart. She asked why I was so dispirited. I told her the reasons, and exhorted her to escape. She did not reject the idea. I begged her to be silent on the matter. She pledged her word. We constantly spoke to one another in whispers, and we floated in suspense between hope and fear. I had in the flock two he-goats of unusual size. These I killed, made their skins into bags,[18] and from their flesh prepared food for the way. Then in the early evening when our masters thought we had retired to rest we began our journey, taking with us the bags and part of the flesh. When we reached the river which was about ten miles off, having inflated the bags and got upon them, we entrusted ourselves to the water, slowly paddling with our feet, that we might be carried down by the stream to a point on the opposite bank much below that at which we embarked, and

that thus the pursuers might lose the track. But meanwhile the flesh became sodden, bits of it fell off, and we could not depend on it for more than three days' sustenance. We drank as much water as we could, preparing for the thirst we expected to endure, then hastened away, constantly looking behind us, and advanced more by night than day, on account both of the ambushes of roaming Saracens, and of the excessive heat of the sun. I grow terrified even as I relate what happened[19] and, although I am now secure, yet my body shudders from head to foot.

9   Three days after we saw in the dim distance two men riding on camels approaching with all speed. At once presaging evil I began to think my master purposed putting us to death, and our sun seemed to grow dark again. In the midst of our fear, and just as we realized that our footsteps on the sand had betrayed us, we found on our right hand a cave which extended far underground. Although we were afraid of venomous animals (for vipers, basilisks, scorpions, and other creatures of the kind often resort to such shady places so as to avoid the heat of the sun), we entered the cave and hastily took shelter in a pit on the left near the entrance, not venturing a step further, lest in fleeing from death we should run into death. We thought thus within ourselves: If the Lord helps us in our misery we have found safety. If He rejects us as sinners, we have found our tomb.[20]

What do you suppose were our feelings? What was our terror, when in front of the cave, close by, there stood our master and fellow-servant, brought by the evidence of our footsteps to our hiding place? How much worse is death expected than death inflicted! Again my tongue stammers with distress and fear; it seemed as if I heard my master's voice, and I hardly dared mutter a word. He sent his servant to drag us from the cavern while he himself held the camels and, with drawn sword, waited for us to come. Meanwhile the servant entered about three or four cubits,[21] and we in our hiding place saw his back though he could not see us (for the nature of the eye is such that those who go into the shade out of the sunshine can see nothing). His voice echoed through the cave: 'Come out, you villains, come out and die. Why do you stay? Why do you delay? Come out, your master is calling and patiently waiting for you.' He was still speaking when behold! through the gloom we saw a lioness seize the man, strangle him, and drag him, covered with blood, further in. Good Jesus! How great was our terror then, how intense our joy! We watched, though our master knew not of it, our enemy perish. He, when he saw that his servant was long in returning, supposed that the fugitives being two to one were offering resistance. Impatient in his rage, and sword still in hand, he came to the cavern, and shouted like a madman as he chided the sluggishness of his slave, but was caught by the beast before he reached our hiding place. Who ever would believe that before our eyes a wild beast would fight for us?[22]

Once that fear was removed, we realized that there was the prospect of a similar death for ourselves, though the rage of a lion was not so bad to bear as the anger of a man. Our hearts failed for fear. Without venturing to stir a step we awaited the issue, having no wall of defence in the midst of so great dangers save the consciousness of our chastity. The lioness, afraid of some snare and aware that she had been seen, took up her cub with her teeth and carried it away early in the morning, leaving us in possession of our retreat. Our confidence was not restored all at once. We did not rush out, but waited for a long time, for as often as we thought of coming out we pictured to ourselves the horror of meeting her.

10   At last we got rid of our fright, and when that day was spent, we sallied forth towards evening, and saw the camels, which are called dromedaries on account of their great speed,[23] quietly chewing the cud. We mounted, and with the strength gained from the new supply of grain, after ten days travelling through the desert arrived at a Roman camp. After being presented to the tribune we told all, and from thence we were sent to Sabianus, who was military commander of Mesopotamia,[24] where we sold our camels. My old abbot was now sleeping in the Lord. I betook myself therefore to this place[25] and returned to the monastic life, while I entrusted my companion here to the care of the virgins, for though I loved her as a sister, I did not commit myself to her as if she were my sister.

All these things the old man, Malchus, told me when I was young. Now I, an old man, have related them to you. I have set them forth as a history of chastity for the chaste. Virgins, I exhort you, guard your chastity. Tell the story to them that come after, that they may know that in the midst of swords, deserts and wild beasts, chastity is never a captive, and that a man who is devoted to the service of Christ may die, but cannot be conquered.

13

THE BIBLICAL SCHOLAR

Preface to the *Book of Hebrew Questions*

INTRODUCTION

Jerome intended to provide as accurate a Latin translation as possible of the Bible. His recourse to the original languages was illuminated and defended in the prefaces to the translated biblical books and in a series of commentaries on the Old and New Testaments. Exegetical letters and treatises dedicated to his Roman friends and other benefactors supplemented his programme of *scientia scripturarum*. Two works in particular should be understood as preparatory studies to his campaign for a new Latin translation of the Old Testament based upon the Hebrew version: the *Liber interpretationis Hebraicorum nominum* or *Liber de nominibus Hebraicis* (*The Book on Hebrew Names*) and the *Quaestiones Hebraicae in Genesim* (*Hebrew Questions on Genesis*).

The latter study, published around 392, is, in Jerome's own words, 'a new work (*opus novum*)' (*QHG* Praef.) and 'a collection of Hebrew questions and traditions (*vel quaestionum Hebraicarum vel traditionum congregatio est*)' (*QGH* 14.18–19). Jerome made a Christian audience familiar with Hebrew teachings that he himself had acquired through philological research and with the assistance of learned Jewish teachers. So, *QGH* is a remarkable example of Christian scholarship, philological expertise, and theological innovation in late antiquity. Jerome advocated his preference for the Hebrew verity (*Hebraica veritas*) over the Septuagint and, at the same time, his use of Jewish tradition.

The *QGH* should be cited according to the edition of P. de Lagarde (Leipzig 1868) or of D. Vallarsi in *PL* 23 (983–1062). The reprint of Lagarde's edition in *CCL* 72 (pp. 1–56) includes some misprints and errors. There is an English translation and fine commentary by Hayward (1995). The authoritative study on *QGH* is by Kamesar (1993) who has also convincingly challenged the view that Jerome, when referring to Jewish sources, only plagiarized Greek sources, especially Origen, Acacius of Caesarea, and Eusebius of Emesa. Although, in some other writings, Jerome borrowed 'Hebrew traditions' from Greek theologians, in _QGH_ he employs a wide range of Jewish material.

TEXT

In the prefaces to my books I ought to set forth the argument of the work which follows; but I am compelled to begin by answering what has been said against me. My case is somewhat like that of Terence, who put on stage the prologues of his plays as a defence of himself. For Luscius Lanuvinus, like our Luscius, pressed him and brought charges against the poet as if he had been a plunderer of the treasury.[1] The poet of Mantua[2] suffered in the same way; he had translated a few verses of Homer very precisely, and they said that he was nothing but a plagiarist from the ancients.[3] But he answered them that it was no small proof of strength to wrest the club of Hercules from his hands. And even Tully, who stands on the pinnacle of Roman eloquence,[4] that king of orators and glory of the Latin language, had charges for expropriation[5] brought against him by the Greeks.

I cannot, therefore, be surprised if a poor little fellow like me is exposed to the gruntings of filthy swines who trample our pearls with their feet,[6] since spite blazed up against the most learned men, who should have conquered envy with glory.[7] It is true, this happened by a kind of justice to men whose eloquence had filled with its resonance the theatres and the senate, the public assembly and the rostra; bravery in the open always courts detraction, and 'the highest peaks invoke the lightning's stroke.'[8] But I am in a corner, remote from the city, the forum, the lawcourts and the crowds; yet, even so (as Quintilian says) 'ill will has discovered the one who has kept out of the public eye.'[9] Therefore, I beseech the reader – 'If one there be, who shall read these lines, held captive by love'[10] – not to expect eloquence or oratorical grace[11] in those Books of Hebrew Questions,[12] which I propose to write on all the sacred books; but rather, that he should himself answer my opponents for me, and tell them that a new work can claim some indulgence. We are poor and of low estate; we neither possess riches nor do we think it right to accept them if they are offered us; and, similarly, they should know that it is impossible for them to have the knowledge of the Scriptures, that is the riches of Christ, and the world's riches as well.

It will be our aim, therefore, first, to point out the mistakes of those who suspect some fault in the Hebrew Scriptures, and, secondly, to correct the faults, which evidently teem in the Greek and Latin copies, by reference to the original authority;[13] and, further, to explain the etymology of things, names, and countries, when it is not apparent from the sound of the Latin words, by giving a paraphrase in the native tongue. To enable the student more easily to take note of an emendation, I propose, in the first place, to set out the witnesses, as they exist among us, and then, by bringing the later readings into comparison with it, to indicate what has been omitted or added or altered. It is not my purpose, as jealous people pretend[14], to convict the Seventy translators of error, nor do I look upon my own labour as a censure of theirs, since they did not want to make known to King Ptolemy of Alexandria all the mysteries which the sacred writings contain,[15] and especially those which give the promise of the advent of Christ, lest the Jews might appear to worship a second God also. For the king, who was a follower of Plato, used to make much of the Jews, on the grounds that they were said to worship one God.

But the Evangelists, and even our Lord and Saviour, and the Apostle Paul, also, bring forward many citations as coming from the Old Testament which are not contained in our manuscripts; and on these I shall dilate more fully in their proper places. But it is clear from this fact that those are the best copies which agree with the authority of the New Testament. Add to this that Josephus, who gives the story of the Seventy translators, reports them as translating only the five Books of Moses;[16] and we also acknowledge that these are more in harmony with the Hebrew than the rest. And, further, those translators who lived afterwards – I mean Aquila and Symmachus and Theodotion[17] – give a version very different from that which we use.

I have but one word more to say, and it may calm my detractors. Foreign goods are to be imported only to the regions where there is a demand for them. Peasants may not buy balsam, pepper, and dates. As to Adamantius,[18] I say nothing. His name (if I may compare small things with great[19]) is even more than my own the object of ill will, because, though following the common version [of the Scriptures] in his homilies, which were spoken to common people, yet, in his tomes,[20] that is, in his fuller discussion of Scripture, he is overcome by the Hebrew verity (*Hebraica veritas*),[21] and, though surrounded by his own forces, occasionally seeks the foreign tongue as his ally.[22] This one thing I say: I should gladly have his knowledge of the

Scriptures (*scientia scripturarum*), even if accompanied with all the ill will which clings to his name, and that I do not care a straw for these images and shadows of ghosts,[23] whose nature is said to be a terror to little children and to chatter in dark corners.

14

THE LITERARY HISTORIAN

Lives of Famous Men

INTRODUCTION

Jerome's first period of literary activity after his settlement in Bethlehem ended with the publication of *de viris illustribus*, a handbook of ecclesiastical writers, which was composed somewhere between 392 and 393 (for 392 or the beginning of 393, cf. e.g. Cavallera [1922] ii 31; Kelly [1975] 174; Booth [1981] 241 n. 17; Barnes [²1985] 235f.; for 393, cf. Nautin [1961] 33f. and [1974] 280ff.). The work is less a literary history than a catalogue of Christian authors, as Erasmus had already noted (Antin [1972]). The motive of the work was apologetic, as Jerome reveals in the preface. Since the great enemies of Christianity – Celsus, Porphyry, and Julian – had always regarded the new religion as vulgar and plebeian, Jerome wanted to exhibit the intellectual, literary, and philosophical qualities of Christian authors.

Although Jerome introduced a new and successful genre into Christian literature (for the manuscript tradition, cf. Feder [1927]), his work was far from being original. In his preface, he mentions many Greek and Latin literary historians, but his most important model was Suetonius (cf. Ceresa-Gastaldo [1979]; [1984]). As Cicero had compiled a list of Latin orators in his *Brutus*, Jerome purposed to enumerate ecclesiastical writers. But he had to face a major problem: for his task, he had no direct predecessor, 'yet I must acknowledge that Eusebius Pamphilus in the ten books of his *Church History* has been of the greatest assistance'. Many scholars have argued cogently that the first seventy-eight chapters are taken almost entirely from Eusebius' ecclesiastical history and the chronicle (cf. e.g. Huemer [1894]; von Sychowski [1894] esp. 18ff.; 49ff.; Bernoulli [1895]; Courcelle [1948] 78ff.; Hagendahl [1958] 138ff.; Barnes [²1985] 6ff. and

236ff.). Their judgement of Jerome's originality has been devastating (cf. also Kelly [1975] 176ff.).

The list begins with the Apostle Peter and ends with Jerome himself, covering the period 'from the Lord's passion down to the fourteenth year of the emperor Theodosius' (*vir.ill.* prol.). Greek, Latin, and a few Syriac authors who had written on theological topics are included. Jerome also mentions a number of heretics like Marcellus, Photinus, and Eunomius (*vir.ill.* 86; 107; 120; cf. Augustine's criticism in Aug. *ep.* 40.7) and even non-Christians. Philo is praised for being a spiritual antecedent of the monastic movement (*vir.ill.* 11); Josephus is inserted because Jerome had read the Christian interpolations about Jesus in *Jewish Antiquities* (*vir.ill.* 13); and the entry on the pagan philosopher Seneca is justified by referring to his exchange of letters with the Apostle Paul (cf. Corsaro [1987]; Mastandrea [1988]; Gamberale [1989]), now regarded as apocryphal (*vir.ill.* 12). The lemmata dealing with the Christian authors of the first three centuries are weighted and reveal Jerome's fondness for certain theologians. They also reflect the tendency of the sources he leaned on. Finally, Jerome's inaccuracies and inconsistencies in copying earlier texts have deformed some of the entries. Jerome devoted most space to Clement of Alexandria (*vir.ill.* 38), Tertullian the presbyter who was harassed 'by the envy and offences of the Roman clergy' (*vir.ill.* 53), the *immortale ingenium* of Origen (*vir.ill.* 54), Hippolytus of Rome (*vir.ill.* 61), and Dionysius of Alexandria (*vir.ill.* 69). The works of Cyprian are not given *cum sole clariora sint* – 'since they are brighter than the sun' (*vir.ill.* 67).

When Jerome moves to the fourth century, and his own time, the presentation is even more biased (*vir.ill.* 79–135). Jerome did not hesitate to canonize his understanding of orthodox staunchness, ascetic championship, and literary brilliance. So, Diodore of Tarsus is criticized for his ignorance of secular literature (*vir.ill.* 119), while Lucifer of Cagliari is praised for his theological constancy and his willingness to meet martyrdom (*vir.ill.* 95). Jerome's personal preferences and his hostility are apparent. He either omitted or chastised contemporaries he disliked. For Ambrose of Milan, whom he detested, Jerome found a particularly malicious phrase: 'He is still writing today. I shall withhold my opinion on him lest I should be blamed either for adulation or for speaking the truth' (*vir.ill.* 124). On John Chrysostom, the rival of Jerome's friend Paulinus, at Antioch, we can read: 'He is said to have composed many books. All I have read of his is his treatise on priesthood' (*vir.ill.* 129). On the other hand, Jerome extolled his patrons and friends. Of course, his teachers Apollinaris of

Laodicea, Didymus the Blind and Gregory Nazianzen received eulogies (*vir.ill.* 104; 109; 117), Damasus' 'fine talent in writing verse' is stressed (*vir.ill.* 103), and Evagrius, Jerome's Antiochene benefactor, is described as 'a man of keen and pungent mind' (*vir.ill.* 125). The praetorian prefect Dexter, to whom the book is dedicated, was a powerful supporter of Jerome (cf. *PLRE* i 251; Matthews [²1990] 133f.; 157ff.); no wonder that his entry is most prominent: 'Dexter is distinguished in secular life and devoted to the Christian faith. He is said to have written a *Universal History*, which I have not yet read' (*vir.ill.* 132). Nummius Aemilianus Dexter was the son of Pacianus (or Pacatianus), bishop of Barcelona, whom Jerome also mentions in *vir.ill.* 106; the Spanish background of the addressee might also explain the fact that Jerome dealt in some detail with the Priscillianist movement, which won a large following in Spain (cf. *vir.ill.* 121–3 and Rebenich [1992a] 213ff.). And even a certain Sophronius, most certainly a mediocre writer, earned the right to be mentioned for his friendship with the author, who apostrophized him as *vir apprime eruditus*, 'a man of outstanding erudition' (*vir.ill.* 134). None of Sophronius' writings have survived, and Erasmus has erroneously attributed a Greek translation of *De viris illustribus* to him (cf. Feder [1927] 68ff.).

The long catalogue of Christian writers who 'founded, built and adorned the church' (*vir.ill.* prol.) culminates in Jerome (*vir.ill.* 135). On the very last page, he gave a detailed account of his literary production (cf. Nautin [1984a]), which was written to reinforce Jerome's image as a prolific author of the western church who continued the work of the most distinguished Christian theologian, in short: to depict Jerome as the Latin Origen (cf. Vessey [1993a]). This extraordinary *laudatio sui ipsius* was, as Kelly (1975) 178 has acutely observed, 'the appropriate place for one who was "as it were an untimely birth, the very least of all Christians" (Hier. *ep.* 47.3.2).'

TEXT

1   I, Jerome, son of Eusebius,[1] of the city of Stridon, which was overthrown by the Goths and was once close to the border of Dalmatia and Pannonia,[2] up to the present year, that is, the fourteenth year of the reign of the emperor Theodosius,[3] have written the following works.[4]

2   *Life of Paul the Monk*,[5] one book of *Letters to different persons*,[6] an *Exhortation to Heliodorus*,[7] *Altercation of a Luciferian with an*

Orthodox,[8] *Chronicle of Universal History*,[9] twenty-eight *homilies of Origen on Jeremiah and Ezekiel*,[10] which I have translated from Greek into Latin, *On the Seraphim*,[11] *On Osanna*,[12] *On the prudent and the prodigal sons*,[13] *On three questions of the ancient law*,[14] two *Homilies on the Song of Songs*.[15]

3   *Against Helvidius, on the perpetual virginity of Mary*,[16] *To Eustochium, on the preservation of virginity*,[17] one book of *Epistles to Marcella*,[18] a consolatory letter *To Paula on the death of a daughter*,[19] three books of *Commentaries on the Epistle of Paul to the Galatians*,[20] three books of *Commentaries on the Epistle to the Ephesians*, one book *On the Epistle to Titus*, one book *On the epistle to Philemon*, *Commentaries on Ecclesiastes*.

4   One book of *Hebrew Questions on Genesis*,[21] one book *On places*, one book of *Hebrew Names*, one book *Didymus on the Holy Spirit*, which I have translated into Latin,[22] thirty-nine *homilies on Luke*,[23] seven tractates *On the Psalms, from the Tenth to the Sixteenth*,[24] *On the captive Monk*,[25] *The Life of the blessed Hilarion*.[26]

5   I have translated the New Testament from the Greek, and the Old Testament from the Hebrew,[27] and the numbers of letters *To Paula and Eustochium* is uncertain, for they are written daily.[28]

6   I have written, moreover, two books of *Explanations on Micah*, one book *On Nahum*, two books *On Habakkuk*, one book *On Zephaniah*, one book *On Haggai*,[29] and many others on the work of the prophets, which I am still at work upon, and are not yet finished.[30]

15

THE TRANSLATOR

The Preface to the Vulgate version of the Pentateuch

INTRODUCTION

Jerome's greatest achievement was his translation of most of Scripture into Latin from the original languages. He also rendered Greek theological writings, especially by Origen and Didymus, and often reflected upon the various difficulties he encountered as a translator. In a letter written in 395–6 and addressed to his influential Roman friend Pammachius, he discussed the best method of translating (*ep.* 57; there is a learned commentary by Bartelink [1980]). Jerome categorically demanded that a translator should render sense for sense and not word for word (*ep.* 57.5.2: *non verbum e verbo, sed sensum exprimere de sensu*; cf. also his preface to the *Chronicle* [Chapter 9]).

Although Jerome agreed, at least in principle, that the sacred writings of the Bible should be rendered word for word, he often advocated a more flexible approach to preserve the characteristic elegance of the Latin language. Even the Apostles and Evangelists, he argued, 'in translating the Old Testament sought to give the meaning rather than the words, and they have not greatly cared to preserve forms or constructions, so long as they could make clear the subject to the understanding' (*ep.* 57.9.8). Still, Jerome felt the dilemma of every translator, for, on the one hand, if he alters anything from a foreign language 'the work becomes less a version than a perversion' and, on the other hand, 'a literal adherence to the original by no means tends to preserve the charm of its eloquence' (*ep.* 84.12.2 – regarding his translation of Origen's *Peri Archon*). For Jerome's translation theory and technique, cf. Winkelmann (1970); Marti (1974), esp. 61ff.; Banniard (1988); D. Brown (1992) 194ff.

In translating Scripture, Jerome soon became aware of the problems arising from the various versions of the Old Testament. He therefore decided to go back to the Hebrew original and, necessarily, to the Hebrew canon and thus anticipated the Reformers' position. In the prologue to the Books of Samuel and Kings, Jerome set forth his principles adopted in all his translations from the Hebrew. This 'helmeted preface (*galeatum pincipium*)' was meant to serve as an exposition to all the books that Jerome translated from Hebrew into Latin. At the same time, he gave a list of twenty-two canonical books and declared that any book outside his catalogue must be regarded as apocryphal (*Vulg. Reg (H)*. prol. [p. 365 Weber/Gryson]).

In his preface to his translation of the five *Books of Moses*, Jerome responded to the harsh criticism his new Latin translation of the Old Testament evoked. He was even accused of forging a new 'Jewish' version. So, Jerome had to defend and explain his disapproval of the common belief, that the Greek Old Testament, the Septuagint, was verbally inspired. For a critical text, cf. the editions of the *Biblia Sacra* by Weber/Gryson (pp. 3–4) and of *Contra Rufinum* (*Apol.* 2.25 [*CCL* 79, pp. 61–3], since Jerome quoted this passage in his apology); for a commentary, cf. Lardet (1993) 217ff.

TEXT

I have received letters so long and eagerly desired from my dear Desiderius[1] who, as if the future had been foreseen, shares his name with Daniel,[2] entreating me to put our friends in possession of a translation of the Pentateuch from Hebrew into Latin. The work is certainly hazardous and it is exposed to the attacks[3] of the detractors, who maintain that it is through contempt of the Seventy translators that I have set to work to forge a new version to take the place of the old. They thus test ability as they do wine, whereas I have again and again declared that I dutifully offer, in the Tabernacle of God, what I can, and have pointed out that the great gifts which one man brings are not marred by the inferior gifts of another.

But I was stimulated to undertake the task by the zeal of Origen, who blended with the old edition Theodotion's translation[4] and used throughout the work as distinguishing marks the asterisk and the obelus, that is the star and the spit, the first of which makes what had previously been defective to beam with light, while the other slaughters and transfixes all that was superfluous. But I was encouraged above all by the authoritative publications of the Evangelists and Apostles, in which we read much taken from the Old Testament which is not found in our manuscripts. For example, 'Out of Egypt have I called my son',[5] 'For he shall be called a Nazarene',[6] 'They shall look on him whom they pierced',[7] 'Rivers of living water shall flow out of his belly',[8] 'Things which eye has not seen, nor ear heard, nor have entered into the heart of man, which God has prepared for those who love him',[9] and many other passages which lack their proper context. Let us ask our opponents then where these things are written, and when they are unable to tell, let us produce them from the Hebrew. The first passage is in Hosea,[10] the second in Isaiah,[11] the third in Zechariah,[12] the fourth in Proverbs,[13] the fifth also in Isaiah.[14] Being ignorant of all this many follow the ravings of the Apocrypha, and prefer to the authentic books the Spanish rubbish.[15] It is not for me to explain the causes of the error.

The Jews say it was deliberately and wisely done to prevent Ptolemy,[16] who was a worshipper of one God, from thinking the Hebrews acknowledged two deities. And that which chiefly influenced them in thus acting was the fact that the king appeared to be falling into Platonism. In a word, wherever Scripture evidenced some sacred truth respecting Father, Son, and Holy Spirit, they either translated the passage differently, or passed it over altogether in silence, so that they might both satisfy the king, and not divulge the secrets of the faith. I do not know whose false imagination led him to invent the story of the seventy cells at Alexandria, in which, though separated from each other, the translators were said to have written the same words.[17] Aristeas, the protector of that same Ptolemy,[18] and Josephus,[19] long after, relate nothing of the kind; their account is that the Seventy assembled in one basilica[20] consulted together, and did not prophesy. For it is one thing to be a prophet, another to be a translator. The former, through the Spirit, foretells things to come; the latter must use his learning and facility in speech to translate what he understands. It can hardly be that we must suppose Tully was inspired with rhetorical spirit when he translated Xenophon's *Oeconomicus*, Plato's *Protagoras*, and the oration of Demosthenes *In Defence of Ctesiphon*.[21] Otherwise the Holy Spirit must have quoted the same books in one sense through the Seventy translators, in another through the Apostles, so that, whereas they said nothing of a given matter, these falsely affirm that it was so written. What then? Are we condemning our predecessors? By no means.[22] But following those who have preceded us we contribute such work in the house of the Lord as lies in our power. They translated before the advent of Christ, and expressed in ambiguous terms that which they knew not. We, after his passion and resurrection, write not prophecy so much as history. For one style is suitable to what we hear, another to what we see. The better we understand a subject, the better we describe it.

Listen then, my rival, listen, my detractor: I do not condemn, I do not censure the Seventy, but I am bold enough to prefer the Apostles to them all. It is the Apostle through whose mouth I hear the voice of Christ, and I read that in the classification of spiritual gifts they are placed before prophets,[23] while interpreters occupy almost the lowest place. Why are you tormented with jealousy? Why do you inflame the minds of the ignorant against me? Wherever in translation I seem to you to go wrong, ask the Hebrews, consult their teachers in different cities. What they have concerning Christ your manuscripts do not contain.[24] The case is different if they have rejected[25] passages which were afterwards used against them by the Apostles, and the Latin texts are more correct than the Greek, the Greek than the Hebrew! But this is said against jealous people. I ask you now, my dearest Desiderius, who encouraged me to undertake such a work and to make a start with the book of Genesis, to support me with your prayers, so that I will be able to translate the books into Latin in the same spirit in which they have been written.

16

THE CONTROVERSIALIST
Against Vigilantius

INTRODUCTION

Throughout his life, Jerome did not hesitate to fight against a large group of opponents whom he lampooned as half-witted heretics and cantankerous backbiters. His major polemical writings assault personal enemies: *Against Helvidius, Against Jovinian, Against John of Jerusalem*, and *Against Rufinus*, some others attack heterodox groups: *Against the Luciferians* and *Against the Pelagians*. Jerome was not content with denouncing his adversaries; at the same time, he depicted himself as a stronghold of orthodoxy and insisted that his scholarship was beyond criticism. His brilliant invectives not only illustrate his nasty character, as scholars have suggested, but also the fierce fight for ideological and material resources fought by Christian intellectuals. Only the fittest were able to survive.

One key issue in the theological debate of the late fourth and the beginning of the fifth century was asceticism. Opposition to monastic practices was common. Also, Vigilantius, a presbyter of Aquitaine, propagated anti-ascetic and anti-monastic views, attacked the cult of the martyrs, ridiculed the vigils at the basilicas of the martyrs, and rejected the cult of the saints. Finally, he criticized the sending of alms to Palestine and proposed to spend them among the poor in each separate diocese. The bishop Exuperius of Toulouse strongly supported Vigilantius, so that his ideas began to spread widely.

Vigilantius was born about 370, at Calagurris, near Convenae (Comminges), which was a station on the Roman road from Aquitaine to Spain. Once, on the recommendation of Paulinus of Nola, he had visited Jerome at Bethlehem where he was involved in the Origenist controversy and left the congregation in great haste, perhaps also shocked by Jerome's fanatic asceticism (cf. E. A. Clark [1992] 36). After his return to the west, he accused Jerome of being a follower of Origen. Jerome first replied in *ep.* 61 deriding his calumniator's intellectual deficiencies. Some years later (404), Riparius, a presbyter from Gaul, asked Jerome to rebuke the heretical notions of Vigilantius. Already, then, Jerome recommended that the monster's 'tongue should be cut out or he should be put under treatment for insanity' (*ep.* 109.2.4). After receiving the latter's work, Jerome started immediately to refute him. In a single night he composed this grim reply, which Georg Grützmacher described as Jerome's 'most venomous invective' ([1901–8] iii 97).

The text of *Against Vigilantius* is to be found in *PL* 23, 339–52 (353–68); a new edition in *CCL* is forthcoming. A short commentary is provided by Opelt (1973) 119ff.; cf. Wiesen (1964) 222ff. Some more conventional remarks on Jerome's heresiological argument are to be found in Jeanjean (1999) 55ff. On Vigilantius, cf. Crouzel (1972); Rebenich (1992a) 240ff.; Hunter (1999); Trout (1999) 97ff.; 220ff. For the context of ecclesiastical politics of the late fourth century Gallic church, cf. Fontaine (1973); Stancliffe (1983) 71ff.; Mathisen (1989); Van Dam (1985); Van Dam (1993).

TEXT

1   The world has given birth to many monsters; in Isaiah[1] we read of centaurs and sirens, screechowls and pelicans. Job, in mystic language, describes Leviathan and Behemoth.[2] Cerberus and the birds of Stymphalus, the Erymanthian boar and the Nemean lion, the Chimaera and the many-headed Hydra, are told of in poetic fables. Virgil describes Cacus.[3] Spain has produced Geryon, with his three bodies.[4] Gaul alone has had no monsters, but has ever been rich in men of courage and great eloquence. All at once Vigilantius, or, more correctly, Dormitantius,[5] has arisen, animated by an unclean spirit, to fight against the Spirit of Christ and to deny that religious reverence is to be paid to the tombs of the martyrs. Vigils, he says, are to be condemned; Alleluia must never be sung except at Easter; continence is a heresy; chastity a hotbed of lust. And as Euphorbus is said to have been born again in the person of Pythagoras,[6] so in this fellow the corrupt mind of Jovinian has arisen;[7] so that in him, no less than in his predecessor, we are bound to meet the snares of the devil. The words may be justly applied to him: 'Seed of

evildoers, prepare your children for the slaughter because of the sins of your father.'[8] Jovinian, condemned by the authority of the church of Rome, amidst pheasants[9] and swine's flesh, breathed out, or rather belched out his spirit. And now this tavern-keeper of Calagurris,[10] who, according to the name of his native village is a dumb Quintilian,[11] is mixing water with the wine.[12] According to the trick which he knows of old, he is trying to blend his perfidious poison with the Catholic faith. He assails virginity and hates chastity. He revels with worldlings and declaims against the fasts of the saints. He plays the philosopher over his cups, and soothes himself with the sweet strains of psalmody, while he smacks his lips over his cheese-cakes; nor could he deign to listen to the psalms of David and Jedutun, and Asaph and the sons of Korah, except at the banqueting table. This I have poured forth with more grief than amusement, for I cannot restrain myself and turn a deaf ear to the wrongs inflicted on Apostles and martyrs.

2   Shameful to relate, there are bishops who are said to be associated with him in his wickedness – if at least they are to be called bishops[13] – who ordain no deacons but such as have been previously married, who credit no celibate with chastity – rather, who show clearly what measure of holiness of life they can claim by indulging in evil suspicion of all men, and, unless the candidates for ordination appear before them with pregnant wives, and infants wailing in the arms of their mothers, will not administer to them Christ's ordinance. What are the churches of the east to do? What is to become of the Egyptian churches and those belonging to the apostolic seat, which accept for the ministry only men who are virgins, or those who practice continence, or, if married, abandon their conjugal rights? Such is the teaching of Dormitantius, who throws the reins upon the neck of lust, and by his encouragement doubles the natural heat of the flesh, which in youth is mostly at boiling point, or rather slakes it by intercourse with women; so that there is nothing to separate us from swine, nothing wherein we differ from the brute creation, or from horses, respecting which it is written: 'They were towards women like raging horses; everyone neighed after his neighbour's wife.'[14] This is what the Holy Spirit says by the mouth of David: 'Do not behave like a horse and a mule which have no understanding.'[15] And again respecting Dormitantius and his friends: 'Bind the jaws of them who do not come near you with bit and bridle.'[16]

3   But it is now time for us to adduce his own words and answer him in detail. For, possibly, in his malice, he may choose once more to misrepresent me, and say that I have trumped up a case for the sake of showing off my rhetorical and declamatory powers in combating it, like the letter which I wrote to Gaul, relating to a mother and daughter who were at variance.[17] This little treatise, which I now dictate, is due to the reverend presbyters Riparius and Desiderius, who write that their parishes have been defiled by being in his neighbourhood, and have sent me, by our brother Sisinnius, the books which he vomited forth in a drunken fit.[18] They also declare that some persons are found who, from their inclination to his vices, assent to his blasphemies. He is a barbarian both in speech and knowledge. His style is rude.[19] He cannot defend even the truth, but, for the sake of laymen, and poor women, laden with sins, ever learning and never coming to a knowledge of the truth, I will spend upon his rubbish[20] a single night's labour, otherwise I shall seem to have treated with contempt the letters of the reverend persons who have entreated me to undertake the task.

4   He certainly well represents his race. Sprung from a set of brigands and persons collected together from all quarters (I mean those whom Gnaeus Pompey, after the conquest of Spain, when he was hastening to return for his triumph, brought down from the Pyrenees and gathered together into one town, whence the name of the city Convenae[21]), he has carried on their brigand practices by his attack upon the church of God. Like his ancestors the Vectones,[22] the Arrebaci, and the Celtiberians,[23] he makes his raids upon the churches of Gaul, not carrying the standard of the cross, but, on the contrary, the ensign of the devil. Pompey did just the same in the East. After overcoming the Cilician and Isaurian pirates and brigands, he founded a city, bearing his own name, between Cilicia and Isauria.[24] That city, however, to this day, observes the ordinances of its ancestors, and no Dormitantius has arisen in it, but Gaul supports a native foe, and sees seated in the church a man who has lost his head and who ought to be put in the strait-jacket which Hippocrates recommended.[25] Among other blasphemies, he may be heard to say, 'What need is there for you not only to pay such honour, not to say adoration, to the thing, whatever it may be, which you carry about in a little vessel and worship?' And again, in the same book, 'Why do you kiss and adore a bit of powder wrapped up in a cloth?' And again, in the same book, 'Under the cloak of religion we see what is all but

a heathen ceremony introduced into the churches: while the sun is still shining, heaps of tapers are lighted, and everywhere a paltry bit of powder, wrapped up in a costly cloth, is kissed and worshipped. Great honour do men of this sort pay to the blessed martyrs, who, they think, are to be made glorious by trumpery tapers, when the Lamb who is in the midst of the throne, with all the brightness of his majesty, gives them light?'

5   Madman, who in the world ever adored the martyrs? Who ever thought man was God? Did not Paul and Barnabas, when the people of Lycaonia thought them to be Jupiter and Mercury, and would have offered sacrifices to them, rend their clothes and declare they were men?[26] Not that they were not better than Jupiter and Mercury, who were but men long ago dead, but because, under the mistaken ideas of the Gentiles, the honour due to God was being paid to them. And we read the same respecting Peter, who, when Cornelius wished to adore him, raised him by the hand, and said, 'Stand up, for I also am a man.'[27] And have you the audacity to speak of 'the mysterious something or other which you carry about in a little vessel and worship'? I want to know what it is that you call 'something or other'. Tell us more clearly (that there may be no restraint on your blasphemy) what you mean by the phrase 'a bit of powder wrapped up in a costly cloth in a tiny vessel'. It is nothing less than the relics of the martyrs which he is vexed to see covered with a costly veil, and not bound up with rags or hair-cloth, or thrown on the dunghill, so that Vigilantius alone in his drunken slumber may be worshipped. Are we, therefore guilty of sacrilege when we enter the basilicas of the Apostles? Was the Emperor Constantius guilty of sacrilege when he transferred the sacred relics of Andrew, Luke, and Timothy to Constantinople?[28] In their presence the demons cry out, and the devils who dwell in Vigilantius confess that they feel the influence of the saints. And in the present day is the Emperor Arcadius guilty of sacrilege, who after so long a time has conveyed the bones of the blessed Samuel from Judea to Thrace?[29] Are all the bishops to be considered not only sacrilegious, but silly into the bargain, because they carried that most worthless thing, dust and ashes, wrapped in silk, in a golden vessel? Are the people of all the churches fools, because they went to meet the sacred relics, and welcomed them with as much joy as if they beheld a living prophet in the midst of them, so that there was one great swarm of people from Palestine to Chalcedon with one voice re-echoing the praises of Christ? They

were, indeed, adoring Samuel and not Christ, whose Levite and prophet Samuel was. You show mistrust because you think only of the dead body, and therefore blaspheme. Read the Gospel: 'The God of Abraham, the God of Isaac, the God of Jacob: He is not the God of the dead, but of the living.'[30] If then they are alive, they are not, to use your expression, kept in honourable confinement.

6 For you say that the souls of Apostles and martyrs have their abode either in the bosom of Abraham, or in the place of refreshment, or under the altar of God, and that they cannot leave their own tombs, and be present where they will. They are, it seems, of senatorial rank, and are not subjected to the worst kind of prison and the society of murderers, but are kept apart in liberal and honourable custody in the isles of the blessed and the Elysian fields. Will you lay down the law for God? Will you put the Apostles into chains? So that to the day of judgment they are to be kept in confinement, and are not with their Lord, although it is written concerning them, 'They follow the Lamb, wherever he goes.'[31] If the Lamb is present everywhere, the same must be believed respecting those who are with the Lamb. And while the devil and the demons wander through the whole world, and with only too great speed present themselves everywhere; are martyrs, after the shedding of their blood, to be kept out of sight shut up in the altar,[32] from whence they cannot escape? You say, in your pamphlet, that so long as we are alive we can pray for one another; but once we die, the prayer of one person for another cannot be heard, and all the more because the martyrs, though they cry[33] for the avenging of their blood, have never been able to obtain their request. If Apostles and martyrs while still in the body can pray for others, when they ought still to be anxious for themselves, how much more must they do so when once they have won their crowns, overcome, and triumphed? A single man, Moses, often wins pardon from God for six hundred thousand armed men;[34] and Stephen, the follower of his Lord and the first Christian martyr, entreats pardon for his persecutors;[35] and when once they have entered on their life with Christ, shall they have less power than before? The Apostle Paul says that two hundred and seventy-six souls were given to him in the ship;[36] and when, after his dissolution, he has begun to be with Christ, must he shut his mouth, and be unable to say a word for those who throughout the whole world have believed in his Gospel? Shall Vigilantius the live dog be better than Paul the

dead lion? I should be right in saying so after Ecclesiastes,[37] if I admitted that Paul is dead in spirit. The truth is that the saints are not called dead, but are said to be asleep. Wherefore Lazarus, who was about to rise again, is said to have slept.[38] And the Apostle forbids the Thessalonians to be sorry for those who were asleep.[39] As for you, when wide awake you are asleep, and asleep when you write, and you bring before me an apocryphal book which, under the name of Esdras, is read by you and those of your feather, and in this book it is written that after death no one dares pray for others.[40] I have never read the book: for what need is there to take up what the church does not receive? It can hardly be your intention to confront me with Balsamus, and Barbelus, and the Thesaurus of Mani,[41] and the ludicrous name of Leusiboras;[42] though possibly because you live at the foot of the Pyrenees, and border on Iberia, you follow the incredible marvels of the ancient heretic Basilides[43] and his so-called knowledge, which is mere ignorance, and set forth what is condemned by the authority of the whole world. I say this because in your short treatise you quote Solomon as if he were on your side, though Solomon never wrote the words in question at all; so that, as you have a second Esdras you may have a second Solomon. And, if you like, you may read the imaginary revelations of all the patriarchs and prophets, and, when you have learned them, you may sing them among the women in their weaving-shops,[44] or rather order them to be read in your taverns, the more easily by this rubbish[45] to stimulate the ignorant mob to replenish their cups.

7 As to the question of tapers, however, we do not, as you in vain misrepresent us, light them in the daytime, but by their solace we would cheer the darkness of the night, and watch for the dawn, lest we should be blind like you and sleep in darkness. And if some persons, being ignorant and simple minded laymen, or, at all events, religious women – of whom we can truly say, 'I allow that they have a zeal for God, but not according to knowledge'[46] – adopt the practice in honour of the martyrs, what harm is thereby done to you? Once upon a time even the Apostles pleaded that the ointment was wasted, but they were rebuked by the voice of the Lord.[47] Christ did not need the ointment, nor do martyrs need the light of tapers; and yet that woman poured out the ointment in honour of Christ, and her heart's devotion was accepted. All those who light these tapers have their reward according to their faith, as the Apostle says: 'Let every one

abound in his own meaning.'[48] Do you call men of this sort idolaters? I do not deny that all of us who believe in Christ have passed from the error of idolatry. For we are not born Christians, but become Christians by being born again. And because we formerly worshipped idols, does it follow that we ought not now to worship God lest we seem to pay like honour to him and to idols? In the one case respect was paid to idols, and therefore the ceremony is to be abhorred; in the other the martyrs are venerated, and the same ceremony is therefore to be allowed. Throughout the whole Eastern church, even when there are no relics of the martyrs, whenever the Gospel is to be read the candles are lighted, although the dawn may be reddening the sky, not of course to scatter the darkness, but by way of evidencing our joy. And accordingly the virgins in the Gospel always have their lamps lighted.[49] And the Apostles are told to have their loins girded, and their lamps burning in their hands.[50] And of John Baptist we read, 'He was the lamp that burns and shines';[51] so that, under the figure of corporeal light, that light is represented of which we read in the Psalter, 'Your word is a lamp unto my feet, O Lord, and a light unto my paths.'[52]

8   Does the bishop of Rome do wrong when he offers sacrifices to the Lord, as we should say, over the venerable bones of the dead men Peter and Paul, but according to you, over a worthless bit of dust, and judges their tombs worthy to be Christ's altars? And not only is the bishop of one city in error, but the bishops of the whole world, who, despite the tavern-keeper Vigilantius, enter the basilicas of the dead, in which 'a worthless bit of dust and ashes lies wrapped up in a cloth,' defiled and defiling all else. Thus, according to you, the sacred buildings are like the sepulchres of the Pharisees, whitened without, while within they have filthy remains, and are full of foul smells and uncleanliness. And then he dares to expectorate his filth upon the subject and to say: 'Is it the case that the souls of the martyrs love their ashes, and hover round them, and are always present, lest haply if any one come to pray and they were absent, they could not hear?' Oh, monster, who ought to be banished to the ends of the earth![53] Do you laugh at the relics of the martyrs, and in company with Eunomius,[54] the father of this heresy, slander the churches of Christ? Are you not afraid of being in such company, and of speaking against us the same things which he utters against the church? For all his followers refuse to enter the basilicas of Apostles and martyrs, so that, indeed, they may worship the dead

Eunomius, whose books they consider are of more authority than the Gospels; and they believe that the light of truth was in him just as other heretics maintain that the Paraclete came into Montanus,[55] and say that Mani himself was the Paraclete. You cannot find an occasion of boasting, even supposing you are the inventor of a new kind of wickedness, for your heresy long ago broke out against the church. It found, however, an opponent in Tertullian, a very learned man, who wrote a famous treatise which he called most correctly *Scorpiacum*,[56] because, as the scorpion bends itself like a bow to inflict its wound, so what was formerly called the heresy of Cain[57] pours poison into the body of the church; it has slept or rather been buried for a long time, but has been now awakened by Dormitantius. I am surprised you do not tell us that there must upon no account be martyrdoms, inasmuch as God, who does not ask for the blood of goats and bulls, much less requires the blood of men. This is what you say, or rather, even if you do not say it, you are taken as meaning to assert it. For in maintaining that the relics of the martyrs are to be trodden under foot, you forbid the shedding of their blood as being worthy of no honour.

9   Respecting vigils and the frequent keeping of nightwatches in the basilicas of the martyrs, I have given a brief reply in another letter[58] which, about two years ago, I wrote to the reverend presbyter Riparius. You argue that they ought to be abjured, lest we seem to be often keeping Easter, and appear not to observe the customary yearly vigils.[59] If so, then sacrifices should not be offered to Christ on the Lord's day lest we frequently keep the Easter of our Lord's Resurrection, and introduce the custom of having many Easters instead of one. We must not, however, impute to pious men the faults and errors of youths and worthless women such as are often detected at night. It is true that, even at the Easter vigils, something of the kind usually comes to light; but the faults of a few form no argument against religion in general, and such persons, without keeping vigil, can go wrong either in their own houses or in those of other people. The treachery of Judas did not annul the loyalty of the Apostles. And if others keep vigil badly, our vigils are not thereby to be stopped; no, rather let those who sleep to gratify their lust be compelled to watch that they may preserve their chastity. For if a thing once done be good, it cannot be bad if often done; and if there is some fault to be avoided, the blame lies not in its being done often, but in its being done at all. And so we should not

watch at Easter-tide for fear that adulterers may satisfy their long pent-up desires, or that the wife may find an opportunity for sinning without having the key turned against her by her husband. The occasions which seldom recur are those which are most eagerly longed for.

10 I cannot traverse all the topics embraced in the letters of the reverend presbyters;[60] I will adduce a few points from the tracts of Vigilantius. He argues against the signs and miracles which are wrought in the basilicas of the martyrs, and says that they are of service to the unbelieving, not to believers, as though the question now were for whose advantage they occur, not by what power. Granted that signs belong to the faithless, who, because they would not obey the word and doctrine, are brought to believe by means of signs. Even our Lord wrought signs for the unbelieving, and yet our Lord's signs are not on that account to be impugned, because those people were faithless, but must be worthy of greater admiration because they were so powerful that they subdued even the hardest hearts, and compelled men to believe. And so I will not have you tell me that signs are for the unbelieving; but answer my question: how is it that poor worthless dust and ashes are associated with this wondrous power of signs and miracles? I see, I see, most unfortunate of mortals, why you are so sad and what causes your fear. That unclean spirit who forces you to write these things has often been tortured by this worthless dust, yes, and is being tortured at this moment, and though in your case he conceals his wounds, in others he makes confession. You will hardly follow the heathen and impious Porphyry[61] and Eunomius, and pretend that these are the tricks of the demons, and that they do not really cry out, but feign their torments. Let me give you my advice: go to the basilicas of the martyrs, and some day you will be cleansed; you will find there many in like case with yourself, and will be set on fire, not by the martyrs' tapers which offend you, but by invisible flames; and you will then confess what you now deny, and will freely proclaim your name – that you who speak in the person of Vigilantius are really either Mercury, for he was greedy of gain; or Nocturnus, who, according to Plautus' *Amphitryon*,[62] slept while Jupiter, two nights together, had his adulterous connection with Alcmena, and thus begot the mighty Hercules; or at all events Father Bacchus,[63] of drunken fame, with the tankard hanging from his shoulder, with his ever ruby face, foaming lips, and unbridled brawling.

11 Once, when a sudden earthquake in this province awoke us all out of our sleep in the middle of the night, you, the most prudent and the wisest of men, began to pray without putting your clothes on, and recalled to our minds the story of Adam and Eve in Paradise; they, indeed, when their eyes were opened were ashamed, for they saw that they were naked, and covered their shame with the leaves of trees; but you, who were stripped alike of your shirt and of your faith, in the sudden terror which overwhelmed you, and with the fumes of your last night's booze still hanging about you, showed your wisdom by exposing your nakedness in only too evident a manner to the eyes of the brethren.[64] Such are the adversaries of the church; these are the leaders who fight against the blood of the martyrs; here is a specimen of the orators who thunder against the Apostles, or, rather, such are the mad dogs which bark at the disciples of Christ.

12 I confess my own fear, for possibly it may be thought to spring from superstition. When I have been angry, or have had evil thoughts in my mind, or some phantom of the night has beguiled me, I do not dare to enter the basilicas of the martyrs, I shudder all over in body and soul. You may smile, perhaps, and deride this as on a level with the wild fancies of weak women. If it be so, I am not ashamed of having a faith like that of those who were the first to see the risen Lord; who were sent to the Apostles; who, in the person of the mother of our Lord and Saviour, were commended to the holy Apostles. Belch out your shame, if you will, with men of the world, I will fast with women; no, with religious men whose looks witness to their chastity, and who, with the cheek pale from prolonged abstinence, show forth the chastity of Christ.

13 Something, also, appears to be troubling you. You are afraid that, if continence, sobriety, and fasting strike root among the people of Gaul, your taverns will not pay, and you will be unable to keep up through the night your diabolical vigils and drunken revels. Moreover, I have learnt from those same letters that, in defiance of the authority of Paul, no, rather of Peter, John, and James, who gave the right hand of fellowship to Paul and Barnabas, and commanded them to remember the poor, you forbid any pecuniary relief to be sent to Jerusalem for the benefit of the saints. Now, if I reply to this, you will immediately give tongue and cry out that I am pleading my own cause. You, indeed, were so generous to the whole community that if you had not come to Jerusalem, and lavished your own money or

that of your patrons, we should all be on the verge of starvation. I say what the blessed Apostle Paul says in nearly all his Epistles; and he makes it a rule for the churches of the Gentiles that, on the first day of the week, that is, on the Lord's day, contributions should be made by every one which should be sent up to Jerusalem for the relief of the saints, and that either by his own disciples, or by those whom they should themselves approve; and if it were thought fit, he would himself either send, or take what was collected.[65] Also in the Acts of the Apostles, when speaking to the governor Felix, he says, 'After many years I went up to Jerusalem to bring alms to my nation and offerings, and to perform my vows, amidst which they found me purified in the temple.'[66] Might he not have distributed in some other part of the world, and in the infant churches which he was training in his own faith, the gifts he had received from others? But he longed to give to the poor of the holy places who, abandoning their own little possessions for the sake of Christ, turned with their whole heart to the service of the Lord. It would take too long now if I purposed to repeat all the passages from the whole range of his Epistles in which he advocates and urges with all his heart that money be sent to Jerusalem and to the holy places for the faithful; not to gratify avarice, but to give relief; not to accumulate wealth, but to support the weakness of the poor body, and to stave off cold and hunger. And this custom continues in Judea to the present day, not only among us, but also among the Hebrews, so that they who meditate in the law of the Lord, day and night,[67] and have no father upon earth except the Lord alone,[68] may be cherished by the aid of the synagogues and of the whole world; that there may be equality – not that some may be refreshed while others are in distress, but that the abundance of some may support the need of others.[69]

14 You will reply that every one can do this in his own country, and that there will never be wanting poor people who ought to be supported with the resources of the church. And we do not deny that doles should be distributed to all poor people, even to Jews and Samaritans, if the means will allow. But the Apostle teaches that alms should be given to all, indeed, especially, however, to those who are of the household of faith.[70] And respecting these the Saviour said in the Gospel, 'Make to yourselves friends of the mammon of unrighteousness, who may receive you into everlasting habitations.'[71] What! Can those poor creatures, with their rags and filth, lorded over, as they are, by raging lust, can they

who own nothing, now or hereafter, have eternal habitations? No doubt it is not the poor simply, but the poor in spirit, who are called blessed; those of whom it is written, 'Blessed is he who gives his mind to the poor and needy; the Lord shall deliver him in the evil day.'[72] But the fact is, in supporting the poor of the common people, what is needed is not mind, but money. In the case of the saintly poor the mind has blessed exercises, since you give to one who receives with a blush, and when he has received is grieved, that while sowing spiritual things he must reap your carnal things. As for his argument that they who keep what they have, and distribute among the poor, little by little, the increase of their property, act more wisely than they who sell their possessions, and once for all give all away, not I but the Lord shall make answer: 'If you wish to be perfect, go, sell all that you have and give to the poor, and come, follow me.'[73] He speaks to him who wishes to be perfect, who, with the Apostles, leaves father, ship, and net. The man whom you approve stands in the second or third rank; yet we welcome him provided it be understood that the first is to be preferred to the second, and the second to the third.

15 Let me add that our monks are not to be deterred from their resolution by you with your viper's tongue and savage bite.[74] Your argument respecting them runs thus: If all men were to seclude themselves and live in solitude, who is there to frequent the churches? Who will remain to win those engaged in secular pursuits? Who will be able to urge sinners to virtuous conduct? Similarly, if all were as silly as you, who could be wise? And, to follow out your argument, virginity would not deserve our appro- bation. For if all were virgins, we should have no marriages, the race would perish, infants would not cry in their cradles, midwives would lose their pay and turn beggars; and Dormitan- tius, all alone and shrivelled up with cold, would lie awake in his bed. The truth is, virtue is a rare thing and not eagerly sought after by the many. Would that all were as the few of whom it is said: 'Many are called, few are chosen.'[75] The prison would be empty. But, indeed, a monk's function is not to teach, but to lament, to mourn either for himself or for the world, and with terror to anticipate our Lord's advent. Knowing his own weakness and the frailty of the vessel which he carries, he is afraid of stumbling, lest he strike against something, and it fall and be broken. Hence he shuns the sight of women, and particularly of young women, and so far chastens himself as to dread even what is safe.

16 Why, you will say, go to the desert? The reason is plain: That I
may not hear or see you, that I may not be disturbed by your
madness, that I may not be engaged in conflict with you, that the
eye of the harlot not lead me captive: that beauty may not lead
me to unlawful embraces. You will reply: 'This is not to fight,
but to run away. Stand in line of battle, put on your armour and
resist your foes, so that, having overcome, you may wear the
crown.' I confess my weakness. I would not fight in the hope of
victory, lest some time or other I lose the victory. If I flee, I
avoid the sword; if I stand, I must either overcome or fall. But
what need is there for me to let go certainties and follow after un-
certainties? Either with my shield or with my feet I must shun
death. You who fight may either be overcome or may overcome.
I who fly do not overcome, inasmuch as I fly; but I fly to make
sure that I may not be overcome. There is no safety in sleep with
a serpent beside you. Possibly he will not bite me, yet it is
possible that after a time he may bite me. We call women
mothers who are no older than sisters and daughters, and we do
not blush to cloak our vices with the names of piety. What
business has a monk in the women's cells? What is the meaning
of secret conversation and looks which shun the presence of witnesses? Holy love has no restless desire. Moreover, what we have
said respecting lust we must apply to avarice, and to all vices
which are avoided by solitude. We therefore keep clear of the
crowded cities, that we may not be compelled to do what we are
urged to do, not so much by nature as by choice.[76]

17 At the request of the reverend presbyters, as I have said, I have
devoted to the dictation of these remarks the labour of a single
night,[77] for my brother Sisinnius is hastening his departure for
Egypt, where he has relief to give to the saints, and is impatient
to be gone. If it were not so, however, the subject itself was so
openly blasphemous as to call for the indignation of a writer
rather than a multitude of proofs. But if Dormitantius wakes up
that he may again abuse me, and if he thinks fit to disparage me
with that same blasphemous mouth with which he pulls to pieces
Apostles and martyrs, I will spend upon him something more
than this short lucubration. I will keep vigil for a whole night on
his behalf and on behalf of his companions, whether they be
disciples or masters, who think no man to be worthy of Christ's
ministry unless he is married and his wife is seen to be with
child.[78]

17

THE THRENODIST
Letter 127 to Principia

INTRODUCTION

Ten letters in Jerome's *opera omnia* are written to offer words of comfort to friends afflicted by grief. Two threnodies were composed in Rome: letter 23 to Marcella to console her for the loss of her friend Lea, and letter 39 to Paula whose daughter Blesilla had died within three months of her conversion to asceticism. Letter 60 is a consolatory letter to Jerome's old friend Heliodorus, now bishop of Altinum, who had lost his nephew Nepotian (on *ep.* 60 there is an excellent commentary by Scourfield [1993]). Letter 66 reached Pammachius after the death of his young wife Paulina, one of Paula's daughters. Letter 75 tries to soothe the grief of the Spanish lady Theodora who had recently lost her husband Lucinus (cf. Rebenich [1992a] 293ff.). Letter 77 to Oceanus is a eulogy of the Roman aristocrat Fabiola, and *epistula* 79 is a letter of consolation to Salvina on the death of her husband Nebridius, who was a member of the imperial court at Constantinople. Letter 108, Jerome's largest consolation, is addressed to Eustochium on Paula's death. Letter 118 is written to the wealthy nobleman Julian whose wife and two daughters had died.

Jerome varied his composition with regard to the individual addressee, the specific situation of the case, and the persons involved. His approach emphasizes the flexibility of the genre. Jerome's consolations, which do not reflect a chronological development (*pace* Guttilla [1980–1] and [1984–5]), illustrate Christian assimilation of pagan consolatory literature. Jerome relies upon the Bible, but he also absorbs the pagan literary tradition and includes a number of classical quotations, *exempla*, and other references. Scourfield (1993) 33 has rightly stressed 'Jerome's conscious and unabashed use of both classical and biblical sources'. For Jerome and the consolatory tradition, cf. also Favez (1937); Duval (1977); and Kierdorf (1980).

Although Jerome's consolations are associated with the expression of sympathy, with exhortation and comfort, he quite often celebrated the ascetic virtues of the deceased and encouraged the bereaved to live a life of renunciation and poverty. The eulogistic element features prominently in consolations to members of the senatorial aristocracy. Here, Jerome propagated a new, Christian concept of nobility that was not based upon illustrious ancestry, but upon ascetic perfection. Paula is praised: *nobilis genere, sed multo nobilior sanctitate* – 'noble in family, she was much nobler still in holiness' (Hier. *ep.* 108.1.1). But the elitist self-fashioning of the Roman aristocrats who perceived themselves as *pars melior generis humani*, 'a better part of mankind' (Symm. *ep.* 1,52), was not challenged by Jerome. On the contrary, the Christianization of the aristocratic family traditions completed and consummated the glorious past of the pagan *gentes*. The social standing and prestige of a noble clan was no longer measured by the number of consuls and praetorian prefects, but by Christian *virtutes* and ascetic castigation. Now the 'holy pride' (*sancta superbia*, cf. Hier. *ep.* 22.16.1) of the Christian ladies excelled the fame of the politicians (cf. Rebenich [1992a] 181ff. and Feichtinger [1997a]).

Letter 127, written about two years after the sack of Rome in 410, should be considered as a memoir, or an obituary, of Jerome's influential patroness Marcella, addressed to her Roman protégée Principia. The Roman aristocrat Marcella (for a new biography, see Letsch-Brunner [1998]), after being widowed at an early age, held firm to her decision, against the opposition of her family, to live an ascetic life and to gather in her palace on the Aventine a circle of Christian women. At the beginning of the fifth century, Jerome had called the Roman matron of rank and her fellow aristocrat, the senator Pammachius, *Christiani senatus lumina*, 'lights of the Christian senate' (Hier. *ep.* 97.3.1). After describing Marcella's biography, character, and intellectual studies, and celebrating her devotion to chastity, Jerome praised her eminent position in the fight against heresy, especially against Origenism (*ep.* 108.9–11; 9–11; cf. also Laurence [1996]). He depicted Marcella as the first Roman lady to adopt the monastic life and she thus becomes a paragon of asceticism and orthodoxy. But Jerome overemphasized her dependence on his theological advice and underrepresented her individualism in doctrinal questions, since Marcella was familiar with the works of various contemporary Christian writers and formed an opinion of her own in theological and church–political issues.

The letter includes a vivid description of the fall of Rome, which is dramatically intervowen with the eve of Marcella's life (*ep*. 108.12–14). For a substantial analysis of the letter, cf. de Vogüé (1991–8) vol. i. 5, 223ff.

TEXT

1   You have begged me often and earnestly, Principia,[1] virgin of Christ, to dedicate a letter to the memory of that holy woman Marcella, and to set forth the goodness we so long enjoyed for others to know and to imitate. And it grieves me that you should spur a willing horse[2] and think that I need your entreaties when I do not yield even to you in love of her. In recording her signal virtues I shall receive far more benefit myself than I can possibly confer upon others. That I have hitherto remained silent and have allowed two years to go over without speaking, has not been due to a wish to ignore her as you wrongly suppose, but rather to an incredible sorrow, which has so overwhelmed my mind that I judged it better to remain silent for the moment than to praise her virtues in inadequate language. Neither will I now follow the rules of rhetoric in eulogizing your, my, or to speak more truly, our Marcella,[3] the glory of all saints and especially of the city of Rome. I will not extol her illustrious family, the splendour of her noble lineage, and the long series of consuls and praetorian prefects who have been her ancestors.[4] I will praise her for nothing but that which is her own and which is the more noble, because despising wealth and rank she has won higher nobility by poverty and humility.[5]

2   Her father's death left her an orphan,[6] and she had been married less than seven months when her husband was taken from her.[7] Then Cerealis, whose name is famous among the consuls,[8] paid court to her with great assiduity since he was attracted by her youth, her ancient family, her beauty – which always is an attraction to men – and her self-control. Being an old man he promised her all his money and offered to transfer his fortune so that she might consider herself less his wife than his daughter. Moreover, her mother Albina tried very hard to secure such an illustrious protector for the widowed household. But Marcella answered: 'If I wished to marry and not rather to dedicate myself to perpetual chastity, I should look for a husband and not for an inheritance.' When Cerealis argued that sometimes old men live long while young men die early, she cleverly retorted: 'A young man may possibly die early, but an old man cannot live long.' This definite

rejection convinced other men that they had no hope of winning her hand.

In the Gospel according to Luke we read the following passage: 'There was also a prophetess, Anna, the daughter of Phanuel, of the tribe of Aser. She was a very old woman and had seen many days. She had lived with a husband seven years from her virginity; and she was a widow of eighty-four years. She never left the temple but served God with fasting and prayer night and day.'[9] It is no marvel that she won the vision of the Saviour, whom she sought so earnestly. Let us then compare her case with that of Marcella. Let us compare the seven years with the seven months. Anna hoped for Christ, Marcella held him fast. Anna confessed him at his birth, Marcella believed in him crucified. Anna did not deny the child, Marcella rejoiced in the man as king. I am not drawing distinctions of merit between holy women, as some people foolishly do between holy men and leaders of churches. The conclusion at which I aim is that, as both have one labour, so both have one reward.

3   In a slander-loving community[10] and in a city such as Rome, which formerly was filled with people from all parts of the world and where it was the triumph of wickedness to criticize the upright and to defile even the pure and the clean, it is hard to escape from the fables of calumnious gossips. A stainless reputation is difficult and almost impossible to attain; the prophet hopes rather than thinks to win it when he says: 'Blessed are the undefiled in the way who walk in the law of the Lord.'[11] The undefiled in the way of this world are those whom no breath of scandal has ever sullied and who have earned no reproach from their neighbours. It is this which makes the Saviour say in the Gospel: 'Be kindly to – or: be favourable to – your adversary while you are in the way with him.'[12] Whoever heard anything displeasing of Marcella that deserved credit? Who believed such without making himself guilty of malice and backbiting? She put the gentiles to confusion by showing them the nature of that Christian widowhood which she set forth in her conscience and look.

For worldly women are wont to paint their faces with rouge and white lead, to wear robes of shining silk, to adorn themselves with jewels, to put gold chains round their necks, to pierce their ears and hang in them the costliest pearls of the Red Sea, and to scent themselves with musk. While mourning for the husbands they have lost they rejoice that they have escaped from their partner's dominion, they look about for new mates, intending not to obey them, as God wills, but to rule over them. With this object in view they choose poor men, who are content with the mere name of husbands and who must patiently put up with rivals. And if they murmur, they will be kicked out at once.[13] Our widow wore clothes that were meant to keep out the cold and not to show her figure. Even her gold seal-ring she rejected and chose to store her money in the stomachs of the poor rather than to hide it in a purse.[14] She went nowhere without her mother, and never visited without witnesses one of the monks, or clergy, as the needs of her large household required her to interview. Her escort was always composed of virgins and widows,[15] and these women were serious; for she knew that the licentious behaviour of the maids speaks ill for the mistress and a woman's character is shown by her choice of companions.[16]

4 Her ardent love for the divine Scriptures was incredible. She always sang: 'Your words have I hid in my heart that I might not sin against you',[17] as well as the words which describe the perfect man: 'His delight is in the law of the Lord; and in his law he does meditate day and night.'[18] This meditation in the law meant for her not a review of the written words, as among the Jews the Pharisees think, but a carrying it out in action[19] according to that saying of the Apostle: 'Whether, therefore, you eat or drink or whatsoever you do, do all to the glory of God.'[20] She remembered also the prophet's words: 'Through your precepts I have got understanding,'[21] and knew that only when she had fulfilled these precepts she would be permitted to understand the Scriptures. So we read elsewhere 'that Jesus began both to do and teach.'[22] However fine someone's teaching may be, it is put to the blush when his own conscience rebukes him; and it is in vain that his tongue preaches poverty or teaches almsgiving, if he himself is swollen with the riches of Croesus[23] and if, in spite of his coarse cloak, he fights to keep the moths from his silk robes.

Marcella practised fasting, but in moderation. She abstained from eating meat, and she knew rather the scent of wine than its taste, for she drank it only for her stomach's sake and her frequent infirmities.[24] She seldom appeared in public and took care to avoid the houses of noble ladies, that she might not be forced to look upon what she had once for all renounced. She frequently visited the basilicas of Apostles and martyrs[25] that she might give herself to quiet prayer, avoiding the throng of people. To her mother she was so obedient that occasionally she did for her sake things of which she herself disapproved. For example, when Albina, who was devoted to her own kin, wished to transfer all her property to her brother's family, since she was without sons and grandsons, Marcella would have preferred to give the money to the poor instead, but still she could not go against her mother. Therefore she handed over her necklaces and other effects to people already rich, content to throw away her money rather than to sadden her mother's heart.

5   In those days no lady of rank in Rome knew anything of the monastic life, or had ventured to call herself a nun. For the thing was strange and the name was commonly viewed as ignominious and degrading.[26] It was from some priests of Alexandria, from pope Athanasius, and subsequently from Peter, who to escape the persecution of the Arian heretics had all fled for refuge to Rome as the safest haven in which they could find communion – it was from these that Marcella heard of the life of the blessed Antony, then still alive, and of the monasteries in the Thebaid founded by Pachomius, and of the discipline laid down for virgins and for widows.[27] She was not ashamed to profess a life which she knew was pleasing to Christ. Many years later her example was followed first by Sophronia[28] and then by others, of whom it may be well said in the words of Ennius: 'Would that never in Pelion's woods!'[29]

Marcella's friendship was also enjoyed by the revered Paula, and in her cell Eustochium, that paragon of virgins, was trained. Thus it is easy to see of what character the teacher was who had such pupils.

The unbelieving reader may perhaps laugh at me for dwelling so long on the praises of weak women. But if he will remember how holy women followed our Lord and Saviour and ministered to him of their substance, and how the three Marys stood before the cross and especially how Mary of Magdala – called 'of the tower'[30] from her earnestness and ardent faith – was privileged to see the risen Christ first, even before the Apostles,[31] he will convict himself of pride sooner than me of folly, who judge of virtue not by sex but by character.[32] It was for this reason that Jesus loved the evangelist John most of all. For he was of noble birth and known to the high priest, and he feared the plots of the Jews so little that he introduced Peter into the high priest's courtyard,[33] and was the only Apostle who stood before the cross and took the Saviour's mother to his own home.[34] It was the virgin son[35] who received the virgin mother as a legacy from the virgin Lord.

6   Marcella then lived an ascetic life for many years, and found herself old before she ever remembered that once she had been young, approving Plato's saying that philosophy consists in meditating on death.[36] So our own Apostle says: 'Every day I die for your salvation.'[37] Indeed according to the old copies our Lord himself says: 'Whosoever does not bear his cross daily and come after me cannot be my disciple.'[38] And ages before, the Holy Spirit had declared by the prophet: 'For your sake are we killed all the day long: we are counted as sheep for the slaughter.'[39] Many generations afterwards the words were spoken: 'Remember the end and you will never go wrong,'[40] as well as that precept of the eloquent satirist: 'Live with death in your mind; the hour flies; the word that I speak is so much taken from it.'[41] Well then, as I was saying, Marcella passed her days and lived always in the thought that she must die. Her very dress reminded her of the tomb, and she presented herself as a living sacrifice, reasonable and acceptable unto God.[42]

7   When the needs of the church at last brought me to Rome in company with the holy bishops Paulinus and Epiphanius – the first of whom ruled the church of the Syrian Antioch while the second presided over that of Salamis in Cyprus – I in my modesty was inclined to avoid the eyes of noble ladies.[43] But Marcella pleaded so earnestly, 'both in season and out of season', as the Apostle says,[44] that at last her perseverance overcame my reluctance. And, as in those days my name was held in some renown as that of a student of the Scriptures, she never came to see me without asking me some question about them, nor would she rest content at once, but on the contrary would dispute them; this, however, was not for the sake of argument, but to learn by questioning the answers to such objections which might, as she saw, be raised.[45] How much virtue and intellect, how much holiness and purity I found in her I am afraid to say, both lest I may exceed the bounds of men's belief and lest I may increase your sorrow by reminding you of the blessings you have lost. This only will I say, that whatever I had gathered together by long study, and by constant meditation made part of my nature, she tasted, she learned and made her own. Consequently, after my departure from Rome, if any dispute arose concerning the testimony of the Scriptures, it was to her verdict that appeal was made. And so wise was she and so well did she understand what philosophers call *to prépon*, that is, propriety of conduct,[46] that when she answered questions she gave her own opinion not as

her own but as from me or someone else, thus admitting that what she taught she had herself learned from others. For she knew that the Apostle had said: 'I do not allow a women to teach',[47] and she would not seem to do a wrong to the male sex, and sometimes even to priests, when they questioned her concerning obscure and doubtful points.

8   I have heard that you immediately took my place as her close companion, and that, as the saying goes, you never left her side even for a finger's-breadth.[48] You both lived in the same house, and had the same cell and bed, so that everyone in the city knew for certain that you had found a mother in her and she a daughter in you. An estate in the suburbs of Rome was your monastery,[49] and you chose the country because of its loneliness. For a long time you lived together, and as many ladies followed your example and joined your company, I had the joy of seeing Rome transformed into another Jerusalem. Monastic establishments for virgins became numerous, and there were countless numbers of monks. In fact so many were God's servants that monasticism, which had before been a term of reproach, became subsequently one of honour. Meantime we consoled ourselves for our separation by exchanging letters of encouragement, and discharged in the spirit the debt which in the flesh we could not pay. Our letters always crossed, surpassed in courtesies, and anticipated in greetings. Not much was lost by a separation thus effectually bridged by a constant correspondence.[50]

9   In the midst of this tranquillity and service rendered to God, there arose in these provinces a tempest of heresy which threw everything into confusion, and finally swelled to such a great fury that it spared neither itself nor anything that was good.[51] And as if it were not enough to have disturbed everything here, it introduced a ship freighted with blasphemies to the port of Rome. There the dish soon found itself a cover;[52] and the muddy feet fouled the clear fountain[53] of the Roman faith. No wonder that in the streets and in the marketplace a painted soothsayer can strike fools on the buttocks and, catching up his stick, knock out the teeth of his objector, when such venomous and filthy teaching found dupes at Rome to lead astray. Next came the scandalous version of Origen's book *On First Principles*, and that 'fortunate' disciple[54] who would have been indeed fortunate if he had never fallen in with such a master. Next followed the ardent[55] confutation set forth by my supporters, which threw the school of the Pharisees[56] into confusion. Finally, the holy Marcella, who had long closed

her eyes to all this lest she should be thought to act from party motives, came forward openly since she found that many people failed to respect the faith which the Apostle once praised.[57] As the heretic was drawing to his cause not only priests, monks and above all laity, but was even imposing on the simplicity of the bishop, who judged other men by himself,[58] she publicly withstood him, choosing to please God rather than men.[59]

10 In the Gospel the Saviour praises the dishonest steward because, although he defrauded his master, he acted wisely for himself.[60] The heretics in the same way, seeing that a small spark had kindled a great fire, and that the flames applied by them to the foundations had now reached the housetops, so that the deception practised on many could no longer be hidden, asked for and obtained letters from the church of Rome, stating that they were in full communion until the day of their departure.[61] Shortly afterwards the distinguished Anastasius succeeded to the pontificate;[62] but Rome was not privileged to have him long, for it was not fitting that the head of the world should be struck off during the episcopate of such a great man.[63] He was removed, no doubt, that he might not seek to turn away by his prayers the sentence which God had passed once for all. For the Lord said to Jeremiah: 'Pray not for this people for their good. When they fast I will not hear their cry; and when they offer burnt-offering and oblation, I will not accept them; but I will consume them by the sword and by the famine and by the pestilence.'[64] You may say: 'What has this to do with the praise of Marcella?' It was she who took the first steps in getting the heretics condemned. It was she who furnished witnesses who first had been taught by them and then had been cured of the error of their heresy.[65] It was she who showed how large a number they had deceived, and who brought up against them the impious books *On First Principles*, which were openly on view after being emended by the hand of the scorpion.[66] It was she, finally, who in a succession of letters called on the heretics to appear in their own defence. They did not venture to come, since they were so conscience-stricken that they preferred to be condemned in their absence rather than appear and be convicted. This glorious victory originated with Marcella; you, too, were the source and cause of great blessings.[67] You, who know that I speak the truth, understand that out of many incidents I only mention a few, lest a tiresome repetition should weary the reader. Moreover, I do not wish ill-natured people to think that under the pretext of praising another I am

giving vent to my own rancour. I will pass now to the rest of my story.

11　The hurricane passed from the west into the east and threatened very many with dire shipwreck. Then were fulfilled the words: 'Do you think, when the son of man comes, will he find faith on earth?'[68] The love of many grew cold,[69] but a few who still loved the true faith rallied to my side. Their lives were openly sought and every means was employed against them, so that indeed 'Barnabas also was carried away with their dissimulation,'[70] and committed plain murder, if not in deed at least in will.[71] But behold! God blew and the tempest passed away, and the prediction of the prophet was fulfilled: 'You take away their breath, they die, and return to their dust.'[72] 'In that very day their thoughts perish.'[73] With it also the Gospel saying was accomplished: 'You fool, this night your soul will be required of you; then whose shall those things be, which you have provided?'[74]

12　While these things were happening in Jebus[75] a dreadful rumour came from the west. Rome had been besieged[76] and its citizens had been forced to buy their lives with gold. Then, thus despoiled, they had been besieged again,[77] so as to lose not only their substance but their lives. My voice sticks in my throat; and, as I dictate, sobs interrupt my utterance. The city which had taken the whole world was itself taken;[78] no, it fell by famine before it fell by the sword, and there were but few citizens left to be made captives. The rage of hunger had recourse to impious food; men tore one another's limbs, and the mother did not spare the baby at her breast, taking again within her body that which her body had just brought forth.[79] 'In the night was Moab taken, in the night did her wall fall down.'[80] 'O God, the heathen have come into your inheritance; they have defiled your holy temple; they have made Jerusalem an orchard. The dead bodies of your servants they have given to be meat unto the fowls of heaven, the flesh of your saints unto the beasts of the earth. Their blood have they shed like water all round Jerusalem; and there was none to bury them.'[81]

> Who can set forth the carnage of that night?
> What tears are equal to its agony?
> Of ancient date a sovereign city falls;
> And lifeless in its streets and houses lie
> Unnumbered bodies of its citizens.
> In many a ghastly shape does death appear.[82]

13 Meanwhile, as was natural in such confusion, one of the blood-stained victors burst his way into Marcella's house. 'Be it mine to say what I have heard,'[83] rather to relate what those holy men have seen who were present at that time, and they say that you too were with her in the hour of danger. When the soldiers entered she is said to have received them with fearless face; and when they asked her for gold and buried treasures she pointed to her coarse dress. However, they would not believe in her self chosen poverty, but beat her with sticks and whipped her. She is said to have felt no pain, but to have thrown herself in tears at their feet and to have begged them that you might not be taken from her, or your youth forced to endure what she as an old woman had no occasion to fear. Christ softened their hard hearts, and even among blood-stained swords an attitude of respect found place. The barbarians conveyed both her and you to the basilica of the Apostle Paul, that you might find there either a place of safety or a tomb. There Marcella is said to have burst into great joy thanking God for having kept you unharmed for her. She said she was thankful too that captivity had found her poor, not made her so, and that she was now in want of daily bread, but that Christ satisfied her needs so that she no longer felt hunger. She was able to say in word and in deed: 'Naked came I out of my mother's womb, and naked shall I return thither. Just as it seemed good to the Lord, so it has been done; blessed be the name of the Lord.'[84]

14 After a few months[85] she fell asleep in the Lord, sound in mind and not suffering from any malady. She made you the heir of her poverty, or rather she made the poor her heirs through you. In your arms she closed her eyes, your lips received her last breath; you shed tears but she smiled[86] conscious of having lived a good life and hoping for her reward hereafter.

In one short night I have dictated this letter to you,[87] revered Marcella, and to you, my daughter Principia, not to show off my own eloquence but to express my deepfelt gratitude to you both. My one desire has been to please both God and my readers.

18

THE ASCETIC EXPERT

Letter 128 to Pacatula

INTRODUCTION

One of Jerome's favourite subjects was asceticism. Many letters and invectives were written to set forth his conception of Christian ascetic life and his monastic ideal. Jerome not only theorized about ascetic perfection, but gave practical advice. Central to his programme was sexual abstinence, and he did not cease to encourage his audience to maintain virginity and chastity, to give alms, to visit the sick, to reject the amenities of civilized life, to keep a strict diet, to neglect clothing, to separate from relatives and friends, to ignore worldly company, and to avoid carnal temptation. More than any other contemporary Latin Christian author, Jerome contributed 'to the definitive sexualization of Paul's notion of *the flesh*' (P. Brown [1988] 376). The praise of virginity was sung in many letters addressed to aristocratic ladies, who were able to support the eloquent ascetic expert. Jerome's most famous treatise on this topic is certainly *ep*. 22 'On the preservation of virginity' (*De virginitate servanda*), written for the young woman Eustochium. Yet, Jerome always insisted that the ascetic *propositum* and monastic life should be based on *lectio divina* (i.e. a systematic study of Scripture and ecclesiastical authors; cf. Gorce [1925]). Therefore, his authority as a learned exegete was vital for his militant campaign for radical seclusion.

Not only women, but also some men, were the victims of Jerome's radical interpretation of Christian asceticism. Nepotianus, for instance, the nephew of Jerome's old friend Heliodorus (for whom cf. *ep*. 14), is the recipient of *ep*. 52, in which Jerome tried to give guidance for those who wanted to combine their ascetic life and their ecclesiastical career (cf. Rousseau [1978] 126). Nepotianus had, like his uncle, abandoned civil or military service (cf. *ep*. 60.9.2) and was now a presbyter at Altinum in the province of Venetia-Istria, where

Heliodorus was bishop. The letter, full of classical quotations and biblical references, is a systematic treatise on how members of the clergy should conduct their life. Asceticism had now become part of the everyday life of the church and laid the spiritual foundation of clerical authority. In *ep.* 125 to Rusticus of Marseille, Jerome also harmonized monastic conduct and ordination to the presbyterate. Although a life in solitude, far away from the cities, remained the ideal of monasticism (*ep.* 125,20,5), the domestic setting was no longer a *conditio sine qua non*, at least for ambitious and wealthy young men. Ascetic perfection is defined as the best preparation for the priesthood and the episcopate (cf. Rebenich [1992a] 289ff.).

The most bewildering pieces of ascetic propaganda are two pedagogical manuals Jerome wrote for his Roman audience. Laeta, daughter-in-law of Paula, was told in *ep.* 107 how she ought to bring up her infant daughter, also called Paula. Some ten years later (after August 410), Jerome gave advice for the training of the Roman girl Pacatula (*ep.* 128). Both girls were consecrated to virginity and to the service of Christ, as soon as they were born. The conduct their mothers had been free to choose was now imposed upon them. Jerome demanded an entirely ascetic education, excluded the study of secular literature, recommended the reading of the Bible from the beginning to the end and of the edifying books written by the Fathers. For this purpose, they should learn Greek and Latin. When the girls get older, boys are to be kept at a distance, they should mortify their bodies by vigils and fasting, be simply dressed and confined to their room, and even shun baths since they 'add fuel to a sleeping fire' (*ep.* 107.11.2). Instead they are told to recite prayers and psalms at night, sing hymns in the morning and spin wool. Finally, Jerome invited Laeta to send Paula to Bethlehem. He seems to have been successful. Although some have applauded this educational scheme, more sensible readers have realized that the little girls were to be forcibly trained up as nuns (cf. Kelly [1975] 275). It should be noted that the Latin boys taught by Jerome himself in his monastery enjoyed a more traditional curriculum: grammar, Virgil, the comic and lyric poets, and the historians (cf. Ruf. *Apol.* 2.11 [*CCL* 20, p. 92]). The harsh precepts for Christian perfection in *ep.* 128, however, are contrasted with a vivid account of the collapsing Roman Empire and the sack of Rome by Alaric in AD 410. In this letter, too, Jerome makes extensive use of classical elements (*pace* Hagendahl [1958] 256).

There are patristic reflections on Jerome's pedagogical expertise (Brunner [1910]; Bardicchia [1925]; Gorce [1932]; Favez [1948]; Faggin [1971], 225ff.), some illuminating remarks by Feichtinger

(1995a) 220ff., and a commentary on *ep*. 107 by Scourfield (1983) 432ff.

TEXT

1   It is difficult to write to a little girl who cannot understand what you say, of whose mind you know nothing, and of whose inclinations it would be rash to prophesy. In the words of a famous orator's preface 'She is to be praised more for what she will be than for what she is.'[1] For how can you speak of self-control to a child who is eager for cakes, who babbles in her mother's arms, and to whom honey is sweeter than any words?[2] Will she hear the deep things of the Apostle when all her delight is in old wives' tales? Will she heed the dark sayings[3] of the prophets when her nurse can frighten her by a frowning face? Or will she comprehend the majesty of the Gospel, when its splendour dazzles all men's intellect? Shall I urge her to obey her parents when with her chubby hand she beats her smiling mother? For such reasons as these my dear Pacatula must read at some other time the letter that I send her now. Meanwhile let her learn the alphabet, spelling, grammar, and syntax. To induce her to repeat her lessons with her little shrill voice, hold out to her as reward a honeycake.[4] She will make haste to perform her task if she hopes afterwards to get some sweetmeats, or a bright bunch of flowers, a glittering bauble, an enchanting doll. She must also learn to spin, shaping the yarn with her tender thumb; for, even if she constantly breaks the threads, a day will come when she will no longer break them. Then when she has finished her lessons she ought to have some recreation. At such times she may hang round her mother's neck, or snatch kisses from her relatives. Reward her for singing psalms that she may love what she has to learn. Her task will then become a pleasure, not a matter of necessity but one of free-will.

2   Some mothers, when they have vowed a daughter to virginity, dress her in dark clothes, wrap her up in a black cloak, and let her have neither linen garments nor gold ornaments on her head and neck. They wisely refuse to accustom her to what she will afterwards have to lay aside. Others act on the opposite principle. 'What is the use,' say they, 'of keeping such things from her? Will she not see them on others? Women are fond of finery[5] and many whose chastity is beyond question dress not for men but

for themselves. Give her what she asks for, but show her that those are most praised who ask for nothing. It is better that she should enjoy things to the full and so learn to despise them, than that from not having them she should wish to have them.' 'This,' they continue, 'was the plan which the Lord adopted with the children of Israel. When they longed for the fleshpots of Egypt he sent them swarms of quails until they gorged themselves and were sick.[6] Those who have once lived worldly lives more readily forego the pleasures of sense than those who from their youth up have known nothing of desire.' 'The former', so they argue, 'trample on what they know, the latter are attracted by what is to them unknown. While the former penitently shun the insidious advances of pleasure from which they have escaped, the latter are allured by the delights of the body and the titillation of the flesh until they find that what they thought to be as sweet as honey is deadly poison.'[7] 'For "the lips of an adulteress drop as an honeycomb",[8] which is sweet indeed in the eater's mouth but is afterwards found more bitter than gall.'[9] 'This' – they argue – 'is the reason that honey is never offered in the sacrifices of the Lord,[10] that the wax in which honey is stored is contemned, and that oil, the product of the bitter olive, is burned in his temple.[11] Moreover it is with bitter herbs that the passover is eaten,[12] and "with the unleavened bread of sincerity and truth."[13] Those who receive these shall suffer persecution in the world. Wherefore the prophet symbolically sings: "I sat alone because I was filled with bitterness" '.[14]

3   What then? Is youth to run riot so that luxury may afterwards be more resolutely rejected? 'Far from it,' they say 'let every man, wherein he is called, therein abide.'[15] 'If a man is called with the marks of circumcision on him' – that is, a virgin – 'let him not become uncircumcised'[16] – that is, let him not seek the coat of marriage given to Adam on his expulsion from the paradise of virginity.[17] 'Is any called in uncircumcision' – that is, having a wife and covered in the skin of matrimony – let him not seek the nakedness of virginity[18] and of that eternal chastity which he has lost once for all. No, let him possess his vessel in sanctification and honour,[19] let him drink of his own wells not out of the dissolute cisterns[20] of the brothels which cannot hold within them the pure waters of chastity.[21] The same Paul also in the same chapter, when discussing the subjects of virginity and marriage, calls those who are married slaves of the flesh, but those not under the yoke of wedlock freemen, who serve the Lord in all freedom.[22]

What I am saying now I am not saying as universally applicable; my treatment of the subject is only partial. I speak of some only, not of all. However my words are addressed to those of both sexes, and not only to 'the weaker vessel.'[23] Are you a virgin? Why then do you find pleasure in the society of a woman? Why do you commit to the high seas your frail patched boat, why do you so confidently face the great peril of a dangerous voyage? You know not what you desire, and yet you cling to her as though you had either desired her before or, to put it as leniently as possible, as though you would hereafter desire her. 'Women,' you will say, 'make better servants than men.' In that case choose an old woman, choose one who is mishappen, choose one whose continence is approved in the Lord. Why should you find pleasure in a young girl, pretty, and voluptuous? You frequent the baths, walk abroad sleek and ruddy, eat flesh, abound in riches, and wear the most expensive clothes; and yet you fancy that you can sleep safely beside a death-dealing serpent. Do you say that you do not live in the same house with her, at least at night? But you spend whole days in conversing with her. Why do you sit alone with her and without any witnesses? By so doing, if you do not actually sin you appear to do so, and you embolden unhappy men by your example, and the authority of your name, to do what is wrong. You too, whether virgin or widow, why do you allow a man to detain you in conversation so long? Why are you not afraid to be left alone with him? At least go out of doors to satisfy the wants of nature, and for this at any rate leave the man. With your brother you did not behave with such liberty as this, and you were more modest with your husband. You have some question, you say, to ask concerning the Holy Scriptures. If so, ask it publicly; let your maidservants and your attendants hear it. 'Everything that is made manifest is light.'[24] Honest words do not look for a corner, or rather they are glad to have hearers and to win praise. He must be a fine teacher who thinks little of men, does not care for the brothers, and labours in secret merely to instruct just one weak woman.

4   I have wandered a little from my immediate subject to discuss other topics; and while it is my object to train, or rather to nurse, the infant Pacatula, I have in a moment drawn upon myself the hostility of many women who will be hard to pacify.[25] But I shall now return to my proper theme.

A woman[26] should associate only with her own sex, she should not know how to play with boys, no, she should be afraid to do so. She should never hear an unclean word, and if amid the bustle of the household she should chance to hear one, she should not understand it. Her mother's nod should be to her as much as speech, her mother's advice equivalent to a command. She should love her as her parent, obey her as her mistress, and reverence her as her teacher. She is now a child without teeth and without ideas, but, as soon as she is seven years old, a blushing girl knowing what she should not say and doubting what she should say, she should commit to memory the Psalter, and until she is grown up, the books of Solomon, the Gospels, the Apostles and the prophets should be the treasure of her heart.

She should not appear in public too freely nor always seek crowded churches. All her pleasure should be in her chamber. She must never look at young men or turn her eyes upon curled fops, who wound the soul through the ears with their sweet voices. The wantonness of other girls must also be kept from her. The more freedom of access such persons possess, the harder is it to avoid them when they come; and what they have once learned themselves they will secretly teach her and will thus contaminate a secluded Danaë by vulgar talk.[27]

Let her teacher be her companion, her pedagogue her guardian, let her be a woman not given to much wine, one who, in the Apostle's words, is not idle nor a tattler,[28] but sober, grave, industrious in spinning wool[29] and one whose words will form a girl's mind to the practice of virtue. For, as water follows a finger drawn through the sand, so one of soft and tender years is pliable for good or evil; she can be drawn in whatever direction you choose to guide her. Moreover, spruce and gay young men often seek access to young ladies by flattering or paying court to nurses, or by bribing them,[30] and when they have thus gently effected their approach they blow up the first spark into a conflagration[31] and little by little advance to the most shameless requests. And it is quite impossible to stop them then, for the verse is proved true in their case: 'You can hardly blame a habit which yourself you have allowed.'[32] I am ashamed to say it, and yet I must. Highborn ladies who have rejected more high born suitors cohabit with men of the lowest grade and even with slaves. Sometimes in the name of religion and under the cloak of continence they desert their husbands, and like another Helen follow their Alexander[33] without the smallest fear of Menelaus. Such things are seen and lamented, but they are not punished, for the multitude of sinners gives licence to sin.[34]

5   Shameful to say, the world sinks into ruin, but our sins still flourish. The renowned city, the capital of the Roman Empire, is swallowed up in one tremendous fire; and there is no part of the earth where Romans are not in exile.[35] Churches once held sacred are now but heaps of dust and ashes; and yet we have our minds set on the desire for gain. We live as though we are going to die tomorrow; yet we build as though we are going to live always in this world.[36] Our walls shine with gold, gold gleams upon our ceilings and upon the capitals of our pillars; yet Christ dies before our doors naked and hungry in the persons of his poor. The pontiff Aaron, we read, faced the raging flames, and by putting fire in his censer checked the wrath of God. The high priest stood between the dead and the living, and the fire dared not pass his feet.[37] God said to Moses, 'Let me alone and I will consume this people,'[38] showing by the words 'let me alone' that he can be withheld from doing what he threatens. The prayers of his servant hindered his power. Who, think you, is there now under heaven able to stay God's wrath, to face the flame of his judgment, and to say with the Apostle, 'I could wish that I myself were accursed for my brethren'?[39] Flocks and shepherds perish together, because as it is with the people, so is it with the priest.[40] Moses spoke in his compassionate love, 'yet now if you will, forgive their sin; and if not, blot me, I pray you, out of your book.'[41] He desires to perish with those that perish and is not satisfied to secure his own salvation; for indeed 'in the multitude of people is the king's honour.'[42]

Such are the times into which our little Pacatula has been born. These are the rattles of her earliest childhood. She is destined to know of tears before laughter and to feel sorrow sooner than joy. And hardly does she come upon the stage when she is called on to make her exit. She thinks that the world has always been what it is now. She knows not of the past, she shrinks from the present, she fixes her desires on what is to come.

These thoughts of mine are but hastily written down. For my grief for lost friends has known no intermission and only recently have I recovered sufficient composure to write an old man's letter to a little child. My affection for you, brother Gaudentius,[43] has induced me to make the attempt and I have thought it better to say a few words than to say nothing at all. The grief that paralyses my will will excuse my brevity; whereas, if I were to say nothing, the sincerity of my friendship might well be doubted.

Part III

BIBLIOGRAPHY

JEROME'S WORKS

For a detailed list of Jerome's *opera*, see:

- CPL = Clavis patrum Latinorum, qua in Corpus Christianorum edendum optimas quasque scriptorum recensiones a Tertulliano ad Bedam commode recludit E. Dekkers. Ed. tertia, aucta, et emendata, Steenbrugge 1995, No. 580–621.
- ThLL = Thesaurus linguae Latinae. Index librorum scriptorum inscriptionum ex quibus exempla afferuntur. Ed. altera, Leipzig 1990, 113–19.
- H. J. Frede, Kirchenschriftsteller. Verzeichnis und Sigel. Repertorium scriptorum ecclesiasticorum latinorum saeculo nono antiquiorum siglis adpositis quae in editione Bibliorum Sacrorum iuxta veterem latinam versionem adhibentur, Vetus Latina, vol. 1.1, 4. Auflage, Freiburg 1995, 510–32 (cf. also R. Gryson, Aktualisierungsheft 1999, Freiburg 1999).

Abbreviations of the major editions:

CCL   = Corpus Christianorum, Series Latina
CSEL = Corpus Scriptorum Ecclesiasticorum Latinorum
GCS   = Griechische Christliche Schriftsteller
PL   = Patrologia Latina, ed. J. Migne
SC   = Sources Chrétiennes (with French translation).

For other abbreviations used in the present work, including classical authors and biblical books, see *The Oxford Dictionary of the Christian Church*, third edition, Oxford 1997; *The Oxford Classical Dictionary*, third edition, Oxford 1996; and *Lexikon der Alten Welt*, Zurich/Stuttgart 1965 (repr. 1990).

The only complete edition of Jerome's works is still that of D. Vallarsi (11 vols, Verona 1734–42), reprinted in *PL* 22–30. Note that the pagination differs in the two editions of Migne's *PL. addenda et corrigenda* are published in *PLS* 2, 18–328. A modern edition in *CCL* (vol. 72–80) is in progress; *CCL* also provides *Instrumenta Lexicologica Latina* and a *Thesaurus Sancti Hieronymi* based on the *opera omnia* of Jerome except the translations (Turnhout 1990).

The most comprehensive English translation of Jerome's writings is to be found in *The Nicene and Post-Nicene Fathers* (*NPNF*), Second Series, vol. 3: Theodoret, Jerome, Gennadius, Rufinus, transl. by E. C. Richardson and W. H. Fremantle, 1892; and vol. 6: St Jerome: Letters and Select Works, transl. by W. H. Fremantle, 1893. There are various reprints and an electronic version of *NPNF* (http://www.ccel.org/fathers2). Some prefaces to Jerome's biblical studies, especially to the Vulgate and his commentaries, are rendered or paraphrased in *NPNF*, Second Series, vol. 6, 483–502.

BIBLE

For Jerome's prefaces to the Vulgate, cf. R. Weber and R. Gryson, *Biblia sacra iuxta Vulgatam versionem*, 2 vols, Stuttgart [4]1994.

For his prefaces to translations from the Septuagint, cf. *PL* 29 and *Biblia sacra iuxta Latinam Vulgatam versionem ad codicum fidem* . . . Rome 1926ff.

COMMENTARIES AND BIBLICAL STUDIES

Quaestiones Hebraicae in Genesim. Ed.: *CCL* 72, 1959, 1–56; P. Lagarde [= 1868]. Cf. *PL* 23, 935 (983) ff. Transl.: Hayward (see Secondary Literature).

Liber interpretationis Hebraicorum nominum (= *Liber de nominibus Hebraicis*). Ed.: *CCL* 72, 57–161; P. Lagarde [= [2]1887]. Cf. *PL* 23, 771 (815) ff.

De locis (= *De situ et nominibus locorum Hebraicorum liber*). Ed. of Jerome's version of Eusebius' *Onomastikon* in *GCS* 11.1 = *Eusebius Werke* 3.1, 1904; E. Klostermann. Cf. *PL* 23, 859 (903) ff.

Commentariolus in psalmos. Ed.: *CCL* 72, 1959, 177–245; G. Morin [= 1895]. Cf. *PLS* 2, 29ff.

Commentarius in Ecclesiasten. Ed.: *CCL* 72, 1959, 249–361; M. Adriaen. Cf. *PL* 23, 1009 (1061) ff.

Commentariorum in Esaiam libri XVIII. Ed.: R. Gryson *et al.*, *Commentaires de Jérôme sur le prophète Isaïe*, 5 vols., Freiburg 1993–9. *CCL* 73 and 73A, 1959–63; M. Adriaen. Cf. *PL* 24, 17 ff.

In Esaiam (1, 1–6) parvula adbreviatio de capitulis paucis. Ed.: Duval (1993). Cf. *CCL* 73A, 801–9; *PL* 24, 937 (973) ff.

In Hieremiam libri VI. Ed.: *CSEL* 59, 1913 = *CCL* 74, 1960; S. Reiter. Cf. *PL* 24, 679 (705) ff.

Commentariorum in Hiezechielem libri XIV. Ed.: *CCL* 75, 1964; F. Glorie. Cf. *PL* 25, 15 ff.

Commentariorum in Danielem libri III. Ed.: *CCL* 75A, 1964; F. Glorie. Cf. *PL* 25, 491 (513) ff. Transl.: G. L. Archer, *Jerome's Commentary on Daniel*, Grand Rapids 1958 [*non vidi*].

Commentarii in prophetas minores. Ed.: *CCL* 76–76A, 2 vols, 1969; M. Adriaen. Cf. *PL* 25, 815 (855) ff.

For Jerome's commentary on Jonah (*Commentariorum in Ionam prophetam liber*), cf. Y-M. Duval, *Jérôme. Commentaire sur Jonas*, *SC* 323, Paris 1985. Transl.: T. M. Hegedus, *Jerome's commentary on Jonah*, PhD, Waterloo, Ont. 1991. N. Pavia, *Commento al libro di Giona*, Rome 1992 (with an Italian translation).

Commentariorum in Evangelium Matheum libri IV. Ed.: *CCL* 77, 1969; D. Hurst and M. Adriaen. E. Bonnard, *Saint Jérôme. Commentaire sur S. Matthieu*, *SC* 242, 259, 2 vols, Paris 1977–9. Cf. *PL* 26, 15 ff.

Commentarii in epistulas Paulinas ad Galatas, ad Ephesios, ad Titum, ad Philemonem. Ed.: *PL* 26, 307–618 (331–656).

HOMILIES AND TRACTATES

Jerome's *Tractatus in psalmos*, his homilies, sermons, and other tractates are edited in *CCL* 78, 1958; G. Morin [cf. *Anecdota Maredsolana* iii. 2–3, 1897–1903], B. Capelle, J. Fraipont.

A translation of Jerome's 59 *Tractatus in Psalmos*, his *Tractatuum in Psalmos series altera*, his *Tractatus in Marci Evangelium*, and of various *homiliae* is to be found in *The Fathers of the Church*, vol. 48 (1964) and vol. 57 (1966), by M. L. Ewald. Cf. also M-H. Stébé, *Marc, commenté par Jérôme et Jean Chrysostome*, Paris 1986, 23–100 (French translation and commentary) and G. Coppa, *Origene – Girolamo, 74 omelie sul libro dei salmi*, Milan 1993 (Italian translation and commentary).

LETTERS

Ed.: *CSEL* 54 (1910), 55 (1912), 56 (1918); I Hilberg. Ed. altera supplementis aucta 1996; Indices comp. M. Kamptner 1996 (= *CSEL* 56.2); cf. S. Rebenich, *Gymnasium* 106 (1999) 75–8.

Letters not published in *CSEL*: Epistula ad Praesidium (= Ps.-Hier. *ep*. 18): G. Morin in *BALAC* 3, 1913, 51–60. Cf. *PL* 30, 182 (188) ff.

Epistula 27* ad Aurelium Papam Carthaginensem: *CSEL* 88, 1981, 130–3; J. Divjak. Cf. J. Divjak and Y-M. Duval, *Bibliothèque Augustinienne* 46B, Paris 1987, 394–401; 560–568 (with a French translation and commentary).

Epistula ad Sophronium de ecclesia Lyddensi: M. van Esbroeck, *Bedi Karthlisa. Révue de karthvélologie* 35, 1977, 127–31.

J. Labourt, *Saint Jérôme. Lettres*, 8 vols, *Collection Budé*, Paris 1949–63 (Latin text with a French translation). S. Cola, *San Girolamo, Le lettere*, 4 vols, Rome 1961–3, ²1996–7 (Italian translation and commentary).

English translations: *NPNF*, Second Series, vol. 6, 1–295, 447. F. A. Wright, *Select Letters of St. Jerome*, *Loeb Classical Library* vol. 262, Cambridge, Mass./London 1933 (various reprints). C. C. Mierow and T. Comerford Lawler, *The Letters of St. Jerome* [*ep*. 1–22], *Ancient Christian Writers* vol. 33, Westminster 1963. P. Carroll, *The Satirical Letters of St. Jerome*, Chicago 1956 [*non vidi*].

The correspondence between Jerome and Augustine is edited by J. Schmid, *SS. Eusebii Hieronymi et Aurelii Augustini Epistulae mutuae*, *Florilegium Patristicum* vol. 22, Bonn 1930. For an English translation, cf. White (1990). There are special studies of some letters which include commentaries and/or translations; cf. e.g. Bartelink (1980); Bastiaensen *et al.* (1975); Scourfield (1983); Scourfield (1993).

POLEMICAL WRITINGS

Altercatio Luciferiani et Orthodoxi. Ed.: *CCL* 79B, 2000; A. Canellis. Cf. *PL* 23, 155 (163) ff. Transl.: *NPNF*, Second Series, vol. 6, 319–34.

Adversus Helvidium de Mariae virginitate perpetua. Ed.: *PL* 23, 183–206 (193–216). Transl.: *NPNF*, Second Series, vol. 6, 334–46. J. N. Hritzu, *Saint Jerome. Dogmatic and Polemical Works*, *The Fathers of the Church*, vol. 53, Washington, DC 1965, 1–43.

Adversus Iovinianum. Ed.: *PL* 23, 211–338 (221–352). Cf. E. Bickel, *Diatribe in Senecae philosophi fragmenta* 1, Leipzig 1915, 382–420 (text of 1, 41–9; 2,5–14). Transl.: *NPNF*, Second Series, vol. 6, 346–416.

Contra Vigilantium. Ed.: *PL* 23, 339–52 (353–68). Transl.: *NPNF* Second Series, vol. 6, 417–23.

Contra Iohannem Hierosolymitanum. Ed.: *CCL* 79A, 1999; J. Feiertag. Cf. *PL* 23, 355 (371) ff. Transl.: *NPNF*, Second Series, vol. 6, 424–47.

Contra Rufinum (Apologia contra Rufinum, libri II and *Epistula adversus Rufinum*

[= *Liber tertius adversus libros Rufini*]). Ed.: *CCL* 79, 1982; P. Lardet.
P. Lardet, *Saint Jérôme. Apologie contre Rufin*, *SC* 303, Paris 1983. Cf.
PL 23, 397 (415) ff. Transl.: *NPNF*, Second Series, vol. 3, 482–541.
J. N. Hritzu, *Saint Jerome. Dogmatic and Polemical Works*, *The Fathers
of the Church*, vol. 53, Washington, DC 1965, 45–220. For a
commentary see Lardet (1993).

Dialogi adversus Pelagianos. Ed. *CCL* 80, 1990; C. Moreschini. Cf. *PL* 23,
495 (517) ff. Transl.: *NPNF*, Second Series, vol. 6, 447–83. J. N.
Hritzu, *Saint Jerome. Dogmatic and Polemical Works*, *The Fathers of the
Church*, vol. 53, Washington, DC 1965, 221–378.

TRANSLATIONS

Chronicon. Ed. of Jerome's translation and continuation of Eusebius'
Chronicle in *GCS* 47 = *Eusebius Werke* 7, [2]1956 ([3]1984); R. Helm.
Transl.: M. D. Donalson, *A Translation of Jerome's Chronicon with His-
torical Commentary*, Lewiston, New York, 1996. Cf. also Brugnoli,
Curiosissimus Excerptor (see Secondary Literature), who reproduces
Helm's edition and comments upon the text (in Italian).

Origenis in Ieremiam homiliae. *Ed.*: *PL* 25, 585–692. *GCS* 33 = *Origenes
Werke* 8, 1925, 290–317; W. A. Baehrens. *SC* 238, 1977, 300–67;
P. Nautin.

Origenis in Ezechielem homiliae. Ed.: *GCS* 33 = *Origenes Werke* 8, 1925,
319–454; W. A. Baehrens. *SC* 352, 1989; M. Borret.

Origenis in Isaiam homiliae. Ed.: *GCS* 33 = *Origenes Werke* 8, 1925, 242–89;
W. A. Baehrens.

Origenis in Canticum Canticorum homiliae. Ed.: *GCS* 33 = *Origenes Werke* 8,
1925, 27–60; W. A. Baehrens. *SC* 37[2], 1966; O. Rousseau.

Didymi Alexandrini liber de Spiritu Sancto. Ed.: *SC* 386, 1992; L. Doutreleau.

Origenis in Lucam homiliae. Ed.: *GCS* 49 = *Origenes Werke* 9, [2]1959;
M. Rauer. *SC* 87, 1962; H. Crouzel, F. Fournier, P. Périchon. Cf.
Fontes Christiani vol. 4.1–2, 1991–2; H-J. Sieben.

Pachomiana. Ed.: A. Boon, *Pachomiana Latina*, Leuven 1932.

OTHER WORKS

Vita S. Pauli. Ed.: *PL* 23, 17–28 (= Vallarsi). Cf. I. S. Kozik, *The First
Desert Hero: St. Jerome's Vita Pauli*, New York 1968 and B.
Dégorski, *Edizione critica della* Vita Sancti Pauli primi eremitae *di
Girolamo*, Rome 1987. Transl.: *NPNF*, Second Series, vol. 6,

299–303. M. L. Ewald, *Early Christian Biographies, The Fathers of the Church*, vol. 15, Washington, DC 1952 (²1964; ³1981), 217–38. For an English commentary, cf. Hoelle (1953).

Vita S. Hilarionis. Ed.: A. Bastiaensen and C. Moreschini, *Vite dei Santi*, vol. 4, Rome 1975, 72–143; 291–317 (with an Italian translation and commentary). Cf. *PL* 23, 29 ff. Transl.: *NPNF*, Second Series, vol. 6, 303–15. M. L. Ewald, *Early Christian Biographies, The Fathers of the Church*, vol. 15, Washington, DC 1952 (²1964; ³1981), 239–80.

Vita Malchi. Ed.: C. C. Mierow, Sancti Eusebii Hieronymi Vita Malchi Monachi Captivi, *The Classical Bulletin*, St Louis 1946 (= Classical Essays Presented to J. A. Kleist), 31–60. Cf. *PL* 23, 55 ff. Transl.: *NPNF*, Second Series, vol. 6, 315–18. M. L. Ewald, *Early Christian Biographies, The Fathers of the Church*, vol. 15, Washington, DC 1952 (²1964; ³1981), 281–97.

De viris illustribus. Ed.: A. Ceresa-Gastaldo, *Gerolamo. Gli uomini illustri*, Florence 1988 (with an Italian translation and commentary). E. Richardson, *Texte und Untersuchungen* 14.1., Leipzig 1896, 1–56. Cf. C. A. Bernoulli, Freiburg 1895 (repr. Frankfurt 1968); G. Herding, Leipzig 1924. Transl.: *NPNF*, Second Series, vol. 3, 359–84. Th. P. Halton, *Saint Jerome. On Illustrious Men, The Fathers of the Church*, vol. 100, Washington, DC 1999.

SECONDARY LITERATURE

NB: Books suggested as a basic reading on Jerome are entered on a tinted background. Periodicals are referred to in abbreviated form according to *L'Année Philologique.* Bibliographies are also provided by: P. Antin in *CCL* 72, viii–lix and G. Sanders and M. van Uytfanghe, *Bibliographie signalétique du Latin des Chrétiens,* CC Lingua Patrum, vol. i, Turnhout 1989, 71–6. Superior figures indicate edition numbers.

Adams, J. D., *The Populus of Augustine and Jerome: A Study in the Patristic Sense of Community,* New Haven 1971.

Adkin, N., Some Notes on the Dream of Saint Jerome, *Philologus* 128, 1984, 119–26.

——, Gregory of Nazianzenus and Jerome: Some Remarks, in M. A. Flower and M. Toher (eds), *Georgica. Greek Studies in Honour of George Cawkwell,* London 1991, 13–24.

——, *Taceo de meis similibus* (Jerome, *epist.* 53,7), *VetChrist* 29, 1992, 261–8.

——, Hierosolymam militaturus pergerem. A Note on the Location of Jerome's Dream, *Koinonia* 17, 1993a, 81–3.

——, The Date of the Dream of Saint Jerome, *SCO* 43, 1993b, 263–73.

——, 'Adultery of the Tongue': Jerome, Epistle 22.29.6f., *Hermes* 121, 1993c, 100–8.

——, Ambrose and Jerome: the Opening Shot, *Mnemosyne* 46, 1993d, 364–76.

——, Jerome, Ambrose and Gregory Nazianzen, *Vichiana* 4, 1993e, 294–300.

——, Juvenal and Jerome, *CPh* 89, 1994, 69–72.

——, Jerome's Use of Scripture Before and After his Dream, *ICS* 20, 1995, 183–90.

——, Who is *accusator meus* at the Start of Jerome's *Liber de optimo genere interpretandi* (Epist. 57)?, *Latomus* 55, 1996a, 876–7.

Adkin, N., Pope Siricius' 'Simplicity' (Jerome, epist. 127,9,3), *VetChr* 33, 1996b, 25–38.

——, Jerome on Ambrose. The Preface of the Translation of Origen's *Homilies on Luke*, *RBen* 107, 1997, 5–14.

——, Jerome's Vow 'Never to Reread the Classics': Some Observations, *REA* 101, 1999a, 161–7.

——, Jerome on Marcella. Epist. 127,10,4, *BStudLat* 29, 1999b, 564–70.

——, *Biblia pagana*: Classical Echoes in the Vulgate, *Augustinianum* 40, 2000a, 77–87.

——, Jerome, Seneca, Juvenal, *RBPh* 78 2000b, 119–28.

Allen, M., The Martyrdom of Jerome, *JECS* 3, 1995, 211–13.

Allgeier, A., Haec vetus et vulgata editio, *Biblica* 29, 1948, 353–90.

Antin, P., *Essai sur saint Jérôme*, Paris 1951.

——, *Recueil de saint Jérôme*, Brüssel 1968.

——, Catalogus chez Jérôme and Érasme, *REAug* 18, 1972, 191–3.

Arnheim, M. T. W., *The Senatorial Aristocracy in the Later Roman Empire*, Oxford 1972.

Arns, E., *La Technique du livre d'après saint Jérôme*, Paris 1953.

Bagnall, R. S., *Egypt in Late Antiquity*, Princeton 1993.

Bammel, C. P. H., Die Hexapla des Origenes: Die *hebraica veritas* im Streit der Meinungen, *Augustinianum* 28, 1988, 125–49.

Bammel, C. P. H., Die Pauluskommentare des Hieronymus: Die ersten wissenschaftlichen lateinischen Bibelkommentare?, in *Cristianesimo Latino e cultura Greca sino al sec. IV.*, Rome 1993, 187–207.

Banniard, M., Jérôme et l''elegantia' d'après le *De optimo genere interpretandi*, in Y-M. Duval (ed.), *Jérôme entre l'Occident et l'Orient*, Paris 1988, 305–22.

Bardicchia, A., *Il pensiero morale e pedagogico di S. Girolamo*, Materna 1925.

Barnes, T. D., *Tertullian. A Historical and Literary Study*, Oxford [2]1985.

——, Angel of Light or Mystic Initiate? The Problem of the *Life of Antony*, *JThS* N.S. 37, 1986, 353–67.

——, *Athanasius and Constantius. Theology and Politics in the Constantinian Empire*, Cambridge, Mass./London 1993.

——, Statistics and the Conversion of the Roman Aristocracy, *JRS* 85, 1995, 135–47.

Bartelink, G. J. M., *Hieronymus*. Liber de optimo genere interpretandi (Epistula 57). *Ein Kommentar*, Leiden 1980.

Bastiaensen, A. A. R., Jérôme hagiographe, in G. Philippart (ed.), *Hagiographies*, vol. i, Turnhout 1994, 97–123.

Bastiaensen, A. A. R. *et al.*, *Vite dei santi*, vol. 4, Milan 1974.

Bernoulli, C. A., *Der Schriftstellerkatalog des Hieronymus. Ein Beitrag zur Geschichte der altchristlichen Literatur*, Freiburg i.Br. 1895.

Berschin, W., *Biographie und Epochenstil*, vol. i, Stuttgart 1986.

Binns, J., *Ascetics and Ambassadors of Christ. The Monasteries of Palestine 314–631*, Oxford 1994.

Booth, A. D., The Date of Jerome's Birth, *Phoenix* 33, 1979, 346–52.

——, The Chronology of Jerome's Early Years, *Phoenix* 35, 1981, 237–59.

Bratok, R., Die Geschichte des frühen Christentums im Gebiet zwischen Sirmium und Aquileia im Licht der neueren Forschung, *Klio* 72, 1990, 508–50.

Braverman, J., *Jerome's Commentary on Daniel: A Study of Comparative Jewish and Christian Interpretations of the Hebrew Bible*, Washington 1978.

Brown, D., *Vir trilinguis. A Study in the Biblical Exegesis of Saint Jerome*, Kampen 1992.

Brown, P., Aspects of the Christianization of the Roman Aristocracy, *JRS* 51, 1961, 1–11 (= id., *Religion and Society in the Age of Saint Augustine*, London 1977, 161–82).

——, *Augustine of Hippo*, Berkeley/Los Angeles 1967.

——, Pelagius and his Supporters: Aims and Environment, *JThS* N.S. 19, 1968, 93–114 (= id., *Religion and Society in the Age of Saint Augustine*, London 1977, 183–207).

——, The Patrons of Pelagius: the Roman Aristocracy between East and West, *JThS* N.S. 21, 1970, 56–72 (= id., *Religion and Society in the Age of Saint Augustine*, London 1977, 208–26).

——, *The Making of Late Antiquity*, Cambridge, Mass. 1978.

——, *The Cult of the Saints. Its Rise and Function in Latin Christianity*, Chicago 1981.

——, *The Body and Society: Men, Women and Sexual Renunciation in Early Christianity*, New York 1988.

——, *Power and Persuasion in Late Antiquity. Towards a Christian Empire*, Madison 1992.

Brown Tkacz, C., *Labor tam utilis*: the Creation of the Vulgate, *VChr* 50, 1996, 42–72.

——, Ovid, Jerome and the Vulgate, *Studia Patristica* 33, 1997, 378–82.

——, *Quid facit cum Psalterio Horatius?* Seeking Classical Allusions in the Vulgate, in D. Kries, C. Brown Tkacz (eds), *Nova doctrina vetusque. Essays on Early Christianity in Honor of F. W. Schlatter*, New York, Bern 1999, 93–104.

Brugnoli, G., *Curiosissimus excerptor. Gli* Additamenta *di Girolamo ai* Chronica *di Eusebio*, Pisa 1995.

Brunner, J. N., *Der hl. Hieronymus und die Mädchenerziehung auf Grund seiner Briefe an Laeta und Gaudentius*, München 1910 (repr. Aalen 1970).

Burstein, E., La compétence de Jérôme en hébreu. Explication de certaines erreurs, *REAug* 21, 1975, 3–12.

Burgess, R. W., Jerome and the *Kaisergeschichte*, *Historia* 44, 1995, 349–69.

Burrus, V. 'In the Theater of Life': The Performance of Orthodoxy in Late Antiquity, in W. E. Klingshirn and M. Vessey (eds), *The Limits of Ancient Christianity. Essays on Late Antique Thought and Culture in Honor of* R. A. *Markus*, Ann Arbor 1999, 80–96.

Burzacchini, G., Note sulla presenza di Persio in Girolamo, *GIF* 27 (= N.S. 6), 1975, 50–72.

Cameron, A., The Latin Revival of the Fourth Century, in W. Treadgold (ed.), *Renaissances before the Renaissance*, Stanford 1984, 42–58.

Cameron, Av., Virginity as Metaphor: Women and the Rhetoric of Early Christianity, in ead. (ed.), *History as Text: the Writing of Ancient History*, London 1989, 181–205.

——, *Christianity and the Rhetoric of Empire. The Development of Christian Discourse*, Berkeley/Los Angeles/Oxford 1991.

——, Early Christianity and the Discourse of Female Desire, in L.J. Archer, S. Fischler and M. Wyke (eds), *Women in Ancient Societies: an Illusion of the Nights*, Basingstoke 1994, 152–68.

Canellis, A., La Composition du Dialogue contre les Lucifériens et du Dialogue contre les Pélagiens de saint Jérôme: à la recherche d'un canon de l'altercatio, *REAug* 43, 1997, 247–88.

Cavallera, F., *Le schisme d'Antioche*, Paris 1905.

——, *Saint Jérôme. Sa vie et son oeuvre*, 2 vols, Louvain/Paris 1922.

Ceresa-Gastaldo, A., La tecnica biografica del *De viris illustribus* di Girolamo, *Renovatio* 14, 1979, 221–36.

——, The Biographical Method of Jerome's *De viris illustribus*, *Studia Patristica* 15.1, 1984, 55–68.

Chadwick, H., *Priscillian of Avila. The Occult and the Charismatic in the Early Church*, Oxford 1976.

——, *Heresy and Orthodoxy in the Early Church*, London 1991.

Chastagnol, A., *Les Fastes de la préfecture de Rome au bas-empire*, Paris 1962.

——, Le Supplice inventé par Avidius Cassius: remarques sur l'Histoire Auguste et la lettre 1 de saint Jérôme, *Bonner Historia Augusta Colloquium* 1970, Bonn 1972, 95–107.

Chromatius Episcopus 388–1988, *AAAd* 34, Udine 1989.

Clark, E. A., *Jerome, Chrysostom, and Friends. Essays and Translations*, New York/Toronto 1979.

——, *Ascetic Piety and Women's Faith. Essays on Late Ancient Christianity*, New York/Toronto 1986.

Clark, E. A., The Place of Jerome's Commentary on Ephesians in the Origenist Controversy: The Apokatastasis and the Ascetic Ideal, *VChr* 41, 1987, 154–71.

——, *The Origenist Controversy. The Cultural Construction of an Early Christian Debate*, Princeton 1992.

——, Ideology, History, and the Construction of 'Woman' in Late Ancient Christianity, *JECS* 2, 1994, 155–84.

Clark, G., *Women in Late Antiquity: Pagan and Christian Lifestyles*, Oxford 1993.

Cloke, G., *'This Female Man of God.' Women and Spiritual Power in the Patristic Age, AD 350–450*, London/New York 1995.

Coleiro, E., St. Jerome's Lives of the Hermits, *VChr* 11, 1957, 161–78.

Comerford Lawler, T., Jerome's First Letter to Damasus, in *Kyriakon. Festschrift J. Quasten*, Münster 1970, 548–52.

Conring, B., *Hieronymus als Briefschreiber. Ein Beitrag zur spätantiken Epistolographie*, Tübingen 2001.

Consolino, F. E., Modelli di comportamento e modi di santificazione per l'aristocrazia femminile d'Occidente, in A. Giardina (ed.), *Società romana e impero tardoantico*, vol. i, Bari 1986, 273–306.

Conybeare, C., *Paulinus Noster. Self and Symbols in the Letters of Paulinus of Nola*, Oxford 2001.

Cooper, K., Insinuations of Womanly Influence: An Aspect of the Christianization of the Roman Aristocracy, *JRS* 82, 1992, 150–64.

——, *The Virgin and the Bride. Idealized Womanhood in Late Antiquity*, Cambridge, Mass./London 1996.

Corsaro, F., Seneca nel Catalogo dei Santi di Gerolamo (vir. ill. xii), *Orpheus* 8, 1987, 264–82.

Courcelle, P., *Les lettres grecques en Occident de Macrobe à Cassiodore*, Paris 1948.

——, *Recherches sur les Confessions de saint Augustin*, Paris [2]1968.

——, Les Lectures de l'Énéide devant les grandes invasions germaniques, *RomBarb* 1, 1976, 25–56.

Cox Miller, P., The Blazing Body. Ascetic Desire in Jerome's Letter to Eustochium, *JECS* 1, 1993, 21–45.

Cracco-Ruggini, L., La cristianizzazione nelle città dell'Italia settentrionale, in W. Eck and H. Galsterer (eds), *Die Stadt in Oberitalien und in den nordwestlichen Provinzen des römischen Reiches*, Cologne 1991, 235–49.

Crouzel, H., Saint Jérôme et ses amis toulousains, *BLE* 73, 1972, 125–46.

——, *Origène*, Paris 1985 (= Origen, Edinburgh 1989).

Dagron, G., *Naissance d'une capitale. Constantinople et ses institutions de 330 à 451*, Paris [2]1984.

de Halleux, A., 'Hypostase' et 'personne' dans la formation du dogme trinitaire, *RHE* 79, 1984, 313–69 and 625–70.

Delehaye, H., *Les origines du culte des martyrs*, Brussels [2]1933.

——, *Les passions des martyres et les genres littéraires*, Brussels [2]1966.

Dölger, F. J., *Die Sonne der Gerechtigkeit und der Schwarze*, Münster [2]1971.

Doignon, J., Oracles, prophéties, on-dit sur la chute de Rome (395–410): les réactions de Jérôme et d'Augustin, *REAug* 36, 1990, 120–46.

Donner, H., *Pilgerfahrt ins Heilige Land. Die ältesten Berichte christlicher Palästinapilger (4.-7. Jahrhundert)*, Stuttgart 1979.

Doutreleau, L., Le prologue de Jérôme au *De Spiritu Sancto* de Didyme, in *AΛΕΞΑΝΔΡΙΝΑ. Hellénisme, judaïsme et christianisme à Alexandrie. Mélanges offerts à C. Mondésert*, Paris 1987, 297–311.

Duval, Y-M., Saint Augustin et le Commentaire sur Jonas de saint Jérôme, *REAug* 12, 1966, 9–40.

——, Sur les insinuations de Jérôme contre Jean de Jérusalem: de l'arianisme à l'origénisme, *RHE* 65, 1970, 353–74.

——, Tertullien contre Origène sur la resurrection de la chair dans le *Contra Iohannem Hierosolymitanum* 23–26 de saint Jérôme, *REAug* 17, 1971, 227–78.

——, *Le Livre de Jonas dans la littérature chrétienne grecque et latine: sources et influence du Commentaire sur Jonas de saint Jérôme*, 2 vols, Paris 1973.

——, Formes profanes et formes bibliques dans les oraisons funèbres de saint Ambroise, in *Christianisme et formes littéraires de l'antiquité tardive en Occident, Entretiens sur l'Antiquité classique 23*, Fondation Hardt, Vandouevres/Geneva 1977, 235–301.

——, Pélage est-il le censeur inconnu de l'*Adversus Iovinianum* à Rome en 393? ou: Du 'portrait–robot' de l'hérétique chez S. Jérôme, *RHE* 75, 1980, 525–57.

——, Jérôme et Origène avant la querelle origèniste. La cure et la guérison ultime du monde et du diable dans l'*In Nahum*, *Augustinianum* 24, 1984, 471–94.

——, Le *Liber Hieronymi ad Gaudentium*. Rufin d'Aquilée, Gaudence de Brescia et Eusèbe de Crémone, *RBen* 97, 1987, 163–86.

—— (ed.), *Jérôme entre l'Occident et l'Orient*, Paris 1988.

——, Chromace et Jérôme, *AAAd* 34, 1989a, 151–83.

——, Les premiers rapports de Paulin de Nole avec Jérôme: Moine ou philosophe? Poète ou exégète?, in *Polyanthema. Studi di letteratura cristiana antica offerti a S. Costanza*, vol. i, Sicania 1989b, 177–216.

——, L'*In Esaia parvula adbreviatio de capitulis paucis* de Jérôme: une homélie (tronquée) et une leçon de méthode aux moines de Bethléem, in R. Gryson (ed.), *Philologia sacra. Biblische und patristische*

Studien für Hermann J. Frede und Walter Thiele zu ihrem siebzigsten Geburtstag, Freiburg i.Br. 1993, 422–82.

Dural, Y-M., *Histoire et historiographie en Occident aux IVe et Ve siècles*, Aldershot 1997.

——, *L'extirpation de l'Arianisme en Italie du Nord et en Occident: Rimini (359/60) et Aquilée (381), Hilaire de Poitiers (367/8) et Ambroise de Milan (397)*, Aldershot 1998.

Elm, S., *'Virgins of God'. The Making of Asceticism in Late Antiquity*, Oxford 1994.

Ensslin, W., *Die Religionspolitik des Kaisers Theodosius des Großen*, München 1953.

Errington, M., Church and State in the First Years of Theodosius I, *Chiron* 27, 1997a, 21–72.

——, Christian Accounts of the Religious Legislation of Theodosius I, *Klio* 79, 1997b, 398–443.

Faggin, G., *La pedagogia. Storia e problemi, maestri e metodi della patristica*, Mailand 1971.

Favez, C., *La Consolation latine chrétienne*, Paris 1937.

Favez, C., Saint Jérôme pédagogue, in *Mélanges J. Marouzeau*, Paris 1948, 173–81.

Feder, A., *Studien zum Schriftstellerkatalog des heiligen Hieronymus*, Freiburg i.Br. 1927.

Feichtinger, B., *Apostolae apostolorum. Frauenaskese als Befreiung und Zwang bei Hieronymus*, Frankfurt a.M. 1995a.

——, Konsolationstopik und 'Sitz im Leben'. Hieronymus' *ep.* 39 *ad Paulam de obitu Blesillae* im Spannungsfeld zwischen christlicher Genusadaption und Lesermanipulation, *JbAC* 38, 1995b, 75–90.

——, Zäsuren, Brüche, Kontinuitäten. Zur aristokratischen Metamorphose des christlichen Askeseideals am Beispiel des Hieronymus, *WS* 110, 1997a, 187–200.

——, *Nec vero sopor ille fuerat aut vana somnia* ... (Hier., *ep.* 22,30,6). Überlegungen zum geträumten Selbst des Hieronymus, *REAug* 43, 1997b, 41–6.

Fischer, B., *Das Neue Testament in lateinischer Sprache*, Berlin 1972 (= id., *Beiträge zur Geschichte der lateinischen Bibeltexte*, Freiburg 1986).

Fontaine, J., L'ascétisme chrétien dans la littérature gallo-romain d'Hilaire à Cassien, *Atti del Colloquio sul tema: La Gallia Romana*, Rome 1973, 87–115.

——, L'aristocratie occidentale devant le monachisme aux IVème et Vème siècle, *RSLR* 15, 1979, 28–53.

—— *et al.* (eds), *Le Monde latin antique et la Bible*, Paris 1985.

——, Un sobriquet perfide de Damase: *matronarum auriscalpius*, in

D. Porte and J-P. Bonniec (eds) *Hommages à Henri Le Bonniec. Res sacrae*, Brussels 1988a, 177–92.

Fontaine, J., L'esthétique littéraire de la prose de Jérôme jusqu'à son second départ en Orient, in Y-M. Duval (ed.), *Jérôme entre l'Occident et l'Orient*, Paris 1988b, 323–42.

Fürst, A., *Veritas Latina*. Augustins Haltung gegenüber Hieronymus' Bibelübersetzungen, *REAug* 40, 1994a, 105–26.

——, Kürbis oder Efeu? Zur Übersetzung von Jona 4,6, *Biblische Notizen* 72, 1994b, 12–19.

——, *Augustins Briefwechsel mit Hieronymus*, Münster 1999.

Fuhrmann, M., Die Mönchsgeschichten des Hieronymus. Formexperimente in erzählender Literatur, in *Christianisme et formes littéraires de l'Antiquité tardive en Occident, Entretiens sur l'Antiquité classique* 23, Vandoeuvres/Geneva 1977, 41–99.

Funke, H., Univira. Ein Beispiel heidnischer Geschichtsapologetik, *JbAC* 8/9, 1964–5, 183–8.

Gamberale, L., Seneca in catalogo sanctorum: considerazioni su Hier. vir.ill. 12, *InvLuc* 11, 1989, 203–17.

Gilliam, J. F., The Pro Caelio in St. Jerome's Letters, *HThR* 46, 1953, 103–7.

Godel, M., Réminiscences de poètes profanes dans les Lettres de Saint Jérôme, *MH* 21, 1964, 65–70.

Gorce, D., *La lectio divina des origines du cénobitisme à saint Benoît et Cassiodore*, vol. i: *Saint Jérôme et la lecture sacrée dans le milieu ascétique romain*, Paris 1925.

——, *Lettera a Leta o dell'educazione della figliuola*, Modena 1932.

Gordini, G., L'oppositione al monachesimo a Roma nel IV secolo, in M. Fois *et al.* (eds), *Dalla chiesa antica alla chiesa moderna*, Rome 1983, 19–35.

Grimm, V., *From Feading to Fasting, the Evolution of Sin. Attitudes to Food in Late Antiquity*, London/New York 1996.

Grützmacher, G., *Hieronymus. Eine biographische Studie zur alten Kirchengeschichte*, 3 vols, Leipzig 1901–8.

Guttilla, G., Tematica cristiana e pagana nell'evoluzione finale della *consolatio* di san Girolamo, *ALGP* 17–18, 1980–1, 87–152.

——, La fase iniziale della *consolatio* latina cristiana, *ALGP* 21–2, 1984–5, 108–215.

Hägg, T. and Ph. Rousseau (eds), *Greek Biography and Panegyric in Late Antiquity*, Berkeley 2000.

Hagendahl, H., *Latin Fathers and the Classics. A Study of the Apologists, Jerome and Other Christian Writers*, Göteborg 1958.

——, Jerome and the Latin Classics, *VChr* 28, 1974, 216–27.

Hagendahl, H., *Von Tertullian zu Cassiodor. Die profane literarische Tradition in den lateinischen christlichen Schriften*, Göteborg 1983.

—— and J. H. Waszink, *s.v.* Hieronymus, in *Reallexikon für Antike und Christentum* 15, 1989, 117–39.

Hamblenne, P., La longévité de Jérôme: Prosper avait-il raison?, *Latomus* 28, 1969, 1081–119.

——, Relectures de philologue sur le 'scandale' du lierre/ricin (Hier. *In Ion.* 4,6), *Euphrosyne* 16, 1988, 183–223.

——, Traces de biographies grecques 'païennes' dans la Vita Pauli de Jérôme?, in *Cristianesimo Latino e cultura Greca sino al sec. IV*, Rome 1993, 209–34.

Hammond, C. P., The Last Ten Years of Rufinus' Life and the Date of his Move South from Aquileia, *JThS* N.S. 28, 1977, 372–429.

Hanson, R. P. C., *The Search for the Christian Doctrine of God. The Arian Controversy 318–381*, Edinburgh 1988.

Harnack, A., *Das Mönchtum. Seine Ideale und seine Geschichte*, Gießen [4]1895.

Hayward, C. T. R., Jewish traditions in Jerome's commentary on Jeremiah and the Targum of Jeremiah, *Proceedings of the Irish Biblical Association* 9, 1985, 100–20.

——, *Jerome's* Hebrew Questions on Genesis. *Translated with Introduction and Commentary*, Oxford 1995.

Heather, P., *Goths and Romans 332–489*, Oxford 1991.

Helm, R., Hieronymus und Eutrop, *RhM* 76, 1927, 138–70 and 254–306.

——, Die neuesten Hypothesen zu Eusebius' (Hieronymus') Chronik, *Sitzungsber. der Preuss. Akad. d. Wiss., Phil.-hist. Kl.* 1929a, 371–408.

——, *Hieronymus' Zusätze in Eusebius' Chronik und ihr Wert für die Literaturgeschichte*, Philologus Suppl. 21.2, 1929b.

Hennings, R., *Der Briefwechsel zwischen Augustin und Hieronymus und ihr Streit um den Kanon des Alten Testaments und die Auslegung von Gal. 2, 11–14*, Leiden 1994.

——, Hieronymus zum Bischofsamt, *ZKG* 108, 1997, 1–11.

Hopkins, K., Social Mobility in the Later Roman Empire: The Evidence of Ausonius, *CQ* 11, 1961, 239–49.

Huber-Rebenich, G., Hagiographic fiction as entertainment, in H. Hofmann (ed.), *Latin Fiction. The Latin Novel in Context*, London/ New York 1999, 187–212.

Huemer, J., Studien zu den ältesten christlichen Literaturhistorikern, *WS* 16, 1894, 121–58.

Hunt, E. D., *Holy Land Pilgrimage in the Later Roman Empire A.D. 312–460*, Oxford 1982.

Hunter, D. G., Resistance to the Virginal Ideal in Late-Fourth-Century Rome: the Case of Jovinian, *ThS* 48, 1987, 45–69.

Hunter, D. G., Helvidius, Jovinian, and the Virginity of Mary in Late Fourth-Century Rome, *JECS* 1, 1993, 47–71.

——, Vigilantius of Calagurris and Victricius of Rouen: Ascetics, Relics, and Clerics in Late Roman Gaul, *JECS* 7, 1999, 401–30.

Inglebert, H., *Les Romains chrétiens face à l'histoire de Rome: histoire, christianisme et romanités en Occident dans l'antiquité tardive*, Paris 1996.

Jay, P., Sur la date de naissance de s. Jérôme, *REL* 51, 1973, 262–80.

——, Jérôme auditeur d'Apollinaire de Laodicée à Antioche, *REAug* 20, 1974, 36–41.

——, Saint Jérôme et le triple sens de l'Ecriture, *REAug* 26, 1980, 214–27.

——, La datation des premières traductions de l'Ancien Testament sur l'hébreu par saint Jérôme, *REAug* 28, 1982, 208–12.

——, *L'Exégèse de saint Jérôme d'après son* Commentaire sur Isaïe, Paris 1985.

——, Saint Jérôme et la prophétie, *Studia Patristica* 18.4, 1990, 152–65.

Jeanjean, B., *Saint Jérôme et l'hérésie*, Paris 1999.

Jenal, G., *Italia ascetica atque monastica. Das Asketen- und Mönchtum in Italien von den Anfängen bis zur Zeit der Langobarden (ca. 150/250–604)*, 2 vols, Stuttgart 1995.

Jones, A. H. M., *The Later Roman Empire 284–602. A Social, Economic and Administrative Survey*, 3 vols, Oxford 1964.

Jungblut, R., *Hieronymus. Darstellung und Verehrung eines Kirchenvaters*, Tübingen 1967.

Kamesar, A., *Jerome, the Hebrew Bible, and Greek Scholarship. A Study of the Questiones Hebraicae in Genesim*, Oxford 1993.

——, The Evaluation of the Narrative Aggada in Greek and Latin Patristic Literature, *JThS* N.S. 45, 1994, 37–71.

Kech, H., *Hagiographie als christliche Unterhaltungsliteratur. Studien zum Phänomen des Erbaulichen anhand der Mönchsviten des hl. Hieronymus*, Göppingen 1977.

Kelly, J. N. D., *Jerome. His Life, Writings, and Controversies*, London 1975.

Kelly, M. J., *Life and Times as Revealed in the Writings of St. Jerome Exclusive of his Letters*, PhD Washington 1944.

Kierdorf, W., *Laudatio funebris. Interpretationen und Untersuchungen zur Entwicklung der römischen Leichenrede*, Meisenheim 1980.

Kinzig, W., Jewish and Jewish-Christian Eschatologies in Jerome, forthcoming in R. Kalmin and S. Schwartz (eds), *Jewish Palestine under Christian Emperors*.

Kopecek, T. A., *A History of Neo-Arianism*, 2 vols, Philadelphia 1979.

Krahwinkler, H., *Friaul im Frühmittelalter. Geschichte einer Region vom Ende des fünften bis zum Ende des zehnten Jahrhunderts*, Vienna 1992.

Kraus, M. A., *Jerome's Translation of the Book of Exodus* iuxta Hebraeos *in Relation to Classical, Christian and Jewish Traditions of Interpretation*, PhD University of Michigan, Ann Arbor 1996.

Krause, J.-U., *Spätantike Patronatsformen im Westen des Römischen Reiches*, München 1987.

——, *Witwen und Waisen im Römischen Reich*, vol. iv: *Witwen und Waisen im frühen Christentum*, Stuttgart 1995.

Lambert, B., *Bibliotheca Hieronymiana Manuscripta. La traduction manuscrite des oeuvres de saint Jérôme*, 7 vols, Steenbrugge/Den Haag 1969–72.

Lardet, P., *L'Apologie de Jérôme contre Rufin. Un commentaire*, Leiden 1993.

Laurence, P., Marcella, Jérôme et Origène, *REAug* 42, 1996, 267–93.

——, *Jérôme et le nouveau modèle féminin. La conversion à la 'vie parfaite'*, Paris 1997a.

——, Rome et Jérôme: des amours contrariées, *RBen* 107, 1997c, 227–249.

——, L'implication des femmes dans l'hérésie: le jugement de saint Jérôme, *REAug* 44, 1998a, 241–67.

——, Ivresse et luxure féminines: les sources classiques de Jérôme, *Latomus* 57, 1998b, 885–9.

——, Les pèlerinages des Romaines sous le regard de saint Jérôme, REL 76, 1998c, 226–40.

Letsch-Brunner, S., *Marcella – discipula et magistra. Auf den Spuren einer römischen Christin des 4. Jahrhunderts*, Berlin/New York 1998.

Lim, R., *Public Disputation, Power, and Social Order in Late Antiquity*, Berkeley 1995a.

——, Religious Disputations and Social Disorder in Late Antiquity, *Historia* 44, 1995b, 204–31.

Lössl, J., Satire, Fiction and Reference to Reality in Jerome's Epistula 117, *VChr* 52, 1998, 172–92.

Loewe, R., The Medieval History of the Latin Vulgate, in *The Cambridge History of the Bible* vol. ii, Cambridge 1969, 102–54.

Lorenz, R., Die Anfänge des abendländischen Mönchtums im 4. Jahrhundert, *ZKG* 77, 1966, 1–61.

McLynn, N. B., Christian Conflict and Violence in the Fourth Century, *Kodai* 3, 1992, 15–44.

——, *Ambrose of Milan. Church and Court in a Christian Capital*, Berkeley 1994.

——, The Other Olympias: Gregory of Nazianzen and the Family of Vitalianus, *ZAC* 2, 1998, 227–46.

Maier, H. O., The Topography of Heresy and Dissent in Late-Fourth-Century Rome, *Historia* 44, 1995a, 232–49.

Maier, H. O., Religious Dissent, Heresy and Households in Late Antiquity, *VChr* 49, 1995b, 49–63.

Maraval, P., *Lieux saints et pèlerinages d'Orient. Histoire et géographie des origines à la conqûte arabe*, Paris 1985.

——, *Petite vie de saint Jérôme*, Paris 1995.

Marti, H., *Übersetzer der Augustin-Zeit. Interpretation von Selbstzeugnissen*, München 1974.

Mastandrea, P., La morte di Seneca nel giudizio di San Gerolamo, in G. Bonamente and A. Nestori (eds), *I cristiani e l'impero nel IV secolo*, Macerata 1988, 205–7.

Mathisen, R., *Ecclesiastical Factionalism and Religious Controversy in Fifth-Century Gaul*, Washington 1989.

Matthews, J., *The Roman Empire of Ammianus*, London 1989.

——, *Western Aristocracy and Imperial Court A.D. 364–425*, Oxford ²1990.

Mayer, W., Constantinopolitan Women in Chrysostom's Circle, *VChr* 53, 1999, 265–88.

Meyvaert, P., Excerpts from an Unknown Treatise of Jerome to Gaudentius of Brescia, *RBen* 96, 1986, 203–18.

Miehe, R., *s.v.* Hieronymus, in *Lexikon der christlichen Ikonographie* 6, 1974, 519–29.

Millar, F., *The Emperor in the Roman World* (31 BC–AD 337), London 1977.

Mohrmann, C., Saint Jérôme et saint Augustin sur Tertullien, *VChr* 5, 1951, 111–12.

Momigliano, A. (ed.), *The Conflict between Paganism and Christianity in the Fourth Century*, Oxford 1963.

Mommsen, Th., Über die Quellen der Chronik des Hieronymus, *Abhandl. d. Kgl. Sächs. Ges. d. Wiss.* 2, 1850, 669–93 (repr. in id., *Gesammelte Schriften* vol. vii, Berlin 1909, 606–39).

——, *Römisches Strafrecht*, Lepzig 1899 (repr. Darmstadt 1955).

Monceaux, P., *Saint Jérôme. Sa Jeunesse. L'Étudiant et l'ermite*, Paris 1932 (English: *St. Jerome: The Early Years*, New York 1933).

Moreschini, C. and G. Menestrina (eds), *Motivi letterari ed esegetici in Gerolamo*, Brescia 1997.

Mouterde, R. and A. Poidebard, *Le Limes de Chalcis*, 2 vols, Paris 1945.

Mras, K., Nachwort zu den beiden letzten Ausgaben der Chronik des Hieronymus, *WS* 46, 1928, 201–8.

Müller, H., Der älteste Brief des heiligen Hieronymus. Zu einem aktuellen Datierungsvorschlag, *WS* 111, 1998, 191–210.

Murphy, F. X., *Rufinus of Aquileia (345–411). His Life and Works*, PhD Washington 1945.

Nauroy, G., Jérôme, lecteur et censeur de l'exégèse d'Ambroise, in Y-M. Duval (ed.), *Jérôme entre l'Occident et l'Orient*, Paris 1988, 173–203.

Nautin, P., La date du *De viris inlustribus* de Jérôme, de la mort de Cyrille de Jérusalem et de celle de Grégoire de Nazianze, *RHE* 56, 1961, 33–5.

——, L'excommunication de saint Jérôme, *AEHE*, Ve Section, 80/81, 1972–3, 7–37.

——, Etudes de chronologie hieronymienne, *REAug* 18, 1972, 209–18.

——, Etudes de chronologie hieronymienne, *REAug* 19, 1973, 69–86 and 213–39.

——, Etudes de chronologie hieronymienne, *REAug* 20, 1974, 251–84.

——, *Origène. Sa vie et son oeuvre*, Paris 1977.

——, La date des Commentaires de Jérôme sur les éptres pauliniennes, *RHE* 74, 1979, 5–12.

——, Le premier échange épistolaire entre Jérôme et Damase: lettres réelles ou fictives? *FZPhTh* 30, 1983a, 331–44.

——, L'activité littéraire de Jérôme de 387 à 392, *RThPh* 115, 1983b, 247–59.

——, La liste des oeuvres de Jérôme dans le *De viris illustribus*, *Orpheus* 5, 1984a, 319–34.

——, La lettre de Paule et Eustochium à Marcelle (Jérôme, Ep. 46), *Augustinianum* 24, 1984b, 441–9.

——, *s.v.* Hieronymus, in *Theologische Realenzyklopädie* 15, 1986, 304–15.

——, La lettre 'Magnum est' de Jérôme à Vincent et la traduction des homélies d'Origène sur les prophètes, in Y-M. Duval (ed.), *Jérôme entre l'Occident et l'Orient*, Paris 1988, 27–39.

——, Notes critiques sur la lettre 27* de Jérôme à Aurélius de Carthage, *REAug* 36, 1990, 298–9.

Nellen, D., *Viri litterati. Gebildetes Beamtentum und spätrömisches Reich im Westen zwischen 284 und 395 nach Christus*, Bochum ²1981.

Nenci, G., Onasus Segestanus in Girolamo, Ep. 40, *RFIC* 123, 1995, 90–4.

Norden, E., *Die antike Kunstprosa*, 2 vols, Leipzig ²1909.

Nürnberg, R., *Non decet neque necessarium est, ut mulieres doceant*. Überlegungen zum altkirchlichen Lehrverbot, *JbAC* 31, 1988, 57–73.

Oberhelman, S. M., Jerome's Earliest Attack on Ambrose: On Ephesians, Prologue (ML 26, 469D–470A), *TAPhA* 121, 1991, 377–401.

O'Brien, M. B., *Titles of Address in Christian Latin Epistolography to 543 A.D.*, Washington 1930.

Oldfather, W. A., *Studies in the Text Tradition of St. Jerome's Vitae Patrum*, Urbana 1943.

Opelt, I., *Hieronymus' Streitschriften*, Heidelberg 1973.

Otto, A., *Die Sprichwörter und sprichwörtlichen Redensarten der Römer*, Leipzig 1890 (repr. Hildesheim 1962).

Paredi, A., San Gerolamo e S. Ambrogio, in *Mélanges E. Tisserant*, vol. v (= *Studi e testi* 235), Rome 1964, 183–98.

Paschoud, F., *Roma Aeterna. Études sur le patriotisme Romain dans l'Occident latin à l'époque des grandes invasions*, Rome 1967.

Penna, A., *San Gerolamo*, Turin 1949.

——, *Principi e carattere dell'esegesi di S. Gerolamo*, Rome 1950.

Peri, V., *Omelie origeniane sui Salmi*, Rome 1980.

Pietri, Ch., *Roma Christiana. Recherches sur l'Eglise de Rome, son organisation, sa politique, son idéologie, de Miltiade à Sixte III (311–440)*, 2 Vols, Rome 1976.

—— and L. Pietri, *Prosopographie de l'Italie chrétienne (313–604)*, 2 Vols, Rome 1999–2000.

PLRE = *The Prosopography of the Later Roman Empire*, vol. i: 260–395; vol. ii: 395–527, Cambridge 1971–80.

PW = A. Pauly and G. Wissowa (eds), *Real-Encyclopädie der classischen Altertumswissenschaft*, Stuttgart 1893–1980.

Preaux, J-G., Procédés d'invention d'un sobriquet par saint Jérôme, *Latomus* 18, 1958, 659–64.

Pronberger, N., *Beiträge zur Chronologie der Briefe des hl. Hieronymus*, Amberg 1913.

RAC = *Reallexikon für Antike und Christentum*, Stuttgart 1950ff.

Rahmer, M., *Die hebräischen Traditionen in den Werken des Hieronymus: Durch eine Vergleichung mit den jüdischen Quellen kritisch beleuchtet*, [Erster Theil: *Die Quaestiones in Genesin*], Berlin 1861.

——, *Die hebräischen Traditionen in den Werken des Hieronymus: Durch Vergleichung mit den jüdischen Quellen und ältesten Versionen kritisch beleuchtet, Die Commentarii zu den zwölf kleinen Propheten*, 2 vols, Berlin 1902.

Ratti, S., Jérôme et Nicomaque Flavien. Sur les sources de la Chronique pour les années 357–64, *Historia* 46, 1997, 479–508.

Rebenich, S., *Hieronymus und sein Kreis. Prosopographische und sozialgeschichtliche Untersuchungen*, Stuttgart 1992a.

——, Der heilige Hieronymus und die Geschichte – Zur Funktion der Exempla in seinen Briefen, *RQA* 87, 1992b, 29–46.

——, Jerome: The *vir trilinguis* and the *hebraica veritas*, *VChr* 47, 1993a, 50–77.

——, Hieronymus und Evagrius von Antiochia, *Studia Patristica* 28, 1993b, 75–80.

——, *Insania circi*. Eine Tertullianreminiszenz bei Hieronymus und Augustin, *Latomus* 53, 1994, 155–8.

Rebenich, S., Asceticism, Orthodoxy and Patronage: Jerome in Constantinople, *Studia Patristica* 33, 1997, 358–77.

——, Der Kirchenvater Hieronymus als Hagiograph: Die *Vita s. Pauli primi eremitae*, in K. Elm (ed.), *Beiträge zur Geschichte des Paulinerordens*, Berlin 2000a, 23–40.

——, Vom dreizehnten Gott zum dreizehnten Apostel? Der tote Kaiser in der christlichen Spätantike, *ZAC* 4, 2000b, 300–24.

——, Wohltäter and Heilige. Von der heidnischen zur christlichen Patronage, in F. A. Bauer and N. Zimmermann (eds), *Epochenwandel? Kunst und Kultur zwischen Antike und Mittelalter*, Mainz 2001, 27–35.

Reichmann, V., *s.v.* Bibelübersetzungen 1.3: Übersetzungen ins Lateinische, in *Theologische Realenzyklopädie* 6, 1980, 172–81.

Reitzenstein, R., *Hellenistische Wundererzählungen*, Leipzig 1906 (repr. Darmstadt 1963).

Rice, E. F., *Saint Jerome in the Renaissance*, Baltimore/London 1985.

Ritter, A. M., *Das Konzil von Konstantinopel und sein Symbol*, Göttingen 1965.

Rousseau, Ph., *Ascetics, Authority, and the Church in the Age of Jerome and Cassian*, Oxford 1978.

Rousselle, A., *Porneia. De la maîtrise du corps à la privation sensorielle IIe–IVe siècles de l'ère chrétienne*, Paris 1983 (= *Porneia. On Desire and Body in Antiquity*, Oxford 1988).

Ruether, R., Misogynism and Virginal Feminism in the Fathers of the Church, in ead. (ed.), *Religion and Sexism. Images of Woman in the Jewish and Christian Traditions*, New York 1974, 150–83.

Salzman, M. R., Aristocratic Women. Conductors of Christianity in the Fourth Century, *Helios* 16, 1989, 207–20.

——, How the West was Won: The Christianization of the Roman Aristocracy in the West in the Years after Constantine, in C. Deroux (ed.), *Studies in Latin Literature and Roman History*, vol. vi, Brussels 1992, 451–79.

Schäublin, C., Textkritisches zu den Briefen des Hieronymus, *MH* 30, 1973, 55–62.

Schmidt, P. L., 'Und es war geschrieben auf Hebräisch, Griechisch und Lateinisch': Hieronymus, das Hebräer–Evangelium und seine mittelalterliche Rezeption, *Filologia mediolatina* 5, 1998, 49–93.

Schöne, A., *Die Weltchronik des Eusebius in ihrer Bearbeitung durch Hieronymus*, Berlin 1900.

Schwind, J., Hieronymus' Epistula ad Innocentium (epist. 1) – ein Jugendwerk?, *WS* 110, 1997, 171–86.

Scourfield, J. H. D., *A Literary Commentary on Jerome, Letters 1, 60, 107*, PhD Oxford 1983.

Scourfield, J. H. D., Jerome, Antioch, and the Desert: A Note on Chronology, *JThS* N.S. 37, 1986, 117–21.

——, Notes on the Text of Jerome, Letters 1 and 107, *CQ* 37, 1987, 487–97.

——, *Consoling Heliodorus. A Commentary on Jerome*, Letter 60, Oxford 1993.

——, A Note on Jerome's Homily on the Rich Man and Lazarus, *JThS* N.S. 48, 1997, 536–9.

Seeck, O., *Geschichte des Untergangs der antiken Welt*, 6 vols. With an introduction by S. Rebenich, Darmstadt 2000 (repr. of the edition Stuttgart [1.2.4]1921–2).

Simonetti, M., Due passi della prefazione di Girolamo alla traduzione del *de spiritu sancto* di Didimo, *RSLR* 24, 1988, 78–80.

Sivan, H., *Ausonius of Bordeaux. Genesis of a Gallic Aristocracy*, London 1993a.

——, On Hymens and Holiness in Late Antiquity. Opposition to Aristocratic Female Asceticism at Rome, *JbAC* 36, 1993b, 81–93.

Smalley, B., *The Study of the Bible in the Middle Ages*, Oxford [3]1983.

Stancliffe, C. E., *St. Martin and his Hagiographer. History and Miracle in Sulpicius Severus*, Oxford 1983.

Steinhausen, J., Hieronymus und Laktanz in Trier, *TZ* 20, 1951, 126–54.

Steininger, C., *Die ideale christliche Frau: virgo – vidua – nupta. Eine Studie zum Bild der idealen christlichen Frau bei Hieronymus und Pelagius*, St Ottilien 1997.

Stemberger, G., *Juden und Christen im Heiligen Land. Palästina unter Konstantin und Theodosius*, München 1987.

Straub, J., Christliche Geschichtsapologetik in der Krisis des Römischen Reiches, *Historia* 1, 1950, 52–81 (= id., *Regeneratio Imperii*, vol. i, Darmstadt 1972, 240–70).

——, Calpurnia univira, *BHAC* 1966–7, 1968, 101–18 (= id., *Regeneratio Imperii*, vol. i, Darmstadt 1972, 350–68).

Strube, Chr., *Die 'Toten Städte'. Stadt und Land in Nordsyrien während der Spätantike*, Mainz 1996.

Sugano, K., *Das Rombild des Hieronymus*, Frankfurt a.M./Bern/New York 1983.

Sutcliffe, E. F., The Name *Vulgate*, *Biblica* 29, 1948a, 345–52.

——, The Council of Trent and the *Authentica* of the Vulgate, *JThS* N.S. 49, 1948b, 35–42.

Sychowski, S. von, *Hieronymus als Literaturhistoriker. Eine quellenkritische*

Untersuchung der Schrift des Hieronymus De viris illustribus, Münster 1894.

Tate, G., *Les campagnes de la Syrie du Nord du IIe au VIIe siècle. Un exemple d'expansion démographique et économique à la fin de l'Antiquité*, Paris 1992.

Tchalenko, G., *Villages antiques de la Syrie du Nord*, 3 vols, Paris 1953–8.

Temkin, O., *s. v.* Hippokrates, in *Reallexikon für Antike und Christentum* 15, 1991, 466–81.

Testard, M., *Saint Jérôme, l'apôtre savant et pauvre du patriciat romain*, Paris 1969.

——, Jérôme et Ambroise. Sur un 'aveu' du 'De officiis' de l'évêque de Milan, in Y-M. Duval (ed.), *Jérôme entre l'Occident et l'Orient*, Paris 1988, 227–54.

Thraede, K., *s.v.* Frau, in *Reallexikon für Antike und Christentum* 6, 1972, 197–269.

Tov, E., *Textual Criticism of the Hebrew Bible*, Assen 1992.

Trout, D. E., *Paulinus of Nola. Life, Letters, and Poems*, Berkeley/Los Angeles/London 1999.

Van Dam, R., *Leadership and Community in Late Antique Gaul*, Berkeley 1985.

——, *Saints and their Miracles in Late Ancient Gaul*, Princeton 1993.

Vessey, M., Jerome's Origen: The Making of a Christian Literary Persona, *Studia Patristica* 28, 1993a, 135–45.

——, Conference and Confession: Literary Pragmatics in Augustine's *Apologia contra Hieronymum*, *JECS* 1, 1993b, 175–213.

——, Erasmus' Jerome: The Publishing of a Christian Author, *Erasmus of Rotterdam Society Yearbook* 14, 1994, 62–99.

——, The Forging of Orthodoxy in Latin Christian Literature: A Case Study, *JECS* 4, 1996, 495–513.

Vidén, G., St. Jerome on Female Chastity: Subjugating the Elements of Desire, *SO* 73, 1998, 139–57.

de Vogüé, A., La *Vita Pauli* de saint Jérôme et sa datation. Examen d'un passage-clé (ch. 6), in *Eulogia. Mélanges offerts à Antoon A.R. Bastiaensen à l'occasion de son soixante-cinquième anniversaire*, Steenbrugge 1991, 395–406.

——, *Histoire littéraire du mouvement monastique dans l'antiquité*, vol. i: *Le monachisme latin*, 5 vols, Paris 1991–8.

Vössing, K., *Schule und Bildung im Nordafrika der römischen Kaiserzeit*, Brussels 1997.

White, C., *The Correspondence (394–419) between Jerome and Augustine of Hippo*, Lewiston 1990.

Wiebel, Chr., *Askese und Endlichkeitsdemut in der italienischen Renaissance*, Weinheim 1985.

Wiesen, D. S., *Saint Jerome as a Satirist. A Study in Christian Latin Thought and Letters*, Ithaca 1964.

Williams, R., *Arius. Heresy and Tradition*, London 1987.

Wimbush, V. L. and R. Valantasis (eds), *Asceticism*, Oxford 1995.

Winkelmann, F., Einige Bemerkungen zu den Aussagen des Rufinus von Aquileia und des Hieronymus über ihre Übersetzungstheorie und -methode, in *Kyriakon. Festschrift J. Quasten*, vol. ii, Münster 1970, 532–47.

Wissemann, M., *Schimpfworte in der Bibelübersetzung des Hieronymus*, Heidelberg 1992.

Yarbrough, A., Christianization in the Fourth Century: the Example of Women, *ChH* 45, 1976, 149–65.

NOTES

1 FROM STRIDON TO AQUILEIA

1 Hier. *Vita Malchi* 1.

2 Cf. McLynn (1992); Lim (1995a); Lim (1995b); Maier (1995b).

3 The exact date of Jerome's birth is subject to scholarly debate. The Chronicle of Prosper of Aquitaine gives the year 331 (*MGH AA* 9, p. 451), cf. Hamblenne (1969) and Kelly (1975) 337–9. There are, however, compelling arguments for dating his birth between 345 and 347–8, cf. Jay (1973) and Booth (1979).

4 Cf. Barnes (1993) 87ff.

5 Hier. *vir.ill.* 135; cf. Chapter 14.

6 Hier. *ep.* 7.5.

7 Hier. *Vulg.Iob (H).* prol. (p. 732 Weber); *ep.* 82.2.2.

8 Cf. Aug. *Conf.* 9.6.14. For Heliodorus and Rufinus, cf. Hier. *ep.* 4.2; Ruf. *Apol. c. Hier.* 1.4 (*CCL* 20, p. 39).

9 Hier. *Apol.* 1.30.

10 Cf. Aug. *Conf.* 1.9.14–15; 1.13.22.

11 Aug. *civ. dei* 21.14. For the educational system in North Africa, cf. now Vössing (1997).

12 Cf. Hier. *ep.* 125.6.1.

13 Hier. *Comm. in Ezech.* 40.5–13 (*CCL* 75, p. 468).

14 Hier. *ep.* 128.5.1.

15 Hier. *Chron. s.a.* 354 (p. 239 Helm).

16 But see Ruf. *Apol. c.*Hier. 2.9 (*CCL* 20, p. 91).

17 Hier. *ep.* 22.30.1.

18 A. Cameron (1984).

19 Aug. *Conf.* 1.10.16.

20 Aus. *Ordo* 28–34 (ed. Green).

21 Hopkins (1961); Matthews ([2]1990) 32ff.; 56ff.; Sivan (1993a).

22 Cf. Hier. *ep.* 5.2.3 (Hilary of Poitiers, *On Synods*).

23 The bishop of Alexandria had spent time in exile there (355–7). I will not discuss here Athanasius' authorship, which has been challenged by Barnes (1986).

24 Aug. *Conf.* 8.6.15. For the *amici principis*, cf. Millar (1977) 110–22.

25 Courcelle (²1968), 181f. Cf. also Steinhausen (1951), esp. 134f.

26 Hier. *ep.* 22.30. Allen (1995) has shown that, in this passage, Jerome describes himself as Christ and Eustochium as the Bride of Christ.

27 Cf. esp. Hagendahl (1958) 91–328; Hagendahl (1983) 89f.; Hagendahl and Waszink (1989) 120 *pace* Adkin (1991) 14f.; Adkin (1995); Adkin (1999a). Hier. *ep.* 22.30 and *Apol.* 1. 31 (*CCL* 79, p. 31f.) are, I believe, clear enough – in the latter case, Jerome defends himself against Rufinus' charge that he had reread the classics by saying the vow was simply a *somnii sponsio*, a promise given in a dream!

28 For a detailed discussion and further reading, cf. Rebenich (1992a) 37ff. I agree, though on different grounds, with Adkin (1984) 121ff.; Adkin (1993a) that the words *Hierosolymam militaturus pergerem* in *ep.* 22.30.1 do not provide a clue to the dream's location. For the literary style of the passage in question, cf. Adkin (1984) 123ff.; Adkin (1993b); Adkin (1993c), who convincingly analyses the language of martyrdom Jerome uses and rightly emphasizes that it is not possible to date the dream. For a post-structuralist interpretation of the dream, cf. Feichtinger (1997b).

29 Cf. Fontaine (1973); Rousseau (1978) 79ff., 143ff.; Stancliffe (1983).

30 Hier. *Chron. s. a.* 374 (p. 247 Helm).

31 Cf. *Chromatius Episcopus* (1989); Duval (1989a); Cracco-Ruggini (1991); Krahwinkler (1992), esp. 67ff., 87ff.

32 Rufin. *Apol. c. Hier.* 1.4 (*CCL* 20, p. 39).

33 Cf. Hier. *ep.* 1.15 (Chapter 7).

34 Hier. *ep.* 7.6.2.

2 ANTIOCH TO CHALCIS

1 Cf. Hunt (1982) *pass.*

2 Hier. *ep.* 3.3.1.

3 On Evagrius, cf. Rebenich (1992a) 57ff.; Rebenich (1993b).

4 I just refer to the famous painting of Albrecht Dürer from about 1496 where Jerome is shown beside a crucifix, holding a rock with which to beat his breast in penance. He keeps a book in his right hand, presumably the Bible. Below this are the cardinal's robe and

hat with which Jerome was traditionally depicted. To his right is the lion, from whose paw Jerome had, according to an early Medieval *vita*, removed a thorn.

5 Grützmacher (1901–8) i 157: 'Durch Handarbeit erwarb er sich wie die anderen Eremiten im Schweiße seines Angesichts täglich seinen kärglichen Unterhalt.'

6 Cavallera (1922) i 46.

7 Kelly (1975) 47 and 56.

8 For this region, cf. Mouterde and Poidebard (1945); Tchalenko (1953–8); Tate (1992); Strube (1996).

9 Cf. e.g. Kelly (1975) 47.

10 Cf. Hier. *ep.* 7.1.2; 15.5.1.

11 Cf. Hier. *ep.* 4 (written in Antioch) and 5.

12 Hier. *ep.* 15 (Chapter 8) and 16.

13 Hier. *ep.* 5.2.4.

14 Cf. Hier. *ep.* 17.3.2.

15 Cf. Grützmacher (1901–8) i 54f. (*pace* Cavallera [1922] i 15f.).

16 Bagnall (1993), 296f.

17 Hier. *ep.* 7.2.1. The reading *barbarus semisermo* seems preferable to *barbarus seni sermo*, which Hilberg suggested in his edition. Cf. also Hier. *ep.* 17.2.4.

18 Hier. *ep.* 125.12.1f.

19 After his return from a diplomatic mission in the west (in 373 or 374), Evagrius had withdrawn from communion with the Meletians; cf. Bas. *ep.* 156.3 and Rebenich (1992a) 72.

20 Cf. Hier. *ep.* 15 (Chapter 8) and 16.

21 Hier. *ep.* 17.3.1f.

22 Maronia is mentioned in Hier. *Vita Malchi* 2 (*PL* 23, 55); cf. Rebenich (1992a) 86ff.

23 Hier. *ep.* 14.6.1.

24 Hier. *ep.* 58.4.2: . . . *si urbibus et frequentia urbium derelicta in agello habites et Christum quaeras in solitudine.*

25 Hier. *ep.* 125.8.1; cf. *C. Vigil.* 16.

26 Hier. *ep.* 117.1.2.

27 Hier. *C. Ioh.* 41 (*CCL* 79A, p. 79).

28 Hier. *ep.* 14.7.2: *monachum perfectum in patria sua esse non posse.*

29 Cf. Hier. *ep.* 14.6.4.

30 Hier. *ep.* 3.1.

31 Hier. *ep.* 84.3.1 and Jay (1974).

32 Hier. *ep.* 24.4.3.

33 Cf. Chapter 4.

34 Hier. *ep.* 43.3.3; cf. Rebenich (1994).

35 Hier. *ep*. 125.7f.

36 Cf. e.g. Rousseau (1978) 118.

37 Cf. Hier. *ep*. 22.22.3.

38 Hier. *ep*. 22.7.

39 Hier. *ep*. 22.30.

40 Hier. *ep*. 125.12.1.

3 CONSTANTINOPLE

1 CTh 16.1.2; cf., moreover, Sozom. *Hist.eccl*. 7.4.5f. and CTh 16.2.25 (which may have been part of the same law).

2 Cf. CTh 16.5.6 and Ensslin (1953) 28f. For church and state at the beginning of Theodosius' reign, cf. Errington (1997a); Errington (1997b).

3 Cf. Socr. *Hist.eccl*. 5.8.

4 I have shown elsewhere that it is very likely that Jerome entered Constantinople shortly after 24 November 380; cf. Rebenich (1992a) 118f.

5 Cf. e.g. Grützmacher (1901–8) i 177 and Cavallera (1922) i 58.

6 Cf. Hier. *ep*. 50.1.3; 52.8.2; *vir.ill*. 117; *adv.Iovin*. 1.13 (*PL* 23, 230); *Apol*. 1.13 (*CCL* 79, p. 12); *Comm. in Is*. 3.6.1 (*CCL* 73, p. 84); *Comm. in Eph*. 5.32 (*PL* 26, 535) and Adkin (1991); Lardet (1993) 71f. *ad Apol*. 1.13.

7 Cf. Antin (1951) 71.

8 Cf. Pietri (1976) 791ff. and McLynn (1994) 139ff.

9 About those rumours, cf. Ritter (1965) 33.

10 Cf. Schöne (1900) 250ff.; Grützmacher (1901–8) i 55ff.; Cavallera (1922) ii 20ff.; Kelly (1975) 72ff.; Rebenich (1992a) 117 and n. 571; Burgess (1995) 351 and 354. The Chronicle itself lacks precise evidence about the date and place of its composition; it can only be dated in the joint reign of the emperors Gratian and Theodosius (i.e. between 379 and 383). Cf. Hier. *Chron*. prol. (p. 7 Helm).

11 Cf. Hier. *Chron. s.a*. 360, 362, 364 (pp. 241–3 Helm).

12 Cf. Hier. *vir.ill*. 128.

13 Cf. Hier. *vir.ill*. 133.

14 Hier. *ep*. 79.

15 Cf. PLRE i 620 (3) and W. Ensslin, *s.v.* Nebridius, in: *PW Suppl*. 7, 1940, 551.

16 In 382–4, he was *comes rei privatae* and became prefect of Constantinople in 386; cf. PLRE i 620 (2); Dagron (1984) 253f.; Matthews (²1990) 109f.

17 Hier. *ep.* 79.1.4.

18 For Olympias, see PLRE i 642f.; Matthews ([2]1990) 132; and Mayer (1999). McLynn (1998) 228–30 has challenged the identification of the Olympias connected with Theodosia and Amphilochius with the famous Constantinopolitan heiress.

19 Cf. Hier. *ep.* 79.2 and 7ff.

20 At least Flavius Rufinus should also be mentioned here, Praetorian Prefect in the east 392–5 and consul of 392, who became Jerome's powerful opponent in the middle of the 390s (cf. Chapter 5).

21 Cf. Rebenich (1992a) 125f. and 214f. For a general evaluation of the westerners at the court of Theodosius in Constantinople, see Matthews ([2]1990) 101ff.

22 For a detailed interpretation of the *Vita Pauli primae eremitae*, cf. Rebenich (2000a) with further reading; for the dating of the life, cf. de Vogüé (1991) and Hamblenne (1993) 210 n. 5.

23 The *Life* was soon translated into Greek, Syriac, Coptic, and Ethiopic; cf. Oldfather (1943) 143ff.

24 Hier. *Vita Pauli* 17 (*PL* 23, 28ff.).

25 Cf. already Harnack (1895) 29.

26 Hier. *ep.* 1 (Chapter 7).

27 Cf. Fontaine (1973) 100.

28 Hier. *ep.* 10.3.3.

29 Cf. e.g. Courcelle (1948) and Nellen (1981) 123ff.

30 Hier. *Hom. Orig. in Ezech.* (*GCS* 33, p. 318). On the work, cf. Grütz-macher (1901–8) i 181ff.; Cavallera (1922) i 68ff., ii 78ff.; Kelly (1975) 75ff; and Nautin (1988).

31 Hier. *Hom. Orig. in Ezech.* (*GCS* 33, p. 318).

32 Cf. Hier. *C. Ioh.* 41 (*CCL* 79A, p. 78).

33 Hier. *Chron.* prol. (*GCS* Eus. 7, p. 1).

34 Cf. Hier. *Chron.* prol. (*GCS* Eus. 7, p. 6).

35 For the *Quellenforschung* on Jerome's *Chronicle*, which has given rise to much controversy, see Mommsen (1850); Helm (1927); Helm (1929a); Helm (1929b); Kelly (1975) 72ff.; Brugnoli (1995); Inglebert (1996) 217ff.; Ratti (1997); and Burgess (1995) who argues that Jerome, for his continuation, used the *Kaisergeschichte* as the single source.

36 Cf. e.g. Grützmacher (1901–8) i 193; Kelly (1975) 75.

37 The example of Meletius has already been mentioned (see note 11); cf. also the entries on Ambrose (p. 247, 16ff. Helm); Athanasius (p. 242, 16ff.); Eusebius of Vercelli (p. 239f.; 242, 19); Hilary (p. 240, 11ff.; 241, 17ff.; 242, 5f.); Liberius of Rome (p. 237, 17ff.),

Lucifer (p. 239f.; 242, 19ff.; 246, 1ff.), on the synods of Ariminum and Seleuceia (p. 241, 10ff., 21ff.) and on the churches of Antioch (p. 232), Constantinople (p. 235) and Jerusalem (p. 237).

38 Cf. Hier. *Chron. s.a.* 356 (p. 240 Helm) on Antony and Paul; *ibid.* 356 and 357 (p. 240) on Antony's disciples Sarmata, Amatas, and Marcarius; *ibid.* 375 (p. 248) on the killing of many monks in the Nitrian desert.

39 Cf. Hier. *Chron. s.a.* 367 (p. 245 Helm).

40 Cf. e.g. Alcimius and Delphidius, *Chron. s.a.* 355 (p. 239 Helm); Euanthius and Chrestus, *ibid.* 358 (p. 241); Victorinus and Donatus, *ibid.* 354 (p. 239); Gennadius und Minervius, *ibid.* 353 (p. 239); Libanius, *ibid.* 368 (p. 245); Nazarius, *ibid.* 324 and 336 (p. 231 and 233); Arnobius, *ibid.* 327 (p. 231); Pater, *ibid.* 336 (p. 233); Tiberianus, *vir disertus* and *Praefectus Praetorio Galliarum*, *ibid.* 336 (p. 233) and Titianus, *vir eloquens* and *Praefectus Praetorio Galliarum*, *ibid.* 345 (p. 236).

41 *Chron. s.a.* 273 (p. 222 Helm).

42 *Chron. s.a.* 354 (p. 239 Helm).

43 *Chron. s.a.* 374 (p. 247 Helm). On Jerome's links with the monastic community in Aquileia, cf. Chapter 1.

44 *Chron. s.a.* 377 (p. 248 Helm).

45 *Chron. s.a.* 374 (p. 247 Helm): 'the noblest of Roman women'. Because of Melania's friendship with Rufinus, Jerome, according to Rufinus (*Apol. c. Hier.* 2.29 [*CCL* 20, p. 105]), erased her name from his personal copies of the *Chronicle* after the outbreak of the Origenist controversy. On other alterations in later years, see Schöne (1900) 96ff., 117ff. and 151ff.

46 Cf. also Inglebert (1996) 276ff., 293ff.

47 Hier. *Chron.* prol. (p. 7 Helm): cf. Chapter 9.

48 Hier. *Chron.* prol. (p. 2 Helm).

49 If the *Altercatio Luciferiani et Orthodoxi* (= *Dialogus contra Luciferianos*) is to be placed in this period, Jerome would have also made his first attempt at a polemical–theological pamphlet in the east. But the dating of the work is controversial, cf. Rebenich (1992a) 99 n. 473, 138 n. 689; more recently, Jeanjean (1999) 21ff. has argued that it was written after Jerome's ordination. For rhetorical elements used in the *Altercatio*, cf. Canellis (1997).

50 Jerome's first commentary on Obadiah, probably composed during his college days in Rome, has not survived; cf. Booth (1979) 349ff.; Rebenich (1992a) 29 and n. 60. He had attempted an allegorical and mystical exegesis of which he was later ashamed (Hier. *comm. in Abd.* prol. [*CCL* 76, p. 350]).

51 Hier. *ep*. 18A and 18B on Is. 6.1–9. On the letter, cf. Grützmacher (1901–8) i 188ff.; Cavallera (1922) i 70ff.; Kelly (1975) 77ff; and Jay (1985) 63f.

52 Cf. Kamesar (1993) 40ff.

4 ROME

1 Cf. McLynn (1994) 142ff.

2 Cf. Lorenz (1966) and Rousseau (1978) 80ff.

3 Cf. Ruf. *Adult*. 13 (*CCL* 20, p. 15f.); Hier. *Apol*. 2.20 (*CCL* 79, p. 56f.); Kelly (1975) 81f.; Vessey (1996) 511ff., who rightly emphasizes, that Rufinus is our only evidence outside Jerome's own writings for his activity in the entourage of bishop Damasus.

4 Hier. *ep*. 123.9.1.

5 Hier. *ep*. 19–20; 21; 35–36. *Contra* Nautin (1983a), who argues that these letters were concocted after the bishop's death, as part of an attack against Ambrose; cf. Rebenich (1992a) 145ff. and Adkin (1993d) 375f. for an authentic address.

6 Cf. Hier. *Hom. Orig. in Cant*. prol. (*GCS* 33, p. 26) and *ep*. 46.1.4, 87.7.4.

7 Hier. *Vulg. Evang*. prol. (p. 1515 Weber/Gryson).

8 Hier. *vir.ill*. 103.

9 P. Brown (1961); Yarbrough (1976); E. A. Clark (1986), esp. 175ff.; Salzman (1989); Cooper (1992); Salzman (1992); Barnes (1995); Feichtinger (1995a), esp. 114ff.; Cloke (1995); Steininger (1997).

10 Hier. *ep*. 22.

11 In recent years, Neil Adkin has studied *ep*. 22 in greatest detail; cf. e.g. *VChr* 37, 1983, 36–40; *Glotta* 62, 1984, 89f.; *Philologus* 128, 1984, 119–26; *RFIC* 112, 1984, 287–91; *GB* 15, 1988, 177–86; *WS* 104, 1991, 149–60; *Arctos* 31, 1992, 5–18; *RSLR* 28, 1992, 461–71; *VChr* 46, 1992, 141–50; *RFIC* 120, 1992, 185–203; *Philologus* 136, 1992, 234–55; *MH* 49, 1992, 131–40; *SO* 68, 1993, 129–43; *RBPh* 71, 1993, 96–106; *Orpheus* 14, 1993, 135–40; *BollClass* 14, 1993, 142–9; *Orpheus* 15, 1994, 154–6; *Hermes* 121, 1993, 100–8; *Sileno* 19, 1993, 361–72; *Emerita* 62, 1994, 43–56; *CPh* 89, 1994, 69–72; *RhM* 137, 1994, 187–95; *SIFC* 3.12, 1994, 120–2; *PP* 279, 1994, 433–76; *Eirene* 30, 1994, 103–7; *SicGymn* 47, 1994 [1997], 315–17; *Helmantica* 45, 1995, 109–14; *C&M* 46, 1995, 237–54; *Athenaeum* 83, 1995, 470–85; *MH* 53, 1996, 56–60; *Hermes* 125, 1997, 240f.

12 Hier. *ep*. 22.16.1, 28.1, 17.1.

13 For various aspects of Jerome's ascetic programme and its place

within Christian tradition, cf. Consolino (1986); P. Brown (1988); Av. Cameron (1989); E. A. Clark (1979) 35ff.; G. Clark (1993); E. A. Clark (1994); Av. Cameron (1994); Feichtinger (1995a); Cooper (1996); Grimm (1996) 157ff.; Laurence (1997a); Laurence (1998a); Vidén (1998) with further reading. For a study of Jerome's theory of sexuality set forth in *ep.* 22, cf. Cox Miller (1993).

14 Hier. *ep.* 22.16.1.

15 Hier. *ep.* 108.1.1; cf. also *ep.* 130.6.1. See Rebenich (1992a) 181ff.; Sivan (1993b); and Feichtinger (1997a).

16 Sym. *ep.* 1.52: *pars melior generis humani.*

17 Hier. *ep.* 97.3.1.

18 For Marcella, cf. Letsch-Brunner (1998) and Chapter 17.

19 Hier. *ep.* 127.4.1: *ardor divinarum scripturarum.*

20 Hier. *ep.* 33.5.

21 Cf. P. Brown (1988) 366ff. and Vessey (1993a).

22 Cf. Ruf. *Apol. c.*Hier. 2.5 (*CCL* 20, p. 86).

23 Cf. Amm. Marc. 28.4.14.

24 Hier. *ep.* 28.1: *ergodióktes.* It should be noted that Origen, too, used this ironic expression to characterize his patron Ambrose, cf. Orig. *Comm. in Ioan.* 5, prol. (*SC* 120, p. 372).

25 Hier. *ep.* 45.3.1: *Damasi os meus sermo erat.*

26 *Ibid.*

27 Still authoritative, Wiesen (1964).

28 Hier. *ep.* 22.16.2–3.

29 Hier. *ep.* 22.32.2.

30 Collectio Avellana No. 1.9 (*CSEL* 35.1, p. 4); cf. Fontaine (1988a).

31 Cf. Hier. *Comm. in Is.* 2.3.12 (*CCL* 73, p. 52).

32 Theodoret. *hist.eccl.* 2.17.1-7 (*GCS* 44, 136f.).

33 CTh. 16.2.20. Cf. Hier. *ep.* 52.6.1 and Ambr. *ep.* 73(18).13.

34 Cf. Hier. *C. Ioh.* 8 (*CCL* 79A, p. 15).

35 Amm. Marc. 27.3.14f; cf. Matthews (1989) 444f.

36 Hier. *ep.* 27.1.1, 27.1.3, 40.2.2; cf. Wiesen (1964) 10 n. 44 and Adkin (1994) 70.

37 Cf. Pietri (1976) 407ff. and Maier (1995a).

38 Cf. Rousselle (1983) 171ff.

39 *De perpetua virginitate beatae Mariae adversus Helvidium liber unus*; cf. Av. Cameron (1991) 117ff.; Hunter (1993).

40 Hier. *ep.* 22.29.4.

41 Cf. Hier. *ep.* 41 and 42.

42 Fontaine (1979) 44.

43 Hier. *ep.* 22.14.1f.

44 Cf. Hier. *ep.* 27.1.

45 Hier. *ep.* 45.2.1; cf. also ep. 45 *pass.* and *ep.* 27.2.

46 Hier. *ep.* 66.13.2f.

47 Hier. *ep.* 66.13.2.

48 Hier. *ep.* 39.6.2. For *ep.* 39 *ad Paulam de obitu Blesillae*, cf. Feichtinger (1995b).

49 Cf. Hier. Didym. *spir.* prol. (*PL* 23, 107f.) and Cavallera (1922) ii 86ff.; Nautin (1983a) 340ff.

50 Students of Jerome have made great efforts to detect shafts against Ambrose throughout his writings. Since he rarely mentioned the bishop by name, the identification and interpretation of invectives are subject to scholarly dispute; cf. Paredi (1964); Nauroy (1988); Testard (1988); Oberhelman (1991); Adkin (1992); Adkin (1993d); Adkin (1993e); McLynn (1994) 289f.; Adkin (1997) with further reading.

51 Cf. Hier. *ep.* 45.6.1.

52 Kelly (1975) 91.

5   BETHLEHEM (I)

1 Cf. Hier. *ep.* 108.14.

2 On the holy land pilgrimage, cf. Donner (1979) 138ff.; Hunt (1982); Maraval (1985); Stemberger (1987) 88ff.; Laurence (1998c).

3 Cf. Hier. *ep.* 71.5.1.

4 Cf. Rebenich (1992a) 209ff. For the important role played by the letter-carriers in the epistolary exchange, cf. also Conybeare (2001) 30ff.

5 Hier. *ep.* 66.6.2: *viri nobiles, viri diserti, viri locupletes.*

6 Paul. Nol. *carm.* 24.481f.

7 Cf. Nautin (1979); Nautin (1983b).

8 Cf. the introduction to Chapter 14. On Jerome's acquaintance with Seneca's work, cf. Adkin (2000b).

9 Cf. Kelly (1975) 180ff. and Hunter (1987); Hunter (1993).

10 Sulp. Sev. *Dial.* 1.9.5.

11 For an authorative analysis, cf. E. A. Clark (1992). A detailed account by P. Lardet is to be found in the introduction to Jerome's *Apologia contra Rufinum* (1983; *SC* 303), esp. 30* ff. with further reading. Cf. also Laurence (1996) and Jeanjean (1999) 128ff.

12 Cf. Hier. *Apol.* 3.18 (*CCL* 79, p. 90).

13 Hier. *vir.ill.* 54.

14 Cf. Hier. *vir.ill.* 135 and note 18 to Chapter 14.

15 Hier. *ep.* 51.3.3.

16 Cf. e.g. Kelly (1975) 198.

17 Cf. P. Brown (1988) 380.

18 Hier. *C. Ioh.* 11 (*CCL* 79A, p. 19f.).

19 Hier. *ep.* 51.

20 Cf. Nautin (1972–3); Nautin (1973) 76ff.

21 Cf. Kelly (1975) 169f. and H. Chadwick in *JThS* 37, 1986, 595f.

22 Cf. Pall. *Hist.Laus.* 36 and 41.

23 Hier. *ep.* 58.4.4. On Jerome's relation to Paulinus, cf. Duval (1989b); Rebenich (1992a) 220ff; and Trout (1999) 90ff.

24 Hier. *ep.* 53.7.1.

25 For an annotated translation of the correspondence, cf. White (1990). There are two recent German studies of this 'unique document in the Early Church' (P. Brown [1967] 247): Hennings (1994) and Fürst (1999). Readers should be aware that the following interpretation clearly contradicts Fürst's thesis that the letters reflect two different characters and two different principles of handling dissent and conflict; cf. S. Rebenich in *Gymnasium* 108 (2001) 267–9. For a more convincing approach, cf. Vessey (1993b) and Burrus (1999).

26 Aug. *ep.* 28 (= Hier. *ep.* 56).

27 Aug. *ep.* 40.9.1 (= Hier. *ep.* 67.9.1).

28 Aug. *ep.* 40.7.1 (= Hier. *ep.* 67.7.1).

29 Aug. *ep.* 67.2.1 (= Hier. *ep.* 101.2.1).

30 Aug. *ep.* 73.1.4 (= Hier. *ep.* 110.1.4).

31 Hier. *ep.* 105.2.1 (= Aug. *ep.* 72.2.1); cf. Hier. *ep.* 102.2.1 (= Aug. *ep.* 68.2.1).

32 Cf. Hier. *ep.* 105.4.2 (= Aug. *ep.* 72.4.2).

33 Hier. *ep.* 105.2.2 (= Aug. *ep.* 72.2.2).

34 On Jerome and Pelagius, cf. Kelly (1975) 309ff. and Jeanjean (1999) 387ff. with further reading. For the significance of patronage networks in the Pelagian movement, cf. P. Brown (1968); P. Brown (1970).

35 Hier. *ep.* 141 (= Aug. *ep.* 195).

36 Hier. *ep.* 57 (*De optimo genere interpretandi*); cf. Bartelink (1980). For various attempts to identify the anonymous accuser of Jerome mentioned in *ep.* 57.1.2, cf. also Adkin (1996a).

37 Rufin. *Praef. in libros Orig. ΠEPI APXΩN* 1.3 (*CCL* 20, p. 246).

38 Cf. Hier. *ep.* 83 (written by Pammachius and Oceanus).

39 Hier. *ep.* 81 and 84.

40 Cf. Hier. *Apol.* 1.12; 3.38 (*CCL* 79, p. 12; 106f.).

41 Hier. *ep.* 86 and 88.

42 Cf. Hier. *ep.* 91–4; 96; 98–100.

43 Hier. *Apol.* 3.7 (*CCL* 79, p. 80).

44 Cf. Hier. *ep.* 127.9–11; cf. Chapter 17.

45 Rufin. *Apol. c. Hier.* 1.21 (*CCL* 20, p. 55).

46 Rufin. *Apologia ad Anastasium* (*CCL* 20, pp. 19–28). On the link between Rufinus and the bishop of Brescia, Gaudentius, see Meyvaert (1986) and Duval (1987).

47 Cf. *ACO* 1.5, p. 3f. (= *PL* 20, 68–73).

48 Rufin. *Apol. c. Hier.* 1.22–44; 2.13–22; 2.28 (*CCL* 20, p. 56ff.; 93ff.; 103f.). Cf. Hier. *Apol.* 3.11 (*CCL* 79, p. 83).

49 Rufin. *Apol. c. Hier.* 2.6f. (*CCL* 20, p. 87ff.). On Jerome's oath, see Chapter 1.

50 Rufin. *Apol. c. Hier.* 1.4–16 (*CCL* 20, p. 39ff.).

51 Hier. *Apol.* 3.3; 44 (*CCL* 79, p. 75; 116).

52 Cf. Aug. *ep.* 73.6-10 (= Hier. *ep.* 110.6–10).

53 Cited in *PL* 21, 175; cf. P. Brown (1970) 210.

54 Cf. Hammond (1977) 412ff.

55 Cf. e.g. Hier. *ep.* 119.11.5; 127.10.3; *Comm. in Hier.* 29.14–20 (*CCL* 74, p. 1047); and Cavallera (1922) ii 131ff.

56 Hier. *Comm. in Ezech.* 1, prol. (*CCL* 75, p. 3f.).

57 Hier. *ep.* 109.1.1; 2.4; cf. also *ep.* 61 and *C. Vigil.* pass. For Jerome's polemical work and his relation to Vigilantius, cf. Rebenich (1992a) 240ff. and Jeanjean (1999) 55ff.

58 Hier. *ep.* 61.2.1–3.

59 For different contemporary perceptions of Jerome, cf. Sulp. Sev. *Dial.* 1.8.4–6; 1.9.1; 4f.; 1.21.5. On Jerome and Sulpicius Severus, cf. Rebenich (1992a) 252ff. with further reading.

60 Hyd. *Chron. s.a.* 415 (p. 84 Burgess).

6 BETHLEHEM (II)

1 On Jerome's representation in art, see Jungblut (1967); Miehe (1974); Rice (1985); Wiebel (1985). The engraving of A. Dürer is, for instance, to be found in the catalogue of the exhibition A. Dürer 1471–1971, Nürnberg 1971, no. 151, fig. 90 and no. 273, fig. 156 .

2 Jerome's Latin translation of the Bible was first called the Vulgate (i.e. *Biblia Sacra Vulgatae Editionis*) at the Council of Trent. During the Middle Ages, Jerome's version was known as *nostra translatio, nostra usitata editio* or *ea translatio qua nostrae ecclesiae passim utuntur*; cf. e.g. Allgeier (1948); Sutcliffe (1948a); Sutcliffe (1948b).

3 Cf. e.g. Loewe (1969) 102ff.; Fischer (1972) 1ff. (156ff.); Reichmann (1980); Smalley (1983); for a general introduction, cf. also *Bible de*

tous les temps, vol. 2: *Le Monde latin antique et la Bible*, Paris 1985 and vol. 3: *Saint Augustin et la Bible*, Paris 1986.

4 Cf. Bammel (1993). On the date of the commentaries, see Nautin (1979).

5 Hier. *vir.ill.* 135: 'I translated the New Testament from the Greek'; cf. Hier. *ep.* 71.5.3; 112.20.5.

6 For Rufinus and Jerome, see Hier. *ep.* 51.2.4; 81.2 (on the identification, see as early as D. Vallarsi, *PL* 22, 736 note (e); and Fischer (1972) 281ff.

7 Cf. Chapter 4.

8 Hier. *Comm. in Tit.* 3.9 (*PL* 26, 630); Hier. *Comm. Ps.* 1.4 (*CCL* 72, p. 180); cf. also Hier. *vir.ill.* 3; 75; 113 and Hier. *Apol.* 3.12 (*CCL* 79, p. 84).

9 Cf. Hier. *Vulg. Ps (G)*. prol. (p. 767 Weber/Gryson).

10 Cf. Hier. *Vulg. Ps (H)*. prol. (p. 768f. Weber/Gryson).

11 Hier. *Vulg. Iob (G)* prol. (*PL* 29, *c*.63f.).

12 Hier. *Vulg. Salom. (G)* prol. (*PL* 29, 425ff.); Hier. *Vulg. Par. (G)* prol. (*ibid.* 423ff.).

13 Cf. e.g. Hier. *ep.* 71.5.3; 106.2.4; 134.2.3 (= Aug. *ep.* 172.2.3); Hier. *Apol.* 2.24; 3.25 (*CCL* 79, p. 61; 97).

14 Grützmacher (1901–8) ii 92ff.

15 Hier. *vir.ill.* 135.

16 Cf. Hier. *Vulg. Ios.* prol. (p. 285f. Weber/Gryson) and Kelly (1975) 283f.

17 See Jay (1982).

18 Cf. e.g. Hier. *Vulg. Par. (H)* prol. (p. 546 Weber/Gryson).

19 Cf. Bammel (1988); Fürst (1994a); and Hennings (1994) 110ff.

20 For Jerome's imitation of classical literature in the Vulgate, cf. Wissemann (1992); Brown Tkacz (1996); Brown Tkacz (1997); Brown Tkacz (1999); Adkin (2000a).

21 *Liber interpretationis nominum Hebraicorum, or Liber de nominibus Hebraicis* in *CCL* 72, pp. 59–116; cf. P. de Lagarde, *Onomastica sacra*, Göttingen [2]1887, 26–116.

22 *De locis* or *Liber de situ et nominibus locorum Hebraicorum* in E. Klostermann, *Eusebius Werke* 3.1, Leipzig 1904 (*GCS* 11.1); P. de Lagarde, *Onomastica sacra*, Göttingen [2]1887, 118–90. The work is a close translation of Eusebius' *Onomasticon*.

23 *Quaestiones Hebraicae in Genesim* in *CCL* 72, pp. 1–56; cf. Kamesar (1993) and Hayward (1995).

24 Hier. *Comm. in Mich.* prol. 2 (*CCL* 76, p. 473).

25 Hier. *Apol.* 3.11 (*CCL* 79, p. 83); cf. Hier. *ep.* 112.5.2 (= Aug. *ep.* 75.5.2) and 119.1.4.

26 Cf. esp. Duval (1973); *SC* 323, 74ff.; Jay (1985); Gryson *et al.* (1993–9) with further reading.

27 Cf. already Rahmer (1861); Rahmer (1902). For a substantial reassessment of Jerome as a Hebrew scholar, cf. Kamesar (1993) with further reading; for Jerome's dependence on Jewish and Jewish–Christian sources, cf. Schmidt (1998) and Kinzig (forthcoming) with further reading. D. Brown (1992) is written without any apprehension of recent scholarship.

28 Cf. already Courcelle (1948) 37ff., esp. 64ff., 83ff., 91ff., Hagendahl (1958); Hagendahl (1974). More recently, Neil Adkin has analysed Jerome's indebtedness to various predecessors and his imitation of classical literature in many articles.

29 Rufin. *Apol. c. Hier.* 2.7 (*CCL* 20, p. 88).

30 Hier. *Apol.* 3.39 (*CCL* 79, p. 108).

31 See Jerome's pointed remark in *Apol.* 3.6 (*CCL* 79, p. 79): 'I am [...] one who knows Hebrew, Greek and Latin, a trilingual man (*ego* ... *hebraeus, graecus, latinus, trilinguis*).'

32 Cf. Hier. *ep.* 17.2.4.

33 E.g. Hier. *Vulg. Tb.* prol. (p. 676 Weber/Gryson); *Vulg. Iud.* prol. (*ibid.* 691); *Vulg. Iob (H)* prol. (*ibid.* 731); *Vulg. Dan.* prol. (*ibid.* 1341); cf. also Hier. *ep.* 18A.10; *Comm. in Dan.* 1.2.4 (*CCL* 75A, p. 785); 1.4.5 (*ibid.* 812).

34 Perhaps with the exception of Jerome's friend Epiphanius of Salamis, the so-called 'pentaglossic', who was said to know the Greek, the Syrian, the Hebrew, the Coptic, and in part also the Latin language (cf. Hier. *Apol.* 2.22; 3.6 [*CCL* 79, p. 58; 79]). For a modern sceptical evaluation of the evidence, cf. e.g. W. Schneemelcher in *RAC* 5, 1962, 910. For Apollinaris of Laodicea's knowledge of Hebrew, see Philost. *Hist. eccl.* 8, 11 (p. 112 Bidez/Winkelmann).

35 Cf. e.g. Aug. *civ.* 18.42; *Contra Iulianum* 1.7.34 (*PL* 44, 665); Sulp. Sev. *Dial.* 1.8.3.

36 Cf. Burstein (1975) and Rebenich (1993a) 56ff. For the modern hypothesis that Jerome was dependent on Greek sources, especially Origen and Eusebius, whenever he referred to Jewish exegesis, and hardly understood a word of Hebrew, cf. esp. Nautin (1977) 214ff., 284ff., 326ff., 344ff., 359ff.; Nautin (1986) 310.

37 Cf. Hier. *Vulg. Dan.* prol. (p. 1341 Weber/Gryson).

38 Hier. *ep.* 84.3.2; cf. Rufin. *Apol. c. Hier.* 2.15 (*CCL* 20, p. 95); Hier. *Apol.* 1.13 (*CCL* 79, p. 12).

39 Hier. *ep.* 84.3.2; cf. Hier. *Vulg. Par (G)* prol. (*PL* 26, 423); *Vulg. Iob*

(H) prol. (p. 731 Weber/Gryson); *Vulg. Dan.* prol. (p. 1341 Weber/ Gryson).

40 Cf. Duval, *SC* 323, 419ff.; Hamblenne (1988); Fürst (1994b).

41 Cf. Hier. *Comm. in Ion.* 4.6 (*SC* 323, 296ff.).

42 *Ibid.*

43 Rufin. *Apol. c. Hier.* 2.39 (*CCL* 20, p. 114). This motif of the Jonah cycle was indeed quite often depicted on early Christian sarcophagi; cf. e.g. *Spätantike und Frühes Christentum. Katalog der Ausstellung im Liebighaus*, Frankfurt/M 1983, 241ff. with bibliography. For Jerome's reply, see Hier. *Apol.* 1.30 (*CCL* 79, p. 29).

44 Hier. *ep.* 104.5 (= Aug. *ep.* 71.5); cf. Duval (1966) and Fürst (1994a).

45 Hier. *ep.* 112.22.1–3 (= Aug. *ep.* 75.22.1–3).

46 Hier. *ep.* 112.20.5; 21.1 (= Aug. *ep.* 75.20.5; 21.1); cf. also Hier. *Vulg. Pent.* prol. (p. 4 Weber/Gryson); *Vulg. Par. (G)* prol. (*PL* 29, 426); *Vulg. Esr.* prol. (*ibid.* 638).

47 Rufin. *Apol. c. Hier.* 2.41 (*CCL* 20, p. 115).

48 Hier. *Apol.* 2.24 (*CCL* 79, p. 60).

49 Cf. e.g. Hier. *Comm. in Eccles.* prol. (*CCL* 72, p. 249); *Apol.* 2.24 (*CCL* 79, p. 60f.); *ep.* 106 to the Goths Sunnia and Fretula.

7   THE NOVELIST

1 The first two paragraphs of the letter are a dedicatory preface. It was conventional for an author to state that he was writing his work in order to conform to the wishes of others; cf. Scourfield (1983) 49ff.

2 Jerome's self-deprecatory expression that he is not able to handle the story is meant to glorify the subject. He likes this kind of affected modesty; for other instances of *recusatio*, cf. Scourfield (1983) 59ff; 67ff.; Scourfield (1993) 77ff.

3 Jerome plays on 'words' (*verba*) and the divine 'Word' (*verbum* or *logos*) of Jn. 1.1.

4 For this rhetorical question, cf. Quint. *inst.* 9.2.11 and Hier. *ep.* 60.2.1; 84.4.1; 130.1.2.

5 Cf. n. 2.

6 Cf. Hier. *ep.* 130.2.3.

7 *scalmum rexi. scalmus* is the peg to which an oar is fastened in rowing, the thole-pin (cf. OLD *s.v.*).

8 The Greek name for the Black Sea. Εὔξεινος (*eúxeinos*) means 'the hospitable', obviously a euphemism, since from a Mediterranean perspective it was cold, deep, and tempestuous.

9 Verg. *Aen.* 3.193.

10 Cf. Verg. *Aen.* 3.194f. and 5.8–11.

11 Jerome's metaphorical use of nautical expressions is reminiscent of Cic. *de Orat.* 1,174 and Quint. *inst.* 12 *prooem.* 3f.; cf. Scourfield (1983) 70ff. and Hagendahl (1958) 100ff., although I doubt whether these lines indicate that 'when writing them Jerome retained a lively recollection of the sea and the experiences of a sea-voyage, [i.e.] his voyage to the East' (Hagendahl [1958] 100f.).

12 Vercellae, a garrison town and *municipium* in the early empire, was a Christian centre of Cisalpine Gaul in the fourth and fifth centuries AD. For the use of a proper name at the beginning of a narrative, cf. Quint. *inst.* 4.2.1f.

13 Cf. Lucan. 1.24–7 and Godel (1964) 68.

14 *Consularis Aemiliae et Liguriae*, the governor of the province of Aemilia and Liguria. His identity cannot be established; cf. PLRE i 1019 (Anonymus 90). Ambrose held the office when he was elected bishop of Milan, cf. PLRE i 52 (Ambrosius 3). For the provincial governorship, see Jones (1964) i 106f.

15 The event can be related to the trials for magic and adultery conducted in senatorial circles by Valentinian I; cf. Amm.Marc. 28.1 and Matthews (1989) 209ff.; Scourfield (1983) 38ff. For the issue of adultery in Late Antiquity, cf. also G. Delling, *s.v.* Ehebruch, *RAC* 4, 1959, 666–77.

16 Cf. G. Thür, *s.v.* Folter, *RAC* 8, 1972, 101–12 and J. Vergote, *s.v.* Folterwerkzeuge, *ibid.* 112–41.

17 *at verior mulier sexu fortior suo.* I follow Hilberg's text (*CSEL* 54, p. 3). Most of the manuscripts have *at verior mulier sexu infirmior virtute fortior* ('But the woman was stronger in virtue, if weaker in sex'). Jerome often stresses the religious strength and ascetic zeal of women; cf. e.g. *ep.* 122.4.3 and Feichtinger (1995a) 152.

18 *eculeus*, an instrument of torture. Apparently, it had the function of stretching the victim; cf. also Prud. *Perist.* 10.109ff. and Scourfield (1983) 87f.

19 In prayer, cf. below *ep.* 1.5.2.

20 Cf. Ps. 7.10. I agree with Scourfield (1983) 89 who suggests *scrutator renum et cordis*, since 'it is the plural form which is regularly found in the Vulgate'. Hilberg (*CSEL* 54, p. 3) reads *scrutator renis et cordis*.

21 The young man.

22 I doubt that this phrase is an echo of Verg. *Aen.* 9.496, as Hilberg (*CSEL* 54, p. 3) indicates.

23 The oxymoron *non moritur, quisquis victurus occiditur* can also be rendered as follows: 'He does not perish, who dies to live again', if *victurus* is derived from *vivere* and not from *vincere*. This understanding

of the passage is to be found in some translations (e.g. *NPNF*² vol. 6, p. 2; Wright in his Loeb edition of *Select Letters of St. Jerome*, p. 7; cf. also Labourt i, p. 4 and 161). But the woman's frank speech alludes to the language of martyrdom: she is prepared to die for her faith and her 'baptism of blood' is a victory over death. Cf. also Scourfield (1983) 90f.

24 Cf. Lucan. 1.327–31 and Godel (1964) 68.

25 Note that in this letter Jerome shifts easily between the historic present and past tenses.

26 Cf. Hier. *ep.* 127.13.2. For a different reading of the text, cf. Schäublin (1973) 56 who objects to *vetuit circa se saevire tormenta*. However, Scourfield's arguments for the text, which is read by all the manuscripts, seem to be compelling ([1987] 488f.).

27 Cf. Scourfield (1983) 100: 'Jerome causes the woman to make her denial not merely on her own behalf but on that of the man whose confession has brought her to this position. But it is only an apparent act of love and self-sacrifice; if one denies adultery, one can hardly avoid denying it for one's alleged lover also. Jerome is employing a trick to build up the woman's stature.'

28 Note that the torturer's groaning contrasts with the woman's firmness, who withstands the torment without wailing.

29 Stories of miracles at the scene of execution can be read in many martyr acts, cf. Delehaye (²1966) 207ff.

30 Jerome uses *lictor* to denote the headsman; cf. Prud. *Perist.* 3.97f. Under the Empire, a military subordinate, normally called *speculator*, put to death the person under sentence, while an officer was responsible for the execution (cf. below *ep.* 1.10). Jerome may have preferred *lictor* to *speculator*, since the former expression obviously reflects the functions of the *lictores* in the Republican era who, carrying the *fasces* of magistrates with *imperium* (the bundle of rods with an axe), arrested, summoned, and executed Roman citizens; cf. Mommsen (1899) 915f. and 923ff.; N. Hyldahl, B. Salomonsen, *s.v.* Hinrichtung, *RAC* 15, 1991, 342–65.

31 *sacramentum trinitatis*.

32 I follow Scourfield's ([1983] 110f.; [1987] 489) reading of the text (*iam igitur et tertium ictum sacramentum frustaverat trinitatis*, etc.); cf. Labourt vol. i, p. 161 *comm. ad loc.*

33 *speculator*.

34 *sarabara*. The Aramaic word seems to refer to some kind of headwear. However, *Hier. Comm. in Dan.* 3.21 (*CCL* 75A, p. 802) considers *sabarara* corrupt and reads *saraballa*; there, the word is said to describe a type of trousers; cf. Scourfield (1983) 116f.

35 Cf. Dan. 3. For Jerome's use of biblical *exempla* adduced from the book of Daniel, cf. Scourfield (1983) 113ff.

36 For the story of Daniel in the pit of lions, cf. Dan. 6, esp. 16ff. and 14 (= Bel).30ff.

37 Text and meaning here are difficult. The translation follows Scourfield (1983) 117f.; (1987) 490: *huc beati Danihelis revocetur historia, iuxta quam* (sc. *historiam*) *adulantibus caudis praedam suam leonum ora timuerunt.* Hilberg (*CSEL* 54, p. 6) reads *iuxta quem* (sc. *Danihelem*) (i.e. 'near (= before) whom the lions wagged their tails and were afraid of the man who was to be their prey').

38 Cf. Dan. 13 (= Sus.). The history of Susanna is found in the Greek text of Daniel, though not in the Hebrew; cf. also 'The Song of the Three Holy Children' and 'The History of the Destruction of Bel and the Dragon'. When Jerome, convinced of the superiority of the Hebrew text, had started on a new Latin version of the Old Testament *iuxta Hebraeos*, he came to regard these stories as apocryphal, but incorporated them into his translation; cf. Hier. *Vulg. Dan.* prol. (p. 1341 Weber/Gryson).

39 Verg. *Aen.* 12.611.

40 Cf. Scourfield (1983) 120: 'Jerome naturally gives the events a Christian slant. He regards the woman's apparent death as another manifestation of God's power and love. God wishes to save the innocent *curator* just as much as the innocent woman, and to do this creates the impression that the execution is, in the end, successful.'

41 The grave-diggers, *fossores* or *fossarii* (from Latin *fodere*, to dig); cf. e.g. Aug. *conf.* 9.31 and Ps.-Hier. *ep.* 12.1 (*PL* 30, 150). They were regarded as minor clergy. In the second part of the fourth and at the beginning of the fifth centuries, the *fossores* organized themselves into powerful corporations, sold grave spaces and controlled the catacombs.

42 I adopt Labourt's conjecture (*misericordia domini celer* [or *celerior*] *ac* [or *et*] *matura nox advenit*), vol. i, p. 7 and 161 (*comm. ad loc.*); cf. Scourfield (1983) 125f.; Scourfield (1987) 491. Hilberg (*CSEL* 54, p. 7) reads *misericordiam domini celatura nox advenit* ('night came on to conceal the mercy of the Lord').

43 Ps. 118 (117).6. Jerome writes *Dominus auxiliator meus*, where the Vulgate has *Dominus mihi adiutor* ('the Lord is on my side').

44 For Christian charities, cf. Krause (1995) with further reading.

45 Cf. Eccles. 12.7 and Hier. *ep.* 77.11.2; *Vita Pauli* 14 (*PL* 23, 26f.).

46 *lictor.* Jerome regards the headsman as a personification of the devil.

47 *erue scilicet ossa.* Scourfield (1983) 128f.; Scourfield (1987) 491f. suggests *erue si licet ossa*: 'dig up the bones, if it is permissible for you'.

48 *ius summum summa malitia*: Terent. *Heaut.* 796; cf. the proverbial *summum ius summa iniuria* in Cic. *off*. 1.10.33 and Otto (1890) 179f.

49 Cf. Chapter 2.

50 Arian bishop of Milan, who probably died in 374, and predecessor of Ambrose; cf. McLynn (1994) 13ff.; 20ff. and 36ff. It has been deduced from this sentence that the letter must have been written after Auxentius' death. But I think Grützmacher (1901–8) i 53f. is right, that *mortuus* does not necessarily refer to the bishop's eternal rest, but can be read as an allusion to his earlier condemnation by a Roman council under Damasus. So *sepultum paene ante quam mortuum* can mean 'buried, so to speak, while yet alive' (i.e. Auxentius was ecclesiastically 'dead' before the time of his death); cf. also Rebenich (1992a) 70 *pace* Cavallera (1922) ii 12f.; Scourfield (1983) 33f.; Scourfield (1986) 118 and Schwind (1997) 171.

51 Damasus (bishop of Rome 366–84). Jerome obviously refers to a successful diplomatic mission by Evagrius to the imperial court, to support Damasus in his fight for the episcopal see against his rival Ursinus, who had also been consecrated bishop in 366. In the bloody struggle more than 100 persons were killed, so that the emperor Valentinian I was forced to intervene; he backed Damasus and banished Ursinus to Cologne, but it was not until the beginning of the 380s that the troubles ceased; cf. Pietri (1976) 407ff.; McLynn (1992) 16ff. and Rebenich (1992a) 64ff.

52 Verg. *Georg.* 4.147f.

53 Valentinian I, emperor of the west from 364 to 375.

8   THE THEOLOGIAN

1 Cf. Jn. 19.23.

2 Cf. Cant. 2.15.

3 Cf. Jer. 2.13.

4 Cf. Cant. 4.12.

5 Cf. Rom. 1.8.

6 Jerome had been baptized at Rome; cf. Hier. *ep.* 16.2.1. For a traditional account of the event, cf. Kelly (1975) 23; for a different chronological setting for Jerome's baptism, cf. Rebenich (1992a) 28ff.

7 Cf. Mt. 13.45f.

8 Lk. 17.37; cf. Mt. 24.28.

9 Cf. Lk. 15.13.

10 Cf. Lk. 8.8.

11 Cf. Mt. 13.22,23.

12 *sol iustitiae*. Cf. Mal. 4.2 and Dölger (²1971).

13 Cf. Lk. 10.18.

14 Cf. Is. 14.12ff.

15 Mt. 15.14.

16 Mt. 15.13.

17 Cf. 2 Tim. 2.20.

18 Cf. Apoc. 2.27; 18.9.

19 *tua beatitudo*. This title was widely used by Christian writers, cf. O'Brien (1930) 3ff.

20 Cf. Mt. 16.18.

21 Cf. Lev. 19.6f.

22 Cf. Gen. 7.23.

23 For the location of Jerome's desert domicile, cf. Hier. *ep*. 5.1; 7.1.1; 16.2.2; *Vita Pauli* 6 (*PL* 23, 21f.); Rebenich (1992a) 85ff. and Chapter 2.

24 *tua sanctimonia*. For the title, given to bishops only, cf. O'Brien (1930) 9.

25 *sanctum Domini*. Most certainly an allusion to the Eucharist that was sent as a symbol of ecclesiastical communion.

26 Probably the 'orthodox' bishops who were exiled at the beginning of the 370s by the emperor Valens; cf. Hier. *ep*. 3.2.1 and Labourt i, p. 163 (*comm. ad ep*. 15.2.2).

27 Cf. Hier. *ep*. 16.2.2: 'Meletius, Vitalis, and Paulinus say that they are on your side, and I could believe the assertion if it were made by one of them only. As it is, either two of them are lying or they all are.'

28 Cf. Lk. 11.23.

29 At the councils of Nicaea (325) and Alexandria (362), Arius and Arianism were condemned. However, at Alexandria, the *homoousios* formula of Nicaea was reinforced (the Son is of one substance [*ousia*] with the Father), and the Origenist distinction of the *hypostaseis* of the three divine persons was admitted. Although the decisions of the synod gave rise to new controversies, Jerome is exaggerating the novelty of the 'three *hypostaseis*' theology to please Damasus.

30 The Meletians were called the 'field community' since they were denied access to the churches of Antioch; cf. as early as *PL* 22, 356 n. (i); Grützmacher (1901–8) i 169 n. 1; Kelly (1975) 52 n. 28 (*contra* Labourt i, p. 164, *comm. ad loc.*).

31 *homo Romanus*; cf. Act. 22.25. For Jerome's image of Rome, cf. Paschoud (1967) 209ff. and Sugano (1983).

32 *tres personas subsistentes.*

33 *cauterio unionis inurimur* (i.e. we are accused of (Sabellian) heresy, uniting the Father and the Son in one person).

34 The teaching about the Trinity that denies the unity of substance in the three divine persons is called tritheism.

35 *nomen essentiae.*

36 Ex. 3.14.

37 *sed quia illa sola est infecta natura.* Some manuscripts read: *sed quia illa (sola) est perfecta natura* (cf. *CSEL* 54, p. 64): 'but because that is (alone) perfect nature' (i.e. God's nature alone is perfect).

38 *deitas,* the translation of the Greek term θεότης (*theótes*), 'divinity' or 'divine nature'.

39 For Ursinus, Damasus' rival for the Roman see, cf. note 51 to Chapter 7.

40 On the Arian bishop of Milan and Ambrose's predecessor, cf. note 50 to Chapter 7.

41 *tres personae subsistentes perfectae, aequales, coaeternae.*

42 Cf. 2 Cor. 11.14.

43 Damasus did not reply, and so Jerome wrote another letter, 'shorter but even more importunate' (Kelly [1975] 53); cf. Hier. *ep.* 16.

44 On Evagrius, cf. Chapter 2.

45 Perhaps the followers of the Arianizing bishop Silvanus of Tarsus.

9   THE CHRONOGRAPHER

1 *Noster Tullius* (i.e. Marcus Tullius Cicero).

2 Cicero is said to have translated Platon's *Protagoras* and *Timaeus*; cf. also Quint. *inst.* 10.5.2; Hier. *ep.* 57.5.2; 106.3.3; *Vulg. Pent.* prol. (p. 4 Weber/Gryson) and Bartelink (1980) 49f. On Jerome's dependence upon Cicero's translations of Greek philosophical texts, cf. Courcelle (1948) 52ff.

3 The *Phaenomena* of the Hellenistic poet Aratus (c. 315 to before 240 BC) are dedicated to the description of the poles, the northern and southern constellations, the circles of the celestial sphere, and weather signs. Latin translations (the so-called *Aratea*) were made by Varro, Cicero, Germanicus, and Avienus. Cicero rendered the work as a young man (cf. Cic. *nat.deor.* 2.41.104); 480 continuous lines and *c.* 70 in quotations are extant from his translation of the *Phaenomena*.

NOTES

4 Cf. Cic. *off.* 2.24.87; Hier. *ep.* 57.5.2; 106.3.3; *Vulg. Pent.* prol. (p. 4 Weber/Gryson) and Bartelink (1980) 50.

5 One may conclude from these lines that Jerome had read the original version of Xenophon's *Oeconomicus*. Jerome, the 'Ciceronian' (cf. Hier. *ep.* 22.30.4), referred to Cicero's authority to sanction his translation theory and his rendering sense for sense and not word for word (*non verbum e verbo, sed sensum exprimere de sensu*); cf. Hier. *ep.* 57.5.2; 106.3.3 and Bartelink (1980) 46ff.; C. Becker, *s.v.* Cicero, *RAC* 3, 1957, 115f.; Courcelle (1948) 42ff.; Winkelmann (1970) 538ff.

6 *tumultuarium opus.*

7 *notarius.* Probably Jerome dictated the historical records, for the chronological tables needed to be copied out; cf. Schöne (1900) 77.

8 Septuagint ('LXX'). The most important Greek version of the Old Testament. Jewish tradition attributes its origin to the initiative of Ptolemy II Philadelphus, king of Egypt (285–46 BC), who asked for a translation of the Hebrew Law and engaged 72 learned Jews (hence the title 'Septuagint') who, on the Island of Pharos, made a Greek version for the royal library at Alexandria. Later, Ptolemy's name was connected with all the Old Testament. Internal evidence indicates that the Septuagint was the work of different translators between the third century BC and the beginning of the Christian era. The Septuagint early became the Old Testament of the Greek-speaking Christians. Cf. also Chapter 13 and Chapter 15.

9 The names represent three Greek versions of the Old Testament that were reproduced in Origen's Hexapla (i.e. in Origen's edition of the Old Testament, in which the Hebrew text, a transliteration into Greek characters and four Greek translations were arranged in parallel columns). Aquila was a native of Sinope in Pontus, who lived under Hadrian (117–38). According to Epiphanius, he became a proselyte to Judaism (*mens. et pond* 14). After learning Hebrew from rabbis, he revised the text of the Septuagint. His translation, which is very literal, was adopted by Greek-speaking Jews. About Symmachus hardly anything is known. He probably lived in the later second century and Jerome called him an Ebionite Christian (*vir.ill.* 54; *Comm. in Hab.* 3.11–3); Epiphanius, however, speaks of him as a Samaritan who later converted to Judaism (*mens. et pond.* 16). Unlike Aquila, Symmachus preferred readable style to verbal accuracy. According to Jerome (*vir.ill.* 54), Theodotion (second century?) was an Ebionite Christian; Irenaeus refers to him as a Jewish proselyte (*Haer.* 3.21.1) and Epiphanius as a follower of Marcion (*mens. et pond.* 17). He translated or revised the Greek

version of the Old Testament which is found in Origen's Hexapla after the Septuagint. Cf. further Tov (1992) 143ff.

10 For certain sections of the Old Testament, up to three further Greek versions were added in the Hexapla.

11 Cultivated Greek and Roman readers often criticized the low literary level of the Bible. Christian writers responded to this problem in two different ways: they either defended the literary quality of the Bible or stressed the importance of the content and minimized the relevance in style; cf. already Norden ([2]1909) ii 516ff. and Kamesar (1993) 46ff. with further reading.

12 Cf. Hier. *ep.* 22.29.7.

13 Horace (Quintus Horatius Flaccus).

14 Different types of Greek and Latin metre. The sapphic and alcaic stanzas are traditionally laid out as four lines, but can also consist of three verses; cf. OCD[3] 970ff., *s.v.* metre, Greek and metre, Latin.

15 For the history of Christian reception of Flavius Josephus, cf. H. Schreckenberg, *s.v.* Josephus, *RAC* 18, 1998, 791ff. with further reading.

16 *minium.* A substance yielding a bright red pigment, properly cinnabar, or the pigment itself (OLD 1112, *s.v.*). On the use of red and black ink and other technical innovations, cf. Schöne (1900) 48ff.; Mras (1928) and R. Helm in *GCS* 47, p. XXI ff.

17 *membrana.* The chronicle was written on parchment, not on papyrus; cf. Schöne (1900) 47f.

18 AD 326.

19 Suetonius (Gaius Suetonius Tranquillus).

20 Jerome's sources are controversial. Various historiographical works and authors have been discussed. For example Eutropius, who wrote a short Roman history from Romulus to the emperor Jovian, the *breviarium* of Festus, *magister memoriae* of Valens, and the so-called *Kaisergeschichte*, which Alexander Enmann first postulated at the end of the nineteenth century (hence 'Enmannsche Kaisergeschichte'). For further reading, see Chapter 3 (note 35).

21 AD 378. The latter emperor mentioned is Valentinian II.

22 Cf. Wiesen (1964) 262f.

23 After the battle of Adrianople in Thrace (9 August 378), in which the emperor Valens and two-thirds of the Roman army were killed, Gothic groups were a permanent threat to the Roman Empire. Gratian and Theodosius, who conducted various campaigns, failed to expel the Goths, so that Theodosius signed a treaty with them (3 October 382), which recognized them as federates and assigned them lands.

10   THE EPISTOLOGRAPHER

1 Cf. Lev. 2.11.

2 Cf. Mt. 7.7.

3 That is the day of his martyrdom, 29 June. From the end of the second century, the anniversary of the martyr's death was kept as the feast of his (heavenly) birthday.

4 For the comparison of oratory to wrestling, cf. e.g. Cic. *Brut.* 37; Quint. *inst.* 2.8.3f.

5 Cf. Ezek. 16.11.

6 Cf. Jer. 36.4ff.; Baruch 6.

7 Cf. Mt. 3.16; Lk. 3.22.

8 Hier. *ep.* 22.

9 Cf. Tim. 2.10.

10 Cf. 2 Cor. 3.2.

11 Cf. Jer. 36.23. Jehoiakim, king of Judah.

12 Hos. 7.11.

13 L. Licinius Lucullus, who had secured the command against Mithridates VI, king of Pontus, defeated the latter's ally, Tigranes, king of Armenia, in a battle near Tigranocerta in 69 BC. Lucullus is said to have brought the cherry tree from Cerasus, a town at the Black Sea, to Italy; cf. Plin. *NH* 15.25.102; Tert. *Apol.* 11.8; Amm.Marc. 22.8.16; F. Olck, *s.v.* Kirschbaum, *PW* 11.1, 1921, 512.

14 Cf. Jer. 24.1ff.

15 *in eo, quo allatum est, id, quod allatum est, praedicamus.* Lit.: 'I will praise in the verse, in which the basket of figs is mentioned, the fruit that has been brought to me.'

16 Jer. 24.3.

17 Apoc. 3.15f.

18 On Jerome's dietary programme and his radical campaign for fasting, cf. Grimm (1996) 157ff.

19 Gal. 1.10.

11   THE SATIRIST

1 For references to physicians and medicine in the writings of Jerome, cf. Kelly (1944) 18ff. For the physician's image in early Christianity, cf. R. Herzog, *s.v.* Arzt, *RAC* 1, 1950, 720–4.

2 Cf. Is. 20.2.

3 Cf. Jer. 13.1–7. Jerome uses the Greek word περίζωμα [*perizoma*] for girdle to show his Greek learning. Letsch-Brunner [1998] 125 n. 226 may be right in comparing the girdle that Jeremiah hid at

the Euphrates with the ascetic life, and the Euphrates with the Roman Tiber.

4 Cf. Ez. 4.9–15.

5 Cf. Ez. 24.15–27.

6 Cf. Am. 7.10–17.

7 Here, Jerome obviously alludes to his own fate: His polemics against theological and ascetic rivals resulted in his expulsion from Rome; cf. also below *ep.* 40.2. Therefore, letter 40 must have been written after Damasus' death on 10 December 384 and Jerome's departure in August 385; cf. already Pronberger (1913) 33f.

8 Gal. 4.16.

9 Cf. Jn. 6.60 and 66.

10 For *cornicula*, the small crow, cf. Hor. *ep.* 1.3.19. For Jerome's imitation of Persius (*Sat.* 1.33; 5.11) in this clause, cf. Preaux (1958) 662 and Burzacchini (1975) 60f.

11 Verg. *Aen.* 6.4.

12 Cf. Pers. *Sat.* 3.82; 5.13 and Burzacchini (1975) 61f.

13 *quadrante dignam eloquentiam nare subsanno.* The expression refers to Onasus' misshapen nose, but Jerome also seems to play with the meaning of *quadrans*, that designated a coin of the value of one quarter of an *as*. The *quadrans*, which was minted until Antoninus Pius (cf. H. Chantraine, *s.v.* quadrans, in *PW* 24, 1963, 660), could also be understood as a token of minimal value, a 'farthing', and F.A. Wright, in his Loeb edition of *Select Letters of St. Jerome* (1933) 169 has translated: 'I sneer scornfully at his eloquence which would be dear at a farthing'; cf. also Labourt ii (1951) 86: 'Je raille une éloquence de quatre sous'. The sentence may be influenced by Pers. *Sat.* 1.40f.; 62 or 5.91; cf. Preaux (1958) 663; Burzacchini (1975) 63.

14 *nummarii sacerdotes.* For Jerome's polemics against money-seeking priests, cf. Hier. *ep.* 52.6.1.; 52.6.4f. (legacy-hunting, cf. *CTh* 16.2.20!); 52.9.1; 66.11.3; *Comm. in Soph.* 3.1–7 (*CCL* 76A, p. 696), and Wiesen (1964) 65ff.; Rebenich, Wohltäter and Heilige (2001).

15 *noctuae* and *bubones* are also mentioned in Hier. *ep.* 22.27.8, which was written before letter 40; cf. Cavallera (1922) ii 24f.

16 Cf. Cic. *Cael.* 50, and Gilliam (1953) 104.

17 Onasus is derived from Onesimus (ὀνήσιμος), which means 'the helpful', 'the profitable', 'the beneficial'. Some have deduced from this passage that Onasus was called Onesimus, or bore a similar name, such as Bonosus or Profuturus, cf. e.g. Labourt ii (1951) 196; Wiesen (1964) 205. Nenci (1995) 93f. tries to show that Jerome's enemy must have been a certain Onasus Faustus of Segesta.

18 Cf. Quint. *inst.* 1.6.34: *lucus a non lucendo.* Wiesen (1964) 205 compares

Jerome's argument with Juv. 8.30–8, 'where the poet warns an aristocrat against believing that nobility consists in high birth alone'.

19 A fine display of traditional erudition. The Latin name for the Fates, *Parcae*, is connected with *parcere*, and the *Furiae* were called *Eumenides* in Greek (i.e. the 'gracious' or the 'well-disposed').

20 Cf. Pers. 2.37f. (altered), and Burzacchini (1975) 52.

12   THE BIOGRAPHER

1 It has been argued that this phrase (*diu tacui*) hints at the date of the *Life of Malchus* (i.e. to its composition immediately after Jerome's settlement in Bethlehem in 386, when he started his literary activity again); cf. Cavallera (1922) ii 26–30. But in paragraph 2 Jerome's old Antiochene patron Evagrius is called *papa* (bishop), an office he did not hold before 388 (cf. Rebenich [1992a] 74). Thus, scholars may be right in dating the work around 390–1; cf. e.g. Kech (1977) 157; Kelly (1975) 170f.

2 Jerome did not write such a history. For Jerome's criticism of the Christian church of his time, cf. Wiesen (1964) 50f.

3 On Maronia and Jerome's patron Evagrius, cf. Chapter 2 and Rebenich (1992a) 52ff.; 89ff. The reference to the place and the well-known bishop are supposed to increase the credibility of the narrative.

4 Cf. Lk. 1.5f.

5 Malchus describes his life in a first-person narrative to emphasize the authenticity of the story.

6 Malchus was a tenant farmer (*colonus*) on an estate of a private landlord and tied to the place where he had been registered.

7 For the 'desert of Chalcis', where Jerome is said to have spent some time, cf. Chapter 2.

8 Cf. Prov. 26.1; 2 Pet. 2.22.

9 Cf. Gen. 3.5.

10 Cf. Lk. 9.62.

11 Cf. Jn. 10.12.

12 Edessa (mod. Urfa) was an important bishopric in northern Mesopotamia.

13 The descendants of Abraham's son Ishmael; cf. Gen. 16.15; 17.20; 21.8ff.; 25.12ff.; Gal. 4.21ff. Early Christian writers used the name to describe nomadic tribes in northern Arabia. Later, Ishmael was considered to be the ancestor of the Arabian bedouins.

14 Cf. Gen. 29ff. and Ex. 2.15ff.

15 Cf. Eph. 6.5.

16 In the early church, women lived associated with men in spiritual marriage. They were called *subintroductae* or *agapetae*. The practice is opposed by Jerome (cf. e.g. *ep.* 22.14 and *ep.* 117.6ff.) and other Christian writers. The councils of Elvira (*can.* 27; AD 306?), Ancyra (*can.* 19; AD 314), and Nicaea (*can.* 3; AD 325) passed canons against it.

17 Cf. Prov. 6.6ff. and 30.25, but also Verg. *Aen.* 4.402ff.

18 *uter.* A leather bag for holding water. It could also be inflated and used to keep a person afloat in water; cf. OLD 2116, *s.v.*

19 Cf. Verg. *Aen.* 2.204.

20 Cf. Sen. *Troad.* 510–12 and Hagendahl (1958) 118.

21 That is the distance from the elbow to the tip of the middle finger (about a foot and a half = 444 mm).

22 A similiar story is to be found in Xenophon of Ephesus (4.6), where Anthia is imprisoned in a ditch by two savage dogs, which do her no harm, since they are fed well by a warder.

23 Derived from *dromas* (running). *dromas camelus* (= *dromedarius*) describes a fast-moving camel.

24 The *dux Mesopotamiae* Sabianus is perhaps to be identified with the *magister equitum per Orientem* 359–60 Sabinianus; cf. PLRE i 788f.

25 Maronia.

13   THE BIBLICAL SCHOLAR

1 Luscius Lanuvinus (that is 'from Lanuvium'), who translated Menander, accused his contemporary Terence (c. 190–59 BC) of plagiarizing Greek plays and destroying the character of the original by integrating foreign material into the 'rendering'. Terence replied to this criticism in his prologues to which Jerome alludes; cf. Ter. *Andr.* prol. 5ff.; *Eun.* prol. 23f. Jerome's opponent cannot be identified, but Luscius Lanuvinus is also mentioned in *Apol.* 1.30 (*CCL* 79, p. 29); cf. Lardet (1993) 122f. and Hayward (1995) 88ff. It is obvious that Jerome wrote these lines to refute charges of plagiarism.

2 Virgil who was born on 15 October 70 BC in Andes, a village near Mantua.

3 Cf. Suet. *Vit.Verg.* p. 66 Reifferscheid.

4 Marcus Tullius Cicero; cf. Quint. *inst.* 12.11.28.

5 Latin *repetundae*. It is a fine play upon the meaning of the word. The *quaestio de repetundis* was a court established in the late Roman

Republic to secure compensation for the illegal acquisition of foreign property by Roman officials.

6 Cf. Mt. 7.6.

7 For Jerome's attacks against the detractors of his scholarly work, cf. Wiesen (1964) 200ff. Rufinus was also called 'swine' and 'grunter' (*Grunnius*); cf. Rebenich (1992a) 207 and n. 417.

8 Hor. *Carm.* 2.10.10–11.

9 Cf. Ps. Quint. *Decl. mai.* 13.2.

10 Verg. *Ecl.* 6.9–10.

11 For 'grace' and 'euphony' in his translations of Hebrew texts, cf. Hier. *ep.* 106.3; 29; 55.

12 Cf. Hagendahl (1958) 130: 'If references to secular authors, unless founded on facts, are rarely to be met with in this work, it is consonant with the warning Jerome expresses in the preface [...]. In the preface, however, he makes up for the loss. It is a cento, composed of open or hidden quotations.' Here, as so often, Jerome rhetorically denies the charge of using rhetoric and utilizes his classical erudition to proclaim his ignorance.

13 Throughout the entire work, Jerome, as Kamesar (1993) 79 has emphasized, 'is completely partial to the Hebrew text'. Therefore, he mentions errors in the Septuagint and expresses his reservations about the Greek Old Testament from the beginning; cf. also Hayward (1995) 92ff.

14 Lit. 'bark' (*latrare*).

15 Cf. note 8 to Chapter 9. The idea that the Seventy translators hid certain things from Ptolemy derives from rabbinical tradition; cf. Hayward (1995) 95.

16 Cf. Jos. *Ant.* 12.11.107–9; *Contra Apionem* 2.46.

17 On the three Greek versions of the Old Testament that were reproduced in Origen's Hexapla; cf. note 9 to Chapter 9.

18 That is Origen. Jerome calls him Adamantius: 'the man of steel'; cf. also Hier. *Comm. in Tit.* 3.9 (*PL* 26, 630D).

19 Cf. Verg. *Georg.* 4.176.

20 From Greek *tómoi* (i.e. detailed commentaries). Jerome divided Origen's exegetical oeuvre in short treatises (*schólia*), homilies, and longer studies (*tómoi*); cf. e.g. his translation *Hom. in Orig. Ezech.* (*GCS* 33, p. 318).

21 For Jerome's use of the expression 'Hebrew verity', cf. *QHG* 13.1–4; 19.14–15; 49.5–6 and Jay (1985) 89ff. and 142ff.

22 On the basis of Jerome's testimony, Kamesar (1993) 6ff. has argued that Origen was not in the first place concerned with the Hebrew

text and that his use of the Hexapla is primarily exegetical (*contra* Nautin [1977] 344ff. and others).

23 This expression may be an allusion to Cicero; cf. Jay (1985) 257f. referring to Cic. *Rep*. 2.30.52; *Off*. 3.17.69; *Tusc*. 3.3; *Rab.Post*. 15.41.

14   THE LITERARY HISTORIAN

1 For Jerome's family and his social standing, cf. Kelly (1975) 5ff. and Rebenich (1992a) 22ff.

2 *Dalmatiae Pannoniaeque confinium. confinium* means a common boundary between two (or more) territories; cf. OLD *s.v.* The exact location of Stridon is still subject to scholarly dispute; it seems that the town was in the province of Dalmatia, not too distant from Aquileia and Emona; cf. Kelly (1975) 3ff.; Bratok (1990); and Rebenich (1992a) 21 and n. 4 .

3 Since Theodosius was proclaimed Augustus on 19 January 379, the fourteenth year of his reign covers the period from 19 January 392 to 18 January 393; cf. Barnes (^{2}1985) 235.

4 According to Nautin (1983b) and (1984a), Jerome organized the following list in four different groups, which cover certain periods of his life: (i) the 'desert period' 374–7; (ii) the stay at Antioch and Constantinople 376–82; (iii) Rome 382–5; (iv) Palestine 386–93. These groups are either arranged chronologically or divided into subgroups that are also presented in chronological order.

5 *PL* 23, 17–28.

6 Perhaps Hier. *ep*. 1–17, but see Schwind (1997) 172 n. 3.

7 Hier. *ep*. 14.

8 *CCL* 79B, ed. A. Canellis.

9 *GCS* 47 = *Eusebius Werke* 7, ed. R. Helm; cf. Chapter 9.

10 *14 Homiliae in Ieremiam* (*PL* 25, 585–692) and *14 Homiliae in Ezechielem* (cf. *GCS* 33, ed. W.A. Baehrens, pp. 318–454; *SC* 352, ed. M. Borret. The Greek text is lost).

11 Hier. *ep*. 18A and B (on Is. 6.1–9) according to Hilberg's edition in *CSEL* 54.

12 Hier. *ep*. (19 and 20) on the meaning of the word 'hosanna'.

13 Hier *ep*. 21 on Lk. 15.11–32.

14 Hier. ep. (35 and) 36 on Gen. 4.15; 15.16 and 27.21ff.

15 That is, the translation of two homilies of Origen (cf. *GCS* 33, ed. W.A. Baehrens, pp. 27–60; *SC* 37bis, ed. O. Rousseau. The Greek text is lost).

16 *PL* 23, 183–206 (193–216).

17 Hier. *ep.* 22.

18 Cf. Hier. *ep.* 23–9; 32; 34; 37–8, and 40–4. Letsch-Brunner (1998) 164ff. argues that *ep.* 43–4 are likely to have been written after Jerome had left Rome. For the hypothesis that *ep.* 33 (to Paula), the famous list of Origen's works, was part of the original collection *To Marcella*, cf. Nautin (1984a) 329f. Jerome's inclusion of the letters among the literary works listed here reveals that they were written for a wider audience.

19 Hier. *ep.* 39. Cf. Feichtinger (1995b).

20 For Jerome's commentaries and biblical studies mentioned here, cf. Chapter 6.

21 Cf. Chapter 13.

22 Cf. *SC* 386, ed. L. Doutreleau; Doutreleau (1987); Simonetti (1988).

23 39 homilies of Origen (cf. *GCS* 49, ed. M. Rauer, pp. 1–222; *SC* 87, ed. H. Crouzel *et al.*; an English translation by J. T. Lienhard in *The Fathers of the Christian Church*, vol. 94, Washington, DC 1996).

24 It seems that all of these tractates disappeared with the exception of two on Psalms 10 and 15, which are part of those fourteen homilies which Dom Germain Morin discovered at the end of the nineteenth century and which constitute an alternate series of Jerome's *tractatus in Psalmos*; cf. *CCL* 78, pp. 353–446; for an English translation (by M. L. Ewald), cf. *The Fathers of the Church*, vol. 57, Washington, DC 1966, 3ff. They have been strongly influenced by Origen; cf. Peri (1980).

25 That is, *The Life of Malchus the Captive Monk*; cf. Chapter 12.

26 A. Bastiaensen, C. Moreschini, *Vite dei santi*, vol. 4, Rome 1975, 72–143; 291–317. Cf. *PL* 23, 29ff.

27 Cf. Chapter 12.

28 For the first period of Jerome's residence at Bethlehem, not one letter addressed to Paula and Eustochium has survived; for earlier letters, cf. Hier. *ep.* 22; 30; 31 (see Chapter 10); 33; 39. So, this statement is obviously a slight exaggeration. On the other hand, many of his commentaries and translations are directed to Paula and Eustochium or other noble women. Jerome was even attacked by some of his opponents for encouraging the scholarly ambitions of women; cf. Wiesen (1964) 118.

29 The sequence of commentaries listed here follows the canonical order. However, some manuscripts (and editions) alter the list as follows: Micah, Zaphaniah, Nahum, Habbakuk, and Haggai. On the order in which these commentaries were written, cf. Duval, *SC* 323, 18ff. They are an extremely important source for the exegetical

tradition of early Christianity, as, for instance, the major studies of Duval (1973), Jay (1985), and Kamesar (1993) have shown.

30 There are many additions to this chapter in later manuscripts mentioning other works of Jerome; cf. Feder (1927) 111ff.

15   THE TRANSLATOR

1 In the Latin text there is a play on words: *Desiderii mei desideratas accepi epistulas*. Desiderius may be identified with the addressee of letter 46 and perhaps also with a correspondent of Paulinus of Nola and Sulpicius Severus who bore this name; cf. Rebenich (1992a) 245 and Pietri and Pietri (1999) 551 (Desiderius 2).

2 That is an allusion to Dan. 9.23 where Daniel, according to the Vulgate, is called *vir desideriorum*: 'man of desires'. It is, however, more likely that the Hebrew original indicates that Daniel was greatly beloved by God.

3 Lit. 'barking' (*latratus*).

4 For Theodotion, cf. note 7 to Chapter 8.

5 Mt. 2.15.

6 Mt. 2.23.

7 Jn. 19.37.

8 Jn. 7.38.

9 1 Cor. 2.9.

10 Hos. 11.1.

11 Is. 11.1.

12 Zech. 12.10.

13 Prov. 18.4.

14 Is. 64.4.

15 The polemic is directed against the teaching of Priscillian, bishop of Avila (381–5), and his followers; cf. Hier. *Comm. in Is.* 17.64.4f. (*CCL* 73A, p. 735); *ep.* 120.10.2; *C. Vigil.* 6 (*PL* 23, 360B–C); and Chadwick (1976) 21f.; Bartelink (1980) 98. Rubbish: *neniae*, lit. songs sung at a funeral, but the expression is applied slightly to literary compositions.

16 Cf. note 8 to Chapter 8.

17 Jerome raises the question of the divine inspiration of the translators and protests against the notion that they were inspired; cf. Chapter 6.

18 Aristeas was an official at the court of Ptolemy. A pseudepigraphic letter is attributed to him in which the genesis of the Septuagint is described ('Letter of Aristeas').

19 Flavius Josephus (AD 37/38 to beginning of second century), the

great Jewish historian, was a Pharisee and member of a priestly
family in Jerusalem. For his *Jewish Antiquities*, in twenty books, he
also adapted Jewish–Hellenistic works like the *Letter of Aristeas*
(12.11.109). He made it clear that the Pentateuch alone had been
translated at Ptolemy's request by the Seventy translators; cf. Jos.
Ant. 12.11.107–109; *Contra Apionem* 2.46.

20 Here, *basilica*, according to its etymology, means 'royal residence'.

21 Jerome mentions Cicero's translations of Plato, Xenophon, and Demosthenes also in *ep.* 57.5.2; cf. Bartelink (1980) 49ff. with further
reading. Demosthenes' speech *In Defence of Ctesiphon*, delivered in
330 BC and also known as *On the Crown*, is an oratorical masterpiece.

22 Jerome had already made this point in his Preface to *Hebrew Questions
on Genesis* to defend himself against his detractors, cf. Chapter 13.
There, he argued that the seventy translators altered the texts of
Scripture because they intended to disguise the mysteries of the
advent of Christ and to prevent King Ptolemy from thinking that
Jews might believe in two deities. Hence, the Hebrew text is
superior to the Septuagint; cf. Kamesar (1993) 68.

23 Cf. 1 Cor. 12.28; Eph. 4.11.

24 Jerome asks his opponents to test the correctness of his version, since
Jewish scholars supported his translating programme; cf. Chapter 6.

25 *Reprobaverunt*. The translation follows an emendation proposed by D.
Vallarsi; cf. *PL* 28, 183 n. 2. The manuscript reading is *probaverunt*
which Weber/Gryson (p. 4) and Lardet (*CCL* 79, p. 63; *SC* 303,
p. 176) have adopted. But, then, as Lardet (1993) 222 has rightly
observed, Jerome has advanced 'arguments par l'absurde'.

16   THE CONTROVERSIALIST

1 Cf. Is. 13.21f. and 34.14–16.

2 Job 3.8; 40.15ff.

3 Verg. *Aen.* 8.193ff.

4 A mythical three-bodied monster who lived in Erythea; cf. Hes.
Theog. 287–94; Apollod. 2.106–9; Verg. *Aen.* 6.289; Hor. *carm.*
2.14.7f.

5 That is, sleepy head; Jerome's favourite play on the name Vigilantius; cf. also *ep.* 61.4.2; 109.1 and 3. Other opponents were also
ridiculed for their name. Jovinian's name, for instance, is derived
from Jove (*Adv. Iovin.* 2.38 [*PL* 23, 352B]); cf. Wiesen (1964) 220
n. 66.

6 Cf. *Adv. Iovin.* 2.37 (*PL* 23, 350B). Euphorbus wounded Patroclus (Hom. *Il.* 16.806ff.) and was killed by Menelaus (*ibid.* 17.45ff.). Pythagoras claimed to have been Euphorbus in a former incarnation; cf. Hor. *carm.* 1.28.9ff.

7 On Jovinian, cf. Chapter 5.

8 Is. 14.21.

9 The *Phasides aves* 'are Jerome's standard symbol of gluttony' (Wiesen [1964] 223).

10 Vigilantius or his father was perhaps the keeper of an inn; cf. *ep.* 61.3.2 (with references to wine and money) and *C. Vigil.* 8.

11 Vigilantius' Aquitanian hometown has the same name as Quintilian's birthplace in Spain, Calagurris (Calahorra); cf. e.g. Crouzel (1972) 193f.

12 Cf. Is. 1.22. The quotation 'has a double significance'. It is 'frequently used by Christian writers to describe the dilution of the wine of true religion with the water of heresy, but Jerome also intends it as a slur on the profession of Vigilantius' father' (Wiesen [1964] 223).

13 Cf. Hier. *ep.* 109.1.1, where Exuperius of Toulouse is also attacked.

14 Jer. 5.8.

15 Ps. 32(31).9.

16 *Ibid.*

17 Hier. *ep.* 117. Cf. Wiesen (1964) 84f.; Rebenich (1992a) 282ff.; Lössl (1998).

18 Jovinian also is said to have vomited forth his work like a sot after a night's debauch; cf. *Adv. Iovin.* 1.1 (*PL* 23, 222A).

19 Cf. Gennad. *vir.ill.* 35.

20 Lit. *neniae*; cf. note 15 to Chapter 15.

21 From Latin *convenire*, to come together. For the history of Convenae (= Lugdunum Convenae), cf. M. Ihm in *PW* 4.1, 1900, 1172.

22 The *Vectones* or *Vettones* were a tribe in north-eastern Lusitania.

23 Greek and Roman writers used the expression Celtiberians to describe different people (such as the *Arrebaci* or *Arevaci*) who lived in middle Spain.

24 The former Soloi. Pompey settled some of the defeated pirates there and called the city Pompeiopolis. It is to be distinguished from Pompeiopolis in Paphlagonia, which was founded by Gnaeus Pompeius Magnus soon afterwards (65–4 BC).

25 *vincula Hippocratis* ('Hippocrates' shackles') are also recommended in Hier. *ep.* 109.2.5; in *ep.* 125.16.3, he refers to *Hippocratis fomenta* ('Hippocrates' foments'). For this medical therapy, cf. Theodoret. *affect.* 1.5 (*SC* 57, p. 105) and Temkin (1991) 475.

26 Cf. Acts 14.11ff.

27 Acts 10.26.

28 Cf. Hier. *vir.ill.* 7; Philost. *Hist.eccl.* 3.2 (p. 31f. Bidez/Winkelmann); Chron.Pasch. *s.a.* 356 und 357 (*CSHB*, ed. L. Dindorf, p. 542); Procp. *aedif.* 1.4.18 and Rebenich (2000b).

29 Cf. Chron.Pasch. *s.a.* 406 and 411 (*CSHB*, ed. L. Dindorf, p. 569ff.). The translation of the remains of Samuel illustrates the importance of the growing collection of relics at Constantinople; cf. Delehaye (²1933) 55 and Dagron (²1984) 408f.

30 Mt. 22.32; Mk. 12.26f.

31 Apoc. 14.4.

32 There is an alternative reading, 'shut up in the coffin' (*arca* instead of *ara*); cf. *PL* 23, 359 and n. 2.

33 Cf. Apoc. 6.10.

34 Cf. Ex. 32.30ff.

35 Cf. Acts 7.59f.

36 Cf. Acts 27.37.

37 Cf. Eccles. 9.4.

38 Cf. Jn. 11.11.

39 Cf. 1 Thess. 4.13.

40 This is an allusion to the fourth book of Esdras/Ezra (7.35ff.), which, like III Esdras, Jerome rejected as uncanonical; cf. Hier. *Vulg. Esd.* prol. (p. 638 Weber).

41 That is Mani (216–77), the founder of the Manichaean religion.

42 Balsamus, Barbelus, and Leusiboras are connected with the origins of Gnosticism. The 'Thesaurus of Mani' is also mentioned by Augustine (cf. e.g. *contra Fel.* 1.14) as part of Mani's writings where Gnostic traditions are adopted; its identification is controversial.

43 Christian authors associated Gnosticism with the teaching of Basilides who taught at Alexandria in the second quarter of the second century.

44 This malicious recommendation is also to be found in other of Jerome's invectives; cf. e.g. Hier. *ep.* 57.13.1 and Bartelink (1980) 121; Wiesen (1964) 223f.

45 Lit. *neniae*; cf. note 15 to Chapter 15.

46 Rom. 10.2.

47 Cf. Mt. 26.8ff.; Mk. 14.4ff.

48 Rom. 14.5 (RV: 'Let each man be fully assured in his own mind').

49 Cf. Mt. 25.1ff.

50 Cf. Lk. 12.35.

51 Jn. 5.35.

52 Ps. 119(118).105.

53 Cf. Cic. *Verr.* 2.1.40 and Hagendahl (1958) 246.

54 Bishop of Cyzicus in Mysia (359–60), who held Anomoean–Arian views, died in 394.

55 The Phrygian Montanus (second half of the second century) initiated an apocalyptic movement. The Montanists lived in expectation of the outpouring of the Paraclete on the church, of which they saw the first manifestation in their own prophets and prophetesses. Montanism soon developed ascetic features.

56 That is, antidote to the scorpion's bite. Tertullian's work *Scorpiace* defends the moral value of martyrdom against Gnostic relativism. For Jerome's view of Tertullian, cf. Mohrmann (1951) 111f.

57 Cainites were a Gnostic sect mentioned by Irenaeus (*haer.* 1.31) and other Christian authors. They argued that the God of the Old Testament was responsible for the evil in the world and applauded those who withstood him, like Cain.

58 Hier. *ep.* 109.

59 Cf. Hier. *Comm. in Mt.* 25.6 (*SC* 259, pp. 214–16).

60 Desiderius and Riparius, who informed Jerome of Vigilantius' work.

61 Neoplatonist philosopher (*c.*232–*c.*305) who, in fifteen books *Against the Christians*, severely attacked Christianity using historical criticism and condemning the leaders of the church for their lack of patriotism. His work was burnt in 448 and has come down only in fragments.

62 Cf. Plaut. *Amph.* 110ff.; 546ff.; Ov. *Am.* 1,13,45f.

63 For the comparision of Vigilantius with *Liber pater*, cf. Wiesen (1964) 224.

64 Cf. Hier. *ep.* 61.3.2. No word about this episode is to be found in Hier. *ep.* 58.11.3 to Paulinus of Nola, who had sent Vigilantius to Bethlehem.

65 Cf. 1 Cor. 16.2ff.

66 1 Acts 24.17f.

67 Cf. Ps. 1.2.

68 Cf. Deut. 18.2f.

69 Cf. 2 Cor. 8.13f.

70 Cf. Gal. 6.10. Cf. Hier. *Comm. in Gal.* 3.5 (*PL* 26, 461f.).

71 Lk. 16.9.

72 Ps. 41(40).2.

73 Mt. 19.21.

74 Jerome often refers to Rufinus as snake (*excetra*) and hydra; cf. Wiesen (1964) 234.

75 Mt. 20.16; 22.14.

76 For Jerome's concept of monastic life, cf. esp. Rousseau (1978) 99ff.

77 Latin *lucubratiuncula*; cf. *C. Vigil.* 3 and note 87 to Chapter 17.

78 Wiesen (1964) 224f. is right in stressing that Jerome, throughout his work, attacks his personal opponent as an enemy of orthodoxy. 'One could hardly find a better illustration of Jerome's exalted conception of his own position in the Church than his virtual inclusion of himself in the ranks of the apostles and martyrs and his designation of Vigilantius' opposition as blasphemy.'

17 THE THRENODIST

1 Principia is also the addressee of Hier. *ep.* 65 explaining Psalm 44 and received a copy of Jerome's commentary on Matthew; she asked Jerome to comment upon the *Song of Songs* (Hier. *Comm. in Mt.* prol. [*CCL* 77, p. 6]). Principia had dedicated herself to a life of chastity and was a friend of Marcella for many years. Cf. PLRE ii 904 and Feichtinger (1995a) 215ff.

2 Cf. Cic. *Att.* 13.45.1.

3 Cf. Hier. *ep.* 60.1.1: *Nepotianus meus, tuus, noster* ('my Nepotianus, yours, ours'), and Favez (1937) 131.

4 For Marcella's family, see PLRE i 542f. (Marcella 2) and 1138 (stemma 13); Letsch-Brunner (1998) 23ff. (with further reading); and 257 (stemma). For Jerome's refusal to praise the lineage of the deceased, cf. Hier. *ep.* 60.8.1; 77.2.3; 79.2.1; 108.3.1; 130.3f.; and Scourfield (1993) 136f.

5 For Jerome's ascetic redefinition of nobility, cf. Hier. *ep.* 1.9.2; 60.8.1; 107.13.4; 108.1.1; 130.7.11.

6 Marcella's mother Albina (PLRE i 32 [Albina 1]) had perhaps married a descendant of Claudius Marcellus (PLRE i 552 [Marcellus 10]), who was *Praefectus urbis Romae* 292–3; cf. Chastagnol (1962) 20f. Marcella was born *c.* 335–40; cf. Barnes (1993) 254 n. 24 and Letsch-Brunner (1998) 29; 237 n. 1.

7 Her husband's name is not known.

8 Naeratius Cerealis (PLRE i 197ff. [Cerealis 2]), *Praefectus urbis Romae* 352–3 and consul 358, descended from one of the most prominent Roman families. He was a brother of Vulcacius Rufinus, consul 347 and praetorian prefect, and of Galla, the wife of Constantine's brother Iulius Constantius and mother of Gallus Caesar; cf. Chastagnol (1962) 135f.; Letsch-Brunner (1998) 29ff.

9 Lk. 2.36f.

10 For *maledicta civitas*, cf. Cic. *Cael.* 38; *Flac.* 68; and Gilliam (1953) 106.

11 Ps. 119(118).1.

12 Mt. 5.25. Here, Jerome offers two translations of the Greek original: ἴσθι εὐνοῶν [*isthi eunoón*] – *esto benevolus* and *esto bene sentiens*. The latter is the literal translation of the Greek expression. In the Vulgate, however, we read: *esto consentiens* – 'come to terms with'.

13 Jerome often juxtaposes the vices of worldly women and the virtues of the saintly ascetics. Clothing and make-up are favourite topics; cf. e.g. Hier. *ep.* 22.16.2; 22.32.1; 38.3f.; 107.5.1; 107.10.1; 128.2.1f.; 128.3.5.

14 Jerome praises Nepotian, Lucinus, Nebridius, Paula and others who gave their possessions to the poor; cf. e.g. Hier. *ep.* 60.120.1; 75.4.1; 79.4.1; 108.5.1. For the theological motivation and social function of almsgiving in late antiquity, cf. Rebenich (2001) with further reading.

15 The conversion to asceticism did not dissolve the traditional structure of an aristocratic household. The number of clients, here described as widows and virgins, still defined the social standing of a member of the Roman nobility. When Paula left Rome in 385, 'many virgins' joined her, and the first inhabitants of her monasteries in Bethlehem were her Roman male and female slaves (*servi et ancillae*); cf. Hier. *ep.* 108.2.2 and 14.4.

16 Cf. Hier. *ep.* 79.9.1.

17 Ps. 119(118).11.

18 Ps. 1.2.

19 For the meditation on the law, cf. also Hier. *ep.* 52.7.1; 60.11.3; 100.3.3.

20 1 Cor. 10.31.

21 Ps. 119(118).104.

22 Acts 1.1.

23 Croesus was a familiar instance adduced to illustrate great wealth; cf. e.g. Hier. *ep.* 53.11.3; 57.12.5; 60.11.2; 84.4.5; 118.5.4; 125.10.1. For Jerome's use of pagan *exempla*, cf. Rebenich (1992b).

24 Cf. 1 Tim. 5.23. For Jerome's attitude to fasting, cf. Grimm (1996) 157ff.

25 Jerome defended the veneration of martyrs in *Against Vigilantius* and in *ep.* 109; cf. Chapter 16.

26 For the pagan and Christian opposition to ascetic conversion, cf. Gordini (1983); Rebenich (1992a) 170ff; and Sivan (1993b).

27 For Athanasius' stay in Rome *c.* 340 and the origins of the monastic movement in Rome, cf. Barnes (1993) 47ff.; Jenal (1995); and Letsch-Brunner (1998) 51ff. with further reading. Peter succeeded Athanasius at Alexandria in 373, but was expelled by his theological

opponents and took refuge with the Roman bishop Damasus. In 377, he attended a synod at Rome. The title 'pope' (Greek: πάππας or πάπας; Latin: *papa*, 'father') was from the third century used as an honorific designation of any bishop; in the eastern part of the Roman Empire, however, it seems to have been confined to the bishop of Alexandria. It was not until the sixth century that the word *papa* was reserved for the bishop of Rome; cf. O'Brien (1930) 85. Antony of Egypt (*c.* 250?–356) was a hermit who lived a life of asceticism and retired completely into the desert; the evidence for his biography is the *Vita Antonii* (*Life of Antony*) often regarded as by Athanasius. Pachomius is the father of coenobitic Christian monasticism. About 320, he founded a monastery at Tabennisi in the Thebaid near the Nile, where he soon attracted large numbers of monks.

28 A noble Roman lady who followed Marcella's example; cf. PLRE ii 1021. For other aristocratic women who adopted the ascetic life, cf. Feichtinger (1995a) 168ff.

29 The phrase comes from the beginning of Ennius' translation of the *Medea* (Ennius, *Medea exul* frg. 1.1: *utinam ne in nemore Pelio securibus/ Caesa accidisset abiegna ad terram trabes* [... /Had the axe these pinetrees felled]). Jerome quotes Ennius to express his grief for the loss of two noble women.

30 Jerome derives Magdala from the Hebrew word for 'tower', מגדל [*migdal*].

31 Cf. Jn. 20.14ff.

32 A manuscript of the twelfth century and some editions add: *contemptaeque nobilitatis ac divitiarum maiorem gloriam ducimus*: 'and hold those to be worthy of higher glory who have renounced both rank and wealth'. Hilberg, in his Vienna edition of Jerome's letter, has not adopted this reading; cf. *CSEL* 56.1, p. 149 *comm. ad loc.*

33 Cf. Jn. 18.15f.

34 Cf. Jn. 19.26f.

35 Tertullian, *De monogamia* 17, called him 'Christ's eunuch'.

36 Cf. Plat. *Phaedo* 64a; 67e; 80e–81a. The dictum is likely to have become known to Jerome through Cic. *Tusc.* 1.30.74; cf. Hagendahl (1958) 250 and 303; Scourfield (1993) 183f.

37 1 Cor. 15.31. The quotation from Paul is connected with the Platonic saying also in Hier. *ep.* 60.14.2 and Ambr. *exc.Sat.* 2.35; cf. Scourfield (1993) 184ff.

38 Lk. 14.27.

39 Ps. 44.22.

40 Ecclus. 7.36.

41 Pers. *Sat.* 5.153. Note the combination of biblical and classical quotations in this paragraph; cf. Hagendahl (1958) 303 and Burzacchini (1975) 54.

42 Cf. Rom. 12.1.

43 For Jerome's journey to Rome in 382, cf. Chapter 4.

44 2 Tim. 4.2.

45 Marcella's scriptural studies can be seen as an intellectual activity which transformed the traditional aristocratic practice of *otium* into an ascetic discipline, cf. Feichtinger (1995a) 173.

46 τὸ πρέπον; Latin: *aptum* (cf. Quint. *inst.* 11.1.1ff.) means 'the suitable, appropriate, fitting', both in morals and in rhetoric (cf. Arist. *rhet.* 3.7; Cic. *Orat.* 70). For integration of this concept into ancient ethics, cf. Cic. *Off.* 1.107ff.; 115ff.; 144.

47 1 Tim. 2.12. On this topic in patristic discourse, cf. Nürnberg (1988).

48 Literally: 'a nail's width' (*unguis*); cf. Cic. *Att.* 13.20.4.

49 There are various theories concerning the location of Marcella's *suburbanus ager*, and some have identified it with an imperial estate at the Via Nomentana; cf. Letsch-Brunner (1998) 41ff.

50 Since Jerome and Marcella did not exchange letters between 385 and 393, Nautin (1984a) 330ff. has conjectured that after Jerome had left Rome in 385 discord was brought into his relation with Marcella who may have supported even Jerome's ecclesiastical rival Siricius. Cf. also Feichtinger (1995a) 175f. However, Letsch-Brunner (1998) 172ff. has recently refuted Nautin's theory.

51 Jerome continues to describe the Origenist controversy; cf. Chapter 5.

52 For the proverbial expression, cf. Hier. *ep.* 7.5; *Apol.* 3.24 (*CCL* 79, p. 96) and Otto (1890) 267f.; Lardet (1993) 323.

53 Cf. Ez. 34.18.

54 Jerome plays upon words: the meaning of ὄλβιος [*ólbios*] is identical with that of μακάριος [*makários*]: 'blessed, happy, fortunate'. Macarius was a Roman noble and supporter of Rufinus who translated Origen's treatise *On First Principles* at his request; cf. E. A. Clark (1992) 160ff.; Lardet (1993) 126; PLRE ii 696 (Macarius 1).

55 Jerome uses the Greek word διάπυρος [*diápyros*].

56 *Pharisaeorum schola* designates the Roman clergy who opposed Jerome; cf. 'the senate of the Pharisees' in Hier. Didym. *spir.* prol. (*SC* 386, p. 136ff.); Cavallera (1922) ii 86ff.; Nautin (1983a) 340ff.

57 Cf. Rom. 1.8.

58 The Roman bishop Siricius (384–99), the successor of Damasus, supported Rufinus, here denounced as *hereticus*. For the literary sources of Jerome's estimate of Siricius, cf. Adkin (1996b).

59 Cf. Gal. 1.10.

60 Cf. Lk. 16.8.

61 Rufinus obtained a letter from Siricius when he left Rome for Aquileia; cf. Hier. *Apol.* 3.21;4 (*CCL* 79, p. 92.96); Cavallera (1922) i 247 n. 2; Nautin (1972; 1973) 21 and n. 104.

62 Siricius' successor Anastasius I (399–402), who backed the ascetic movement, showed favour to Jerome and his Roman circle. Obviously, Marcella and Pammachius had pressed him to convoke a synod at Rome in 400 which condemned Origen's blasphemies; cf. Kelly (1975) 246ff.; Pietri (1976) 905ff.; 1288ff.

63 The 'head of the world' (*orbis caput*) is Rome. Jerome alludes to the fall of Rome in 410. Anastasius died in 402. For Jerome's sentiments towards Rome, cf. Sugano (1983) and Laurence (1997c).

64 Jer. 14.11f. The words concerning Israel are applied to Rome.

65 Some manuscripts read: *postea ab heretico fuerant errore correpti* instead of *correcti* (i.e. 'then they had been corrupted by their heretical teaching'); cf. Hilberg in *CSEL* 56.1, p. 153.

66 Rufinus. Since the Origenist controversy, Jerome had called his former friend 'the scorpion', 'the gross swine', and the 'grunting pig' (*Grunnius*); cf. Cavallera (1922) ii 131ff.

67 Cf. Verg. *Aen.* 11.361 and Adkin (1999b).

68 Lk. 18.8.

69 Cf. Mt. 24.12.

70 Cf. Gal. 2.13.

71 A vitriolic onslaught typical of Jerome. It is difficult to decide whom Jerome refers to as Barnabas. John of Jerusalem has been supposed, who was an ally of Rufinus and excommunicated Jerome and his community at Bethlehem in 395 (cf. Chapter 5). But the allusion is perhaps to Rufinus again; cf. *PL* 22, 1094 n. (d).

72 Ps. 104(103).29.

73 Cf. Ps. 146(145).4.

74 Lk. 12.20.

75 The Canaanite name for Jerusalem.

76 By Alaric in AD 408; cf. Matthews ([2]1990) 284ff. and Heather (1991) 213ff.

77 Again by Alaric, AD 409.

78 By Alaric on 24 August AD 410. For Christian reactions on the fall of Rome, cf. Straub (1950) 249ff.; Paschoud (1967) 218ff.; Doignon (1990). When Jerome heard for the first time that Rome was besieged by Alaric, he exclaimed: *quid salvum est, si Roma perit* – 'If Rome be lost, where shall we look for help?' (Hier. *ep.* 123.16.4).

For a detailed description of the events, cf. e.g. Seeck (1921/2) v, 391ff.

79 Cannibalism is also attested by other writers; cf. e.g. Olymp. frg. 7.1 Blockley and Procop. *Bell.Vand.* 1.2.27.

80 Is. 15.1.

81 Cf. Ps. 79(78).1–3. The first verse is translated according to the text of the Septuagint; the Hebrew original reads: '[...] they have defiled your holy temple and laid Jerusalem in ruins.'

82 Cf. Verg. *Aen.* 2.361–5 and 369. Jerome quotes the whole of vv. 361–4 and combines vv. 365 and 369. He causes a dramatic effect 'by placing together without any prelude, and without any intermediary link, two Bibl[ical] texts and the sublime Virgilian lines about the ruin of Troy' (Hagendahl [1958] 259). For the use of Vergil's Aeneid to illustrate the barbarian incursions into the Roman Empire, cf. Courcelle (1976).

83 Verg. *Aen.* 6.266.

84 Job 1.21 according to the Septuagint. The Hebrew text reads: 'Naked came I out of my mother's womb, and naked shall I return whence I came. The Lord gives and the Lord takes away; blessed be the name of the Lord.'

85 Some manuscripts have *post aliquot dies*: 'after a few days'.

86 Nepotianus too died smiling, while everyone around him wept; cf. Hier. *ep.* 60.13.2.

87 Jerome quite often mentions that his work was done by lamplight late at night (Latin: *lucubratiuncula* or *lucubratio*) or that he had to dictate in great hurry, to emphasize his scholarly restlessness and literary assiduity. For Jerome's redaction of his writings, cf. Arns (1953) 37ff.

18 THE ASCETIC EXPERT

1 Cf. Cic. *Rep.* frg. 5 (p. 137 Ziegler).

2 Cf. Hom. *Il.* 1.2549 = Cic. *Sen.* 10.31; Ps. 119(118).103.

3 *Prophetarum αἰνίγματα*. A nice example of Jerome's effort to demonstrate his knowledge of Greek.

4 Cf. Hor. *Sat.* 1.1.25f.

5 *φιλόκοσμον genus femineum est*. Again, Jerome inserts a Greek word to show his erudition.

6 Cf. Num. 11.

7 Cf. Ov. *Am.* 1.8.104.

8 Prov. 5.3 (according to the Septuagint).

9 Cf. Apoc. 10.9f.

10 Cf. Lev. 2.11.

11 Cf. Ex. 25.6; 27.20.

12 Cf. Ex. 12.8.

13 1 Cor. 5.8.

14 Jer. 15.17 (according to the Septuagint).

15 Cf. 1 Cor. 7.20; 7.24.

16 1 Cor. 7.18.

17 Cf. Gen. 3.21ff.

18 Cf. Gen. 3.25.

19 Cf. 1 Thess. 4.4.

20 Jer. 2.13.

21 Cf. Prov. 5.15.

22 Cf. 1 Cor. 7.21ff.

23 1 Pet. 3.7.

24 Eph. 5.13.

25 A play on words: *dum infantem Pacatulam instituo [...] multarum subito male mihi pacatarum bella suscepi.*

26 *sexus femineus.* For Jerome, Pacatula is a young woman; therefore, his main concern is feminine training and not the education of a child.

27 Cf. Hor. *Carm.* 3.16.1. Danaë was the mythological daughter of Acrisius, king of Argos, and Eurydice. Acrisius imprisoned her in a bronze chamber to protect her virginity, since he had been warned by an oracle that his daughter's son would kill him. But Zeus visited Danaë in a shower of gold, and she gave birth to Perseus.

28 Cf. 1 Tim. 5.13.

29 The Christian ideal of womanhood has integrated traditional elements of female conduct praised by pagan authors (e.g. chastity, sexual purity, gravity); cf. e.g. Liv. 1.58.5; Plin. *ep.* 7.19.4; Funke (1964/5); Straub (1968). Wool-working and spinning were part of the traditional occupation of a Roman matron.

30 Cf. Hier *ep.* 130.19.1.

31 Cf. Curt. 6.3.11.

32 Pub. Syr. *Sent.* 52 (p. 180 Ribbeck, *Comicorum Romanorum Fragmenta*). Also quoted in Hier. *ep.* 107.8.1.

33 That is, Paris, the son of Priam, who abducted Helen to Troy, which was the cause of the Trojan War. He is also called Alexander.

34 For Jerome's critical statement of the ascetic practices of noble women, cf. Wiesen (1964) 145; on Christian polemics against women in general, see Thraede (1972) 256ff.; on the traditional sources of Jerome's criticism, cf. Laurence (1998b).

35 For Jerome's reaction to the sack of Rome by Alaric, cf. also *ep.*

126.2; 127.11f. (Chapter 17); and *Comm. in Ezech.* 3, prol. (*CCL* 75, p. 79f.). Shortly before Rome was sacked, he asked: 'Where shall we look for help, if Rome be lost (*quid salvum sit, si Roma perit*)?' (*ep.* 123.16.4); cf. also Straub (1950); Wiesen (1964) 45f.; and Sugano (1983) 54ff.

36 Cf. Hier. *ep.* 123.14.6 and Tert. *Apol.* 39.15.

37 Cf. Num. 16.46ff.

38 Ex. 32.10.

39 Rom. 9.3.

40 Cf. Is. 24.2.

41 Ex. 32.32.

42 Prov. 14.28.

43 Gaudentius was Pacatula's father. Nothing else is known of him; cf. PLRE ii 493 (Gaudentius 4) and Pietri and Pietri (1999) 892 (Gaudentius 10). In older editions, the letter is addressed to him (*Ad Gaudentium*), but according to I. Hilberg's critical edition (*CSEL* 56.1, p. 156) Pacatula was its recipient.

INDEX